On Account of Sex

An Annotated Bibliography
on the Status of Women
in Librarianship
1977–1981

Kathleen Heim and Katharine Phenix
FOR THE
Committee on the Status of
Women in Librarianship
AMERICAN LIBRARY ASSOCIATION

American Library Association
CHICAGO 1984

Text composed by Caron Communications
  in Roman P.S. on a Xerox 630 Word
  Processor. Display type, Helvetica,
  composed by Pearson Typographers

Printed on 50-pound Glatfelter, a
  pH-neutral stock, and bound in
  10-point Carolina cover stock by
  BookCrafters

Library of Congress Cataloging in Publication Data

Heim, Kathleen M.
  On account of sex.

  Includes bibliographical references and indexes.
  1. Women in library science--United States--Bibliography. 2. Women in information science--United States--Bibliography. 3. Women librarians--United States--Bibliography. 4. Women information scientists--United States--Bibliography. I. Phenix, Katharine, 1952-
II. Title.
Z682.4.W65H44   1984   016.010'88042   83-15641
ISBN 0-8389-3287-8

Copyright ©1984 by the American Library Association. All rights reserved except those which may be granted by Sections 107 and 108 of the Copyright Revision Act of 1976.
Printed in the United States of America.

This book is dedicated to our friends,
Sally Eakin and Kathryn Painter,
clerical support staff at the University of Illinois
Graduate School of Library and Information Science
at Urbana-Champaign. To us they stand for
the thousands of dedicated support-staff women
who make libraries work.

"Equality of rights under the law shall not be denied
or abridged by the United States or by any State
on account of sex."--proposed Equal Rights
Amendment to the U.S. Constitution.

Contents

Foreword   vii

Acknowledgments   ix

The Women's Movement
  within Librarianship, 1977-1981   xi

Introduction   xxxvii

Annotated Bibliography   1

Author Index   141

Title Index   149

Subject Index   169

Index to Preliminary Pages   185

Foreword

The Committee on the Status of Women in Librarianship of the American Library Association is charged with the responsibility of promoting and initiating the collection, analysis, dissemination, and coordination of information on the status of women in librarianship. As a result of this charge the Committee has supported the continuation of the annotated bibliography <u>The Role of Women in Librarianship 1876-1976: The Entry, Advancement, and Struggle for Equalization in One Profession</u>. This new volume, <u>On Account of Sex</u>, provides over 900 items about women in the library and information professions and updates the earlier work with items missed between 1918 and 1976. <u>On Account of Sex</u> facilitates the study of women within the profession and will be an invaluable aid to those doing research on issues affecting the status of women. Additionally it enhances the quality of services to women as library users.

The introductory essay provides an excellent summary of the past five years of active participation of women within a women's profession, especially within the American Library Association. All too often the active participants in any movement are too busy effecting change to provide sound documentation and to organize the historical records. However, this has not been true of the feminist movement in librarianship due to the excellent efforts of the activist women who compiled this annotated bibliography--Kathleen M. Heim and Katharine Phenix.

Heim and Phenix have spent countless hours gathering and organizing the items in this volume while the documentation was fresh and relevant to the times in which it was written. This was especially critical in a time that saw much political activity as librarians sought to gain constitutional rights for women. The compilers maintained the high standards established by Weibel and Heim in <u>The Role of Women in Librarianship 1876-1976</u>.

The scope of subject identified in this volume accurately reflects the diverse interests of women within a "women's profession" as the struggle to achieve full opportunity and recognition enters its second century. One can readily trace the early involvement of all librarians in the pay equity/comparable worth issue--"the issue of the 80s"--and see librarians laying the ground work in the mid-1970s.

The Committee on the Status of Women is proud to have sponsored this annotated bibliography and to have been associated with Kathleen M. Heim and Katharine Phenix.

>Cynthia J. Johanson, Chair
>Committee on the Status of Women
>in Librarianship, 1982/83

Acknowledgments

We are grateful to a number of individuals who helped to ensure comprehensivity in this project: Margaret Myers, ALA staff liaison to the Committee on the Status of Women in Librarianship who provided citations, advice, and encouragement for the duration; Kathleen Weibel, Maxine K. Rochester, Norman Horrocks, Peter Hiatt, David S. Zubatsky, Suzanne Hildenbrand, Pat Stenstrom, Walter Allen, Terry Weech, Linda C. Smith, Katherine Dickson, Herbert Goldhor, Deborah Beckel, Johnna Holloway, William M. McClellan, Donald Krummel, John Littlewood, and Karen L. Stanfield, who identified elusive citations; Jorg Jemelka who translated Dutch citations; June Pachuta who translated Russian citations; Pamela R. Broadley, Bernadette Szczech, Marsha K. Fulton, Julia Koehler, and Carol Gates, research associates of Kathleen Heim from 1978 to 1983, who assisted in obtaining material for annotation; Sally Ann Eakin who typed the majority of the manuscript; Kathryn Anne Painter who typed correspondence relating to the project; Janet Frederick who duplicated materials; Mary Mallory who organized the deposit collection; and the members of the ALA Committee on the Status of Women in Librarianship from 1980 to 1983.

THE WOMEN'S MOVEMENT WITHIN LIBRARIANSHIP, 1977-1981

Outline

Organized Activity for Equality and Status Gains
    American Library Association
        SRRT Task Force on Women
        Committee on the Status of Women in Librarianship
        Divisional Attention to Women's Issues
            RASD Discussion Group
            LAMA Discussion Group
        Cutting Across Women's Concerns
            Racism and Sexism Awareness
            Equal Rights Amendment
    Special Libraries Association
    Society of American Archivists
    Association of American Library Schools
    Library of Congress Women's Program Office
    Women Library Workers
        National Activity
        Chapter Action
        A Regional Show of Solidarity
The Future for Women in Libraries
    Career Development
    Comparable Worth
    Women in the Community
Conclusion

The Women's Movement within Librarianship, 1977–1981

Important activities in the various library associations have affected women's status. A recent one was commitment to ratification of the Equal Rights Amendment within the American Library Association.[1] The all-encompassing nature of this commitment imbues the period 1977-81 with a solidarity among women's groups not found in the first century of the women's movement in librarianship. In fact, involvement in the national ratification effort has been characterized as a turning point in the attitudes of many librarians towards political involvement.[2] Following were steps to combat prejudice, stereotyping, and discrimination. The complex interrelationships of committees and caucuses devoted specifically to the advancement of women have had an impact on their parent organizations.

ORGANIZED ACTIVITY FOR EQUALITY AND STATUS GAINS

Women working in groups both within associations and within large organizations have steadily worked to change policies and attitudes. The rise of a variety of committees and discussion groups with special interests in many associations indicates the breadth and diversity of concerns that relate to the status of women in the profession. In this section the response of major associations and organizations to women's concerns is reviewed.

American Library Association

At the outset of the 1977-81 period one group of feminists had succeeded in gaining for women a forum to make policy within the American Library Association. The Social Responsibilities Round Table (SRRT) Task Force on Women, begun in 1970, presented a successful resolution at the 1976 Annual Conference in Chicago to create a status of women in librarianship committee as a standing committee of Council. It is difficult to sort out ALA women's activities without differentiating between the two groups, the Task Force and the Council Committee.

SRRT Task Force on Women

The SRRT Task Force on Women worked tirelessly through the seventies to equalize the position of women in libraries. It sponsored resolutions to support the ERA; to develop guidelines for horizontal as well as vertical career development; to request that the Committee on Accreditation use affirmative action criteria; and to eliminate sexist terminology in ALA publications and advertising. Its projects included a 1974 pre-conference on women; a list of non-sexist subject headings; a bibliography of women in librarianship; a job information service; and programs focusing on women at ALA conferences.[3] Since 1970 the Task Force newsletter, Women in Libraries [1970-24; 1970-30; 1971-17; 1972-11; 1972-42; 1974-51] has documented the women's movement within the Association. An index to the newsletter from 1970 to 1977 permits access to the events of that period.[4]

With the creation of the Committee on the Status of Women in Librarianship (COSWL) in 1976, the Task Force redefined its goals at the 1977 Midwinter Meeting. Its statement of purpose was developed:

> The SRRT Task Force on Women serves as a membership forum within the American Library Association for the exchange of information, concerns, experience and resources on women's issues and as a vehicle for activism within the profession, particularly within the Association, on these same women's issues.[5]

Major Task Force accomplishments during the period 1977-81 included support for the publication of Joan Marshall's book, On Equal Terms (assisted by a Task Force on Women Committee on Non-Sexist Subject Headings); monitoring exhibits for sexism; forums for ALA presidential candidates; ERA-related support; a 1980 pre-conference, "Women in a Woman's Profession--Strategies II"; and building coalitions with groups outside the library community. Programs sponsored by the Task Force included speakers such as Gail Sheehy, authors of Our Bodies Ourselves, Rita Mae Brown, Alix Kates Shulman, Marcia R. Fox, Barbara Haber, Dorothy Bryant, Susan Griffith, and Alice Walker. Workshops at conferences on career decisions and life/work planning were also presented by the Task Force.

In 1980 the Task Force changed its name to the Feminist Task Force and noted, "We expect to change our direction as well. We need no longer be the spokeswoman for the national library association. This role is taken by COSWL."6 Whatever the future role of the Task Force, it is evident that since its inception it has been the basis for the movement for equality in the Association. As its leaders have moved into other positions of importance within ALA, this sensibility has gained an even larger audience. The Task Force is the feminist conscience of the Association and has been the basis for political action. From the Task Force's deliberations have come most of the resolutions fostering equality between the sexes put before ALA's governing bodies. The Task Force's insistence on the creation of a Council committee on the status of women in librarianship added another level to the strength of women's concerns within the ALA hierarchy.

Committee on the Status of Women in Librarianship

The Committee on the Status of Women in Librarianship (COSWL) held its first meetings at Midwinter, 1977. Its charge is:

> To officially represent the diversity of women's interests within ALA and to ensure that the Association considers the rights of the majority (women) in the library field. To promote and initiate the collection, analysis, dissemination, and coordination of information on the status of women in librarianship. To coordinate the activities of ALA units that consider questions having special relevance for women. To identify lags, gaps, and possible discrimination in resources and programs relating to women. To help develop evaluative tools, guidelines, and programs in cooperation with other ALA units designed to enhance the opportunities and the image of women in the library profession, thus raising the level of consciousness concerning women. To establish contacts with committees on women within other professional groups and to officially represent ALA concerns at interdisciplinary meetings on women's equality. To provide Council and Membership with reports needed for the establishment of policies and actions related to the status of women in librarianship, and monitor ALA units to ensure consideration of the rights of women.[7]

Appointments to COSWL are made by the ALA president-elect, and thus it may have a more middle-of-the-road composition than the Feminist Task Force. However, since its creation COSWL has always included a core of members trained in the Task Force and it has maintained good linkage with grass-roots feminists. COSWL was fortunate from its beginning with the designation of Margaret Myers as ALA staff liaison. Myers, director of the Office for Library Personnel Resources (OLPR), has been able to assist in the linkage of concerns of COSWL with general personnel issues. Her consistent commitment to the COSWL charge as well as her organizational skills and understanding of overriding societal movements in such areas as affirmative action [1978-08] and pay equity[8] have been the mainstay of COSWL's efforts.

In its first Annual Report COSWL noted that making itself visible both within and without the library profession was a primary concern. Other long-term goals included provision for an in-depth profile of women in the profession and development of a pamphlet about equality in the field.[9] During its second year COSWL submitted a proposal for an ALA goal award to develop a profile of women librarians. Although it did not receive funding, the committee continued the effort to get this project under way. Liaison between ALA and other professional associations was maintained from 1977 to 1978 and three members of COSWL attended the National Women's Conference in Houston, Texas. Coordination of women-related meetings and programs within ALA was a continued emphasis of COSWL. Schedules of sessions on women's issues were distributed at conferences and COSWL worked closely with all ALA women's groups toward common goals. Resolutions on comparable worth, acceptance of the National Plan of Action, and the inclusion of salary ranges in job advertisements in ALA journals were brought to Council.[10]

During its third year COSWL received funding for its long-planned profile of ALA members; participated with COALITION[11] members and other women's groups to move ALA meetings out of states that had not ratified the Equal Rights Amendment; co-sponsored programs with other groups; represented ALA at the National Women's Studies Association, Women's Action Alliance, Women Library Workers, Federation of Organizations for Professional Women, and Coalition for Women in the Humanities and Social Sciences.[12]

In 1980 the profile project (familiarly called the "COSWL Study") investigators began to issue preliminary findings. Not only were women in ALA earning less, they also had a record of fewer publications and less participation in national and state activities than male ALA members.[13] COSWL action to rectify these findings included the Pay Equity Project carried out in collaboration with OLPR and work on an information brochure on discrimination.[14]

COSWL was working on two major fronts in 1981: enhancing and monitoring the status of women within the profession (both within ALA and within other professional library and information science associations) and maintaining linkages with women in the larger society. Enhancement and monitoring were advanced through internal reports on salary issues and ALA Council composition; publication of Equality in Librarianship: A Guide to Sex Discrimination Laws [1981-37]; successful submission of a third ALA Goal Award proposal for a project on women reentering the profession; and continued co-sponsorship of programs. Better external linkages were forged with the initiation of the Directory of Library and Information Profession Women's Groups [1981-94]; formal liaison with the ALA Washington

The Women's Movement   xv

Office to monitor women's issues; continued designation of COSWL representatives to attend national conferences; and development of an information brochure on libraries and library service to women for use at women's conferences, written for COSWL by Kathleen Weibel.[15]

Divisional Attention to Women's Issues

Other groups within the American Library Association have organized to focus on special aspects of feminist concerns. The Reference and Adult Services Division (RASD) and the Library Administration and Management Association (LAMA) have each developed discussion groups with unique approaches to important issues.

RASD Discussion Group Special attention to women as library users as a topic of concern arose from discussions within the SRRT Task Force on Women. Lynne Erickson organized a petition drive to institute a discussion group on the topic which Helen Josephine successfully presented to the RASD Board of Directors. At the 1977 Annual Conference in Detroit the first official meeting of the RASD Women's Materials and Women Library Users Discussion Group was held to "define concerns and constituencies." Its purposes were to "examine the growing body of research on women for implications for library usage by women; and, to serve as a forum for information exchange on library programs, services and collections which relate to women specifically, and on media useful to women."[16] The Discussion Group's programs at Annual Conference and Midwinter Meetings have focused on such topics as women's history sources, women's collections, information services to women, women as an underserved population, and indexing women's materials.[17] Proposed projects of the groups have been to create a union list of women's serials, to index women's periodicals and to develop an online database of women's materials.[18]

LAMA Discussion Group Women administrators have been meeting unofficially since June 1976.[19] At the Midwinter Meeting in 1977, 60 women met to discuss ways "to open the way for other qualified women; and, to facilitate a mechanism for knowing who is job-hunting when an opening in management comes up."[20] At the 1977 Annual Conference, coordinators Sherrie Bergman and Kay Cassell met with the discussion group to develop strategy for their upcoming meeting with the LAD Executive Board.* The group formulated goals to increase the influence of women in the profession and to put more wom-

---

*The change of division title from Library Administration Division (LAD) to Library Administration and Management Association (LAMA) in 1979 did not affect the Discussion Group's status. It continues within LAMA.

en into decision-making positions in ALA. They planned to develop a women's talent pool and a network of women administrators to provide women with better access to management-level jobs. Plans for workshops on resume writing, interview techniques, and career counseling were also considered.[21]

The LAD Executive Board approved the petition and designated the group as an official discussion group, Women Administrators Discussion Group.[22] Since then panel discussions on women and power, professional networking, career directions, administration in non-library settings, and comparable worth have been sponsored by the group. After most meetings women share information on job openings.[23]

Cutting across Women's Concerns

In addition to committees, task forces, and discussion groups with a specific focus on women's issues, two major issues surfaced during the period from 1977 to 1981 which generated support from many sectors of the Association. The first was the issue of racism and sexism; the second, the struggle for the Equal Rights Amendment.

Racism and Sexism Awareness At its 1976 Annual Conference ALA membership passed a resolution on Racism and Sexism Awareness which had far-ranging effects within the Association:

> Whereas, during the last 200 years the United States has failed to equalize the status of racial minorities and of women, and
>
> Whereas, the American Library Association has professed belief in the principle of equality yet has failed to aggressively address the racism and sexism within its own professional province;
>
> Therefore, be it resolved, That the American Library Association actively commit its prestige and resources to a coordinated action program that will combat racism and sexism in the library profession and in library service by taking the following steps:
>
> The ALA will survey library schools to determine the extent to which racism and sexism awareness training form a part of the curricula and urge that such training be added to the curricula in every library school where it is not now included.
>
> The Library Administration [Division]--Personnel Administration Section will develop a model in-service program providing racism and sexism awareness training for library personnel.
>
> The Public Library Association, the American Association of School Librarians, the Children's Services Division, the Young Adult Services Division, the Reference and Adult Services Division, and the Association of College and Research Libraries will be urged to develop a program to raise the awareness of library users to the pressing problem of racism and sexism.

The Resources and Technical Services Division will develop a coordinated plan for the reform of cataloging practices that now perpetuate racism and sexism.

<u>Be it further resolved,</u> That the President and Executive Board assess the extent of implementation of these steps and report on progress by the 1977 Annual Conference.[24]

Each step of the resolution resulted in various actions to combat sexism and racism. The survey of library schools was conducted by Maurice Marchant to determine how the schools were dealing with sexism, racism, and discrimination.[25] Marchant queried 64 library education programs to discover if they (1) offered a course specific to racism/sexism/discrimination awareness; (2) incorporated the topics in general courses; (3) covered the topics adequately; (4) had a faculty prepared to consider the topics; and (5) would consider changing their curricula. Marchant concluded that library schools felt they were responding to the need for discrimination awareness and that students were encouraged to explore the problems of discrimination.

The Library Administration and Management Association/Personnel Administration Section established an ad hoc Racism and Sexism Awareness Training Committee chaired by Mary A. Hall which developed two workshops. Sexism awareness was the focus of the Dallas Conference where in-service programs called SMARTS (Sexism: Monitor Awareness--Review Thinking Sessions) were held.[26]

The Divisions, directed to develop programs to raise the awareness of library users to racism and sexism, responded in a variety of ways. The Young Adult Services Division Sexism in Adolescent Literature Committee, chaired by Carol Starr, developed a bibliography of role-free books for teenagers and a media presentation of record and book jackets and ads depicting sexist attitudes. The American Association of School Librarians held a pre-conference in 1978, "Focus on Change: Sexism Awareness," covering materials, practices, and procedures for promoting educational equity in schools and libraries.

The final step, reform of cataloging practices which perpetuate racism and sexism, was addressed by the Racism and Sexism in Subject Analysis Subcommittee of the Resources and Technical Services/Cataloging and Classification Section chaired by Elizabeth M. Dickinson. The Committee's final report (available as ERIC Document ED 192730) was submitted at the June 1980 Annual Conference. Its findings reflected dissatisfaction with LC and Dewey schedules as well as with <u>Library of Congress Subject Headings</u>.[27]

By the end of 1981 ALA's efforts to combat sexism had been "mainstreamed" throughout the Association. COSWL continued to monitor these issues.

Equal Rights Amendment In 1974 the American Library Association Council resolution supporting ERA ratification was passed. The resolution, introduced by the Social Responsibilities Round Table Task

xviii The Women's Movement

Force on Women, was the immediate result of discussion at the Task Force's pre-conference, "Women in a Women's Profession: Strategies" [1975-01; 1975-02].[28] No other ALA action in support of the ERA took place until 1977.[29]

At the 1977 Annual Conference in Detroit both the membership and Council passed a resolution on ERA and conference sites which mandated that the Association "add its voice and efforts to the passage of the Amendment by committing future conferences only to states that have ratified the Equal Rights Amendment."[30] Because of the lead time for the ALA conference site selection, this resolution was not to take effect until 1981. However, the fact that many more conferences were to be held in Illinois, a state which had unyieldingly refused to ratify the ERA (voting it down only a week before the 1978 Conference held in Chicago), so angered the membership that a resolution was passed to move the 1979 Midwinter Meeting from Chicago.[31] At that same 1978 Conference the Association passed a resolution supporting extension of the period of time for ratification of ERA. In a letter to Congress dated March 10, 1978, ALA Washington Office director Eileen D. Cooke wrote:

> On behalf of the American Library Association, a nonprofit educational association of some 35,000 members, I am writing to urge you to vote support . . . in recognition of the fact that efforts in support of equal rights for women must be on the national scale to be effective, and in recognition of the fact that pursuit of equal rights can have no deadline.[32]

At the 1979 Midwinter Meeting in Washington, D.C., an effort was made to change the site of the 1980 Midwinter Meeting, slated to be held in Chicago. Although the Executive Board affirmed the Chicago site for 1980, a dramatic vote on the floor of Council resulted in a tie and president Russell Shank cast the deciding vote to move the meeting from Chicago. Anti-ERA members organized a petition drive to take the issue to membership with a mail vote and received the required 200 signatures. Thus a mail vote was scheduled for March 1979.

In February 1979 a coalition of organizations and individuals was formed "to support ALA's commitment to the ERA."[33] Names which appeared on a letter sent to supporters included past presidents Clara S. Jones and Eric Moon, president Russell Shank, president-elect Thomas J. Galvin, Peggy A. Sullivan and Alice Ihrig, (both candidates for the 1979 presidency); ALA councilors E. J. Josey, Patricia G. Schuman, Suzanne LeBarron, Miriam Crawford, and Marilyn Hinshaw; and organizations such as the Social Responsibilities Round Table, the Black Caucus, REFORMA, Women Library Workers, and the ALA Committee on the Status of Women in Librarianship.

The letter described tactics for lobbying ALA members and a variety of options to support the effort to keep ALA out of Chicago.

Working from Middleton, Wisconsin, COALITION staffer Betty Lowe coordinated efforts to inform voters about the need to move ALA meetings from Chicago. Mailings were sent to SRRT members by Bob Baer; to Women Library Workers by Neel Parikh and Helen Josephine; to the Black Caucus by George Grant; and to those receiving the <u>Young Adult Alternative Newsletter</u> by Carol Starr.[34] A detailed fact sheet was also provided. The ballot included a statement prepared by Helen Tuttle, Rose Vainstein, and Allen Veaner explaining that a "yes" vote (to keep meetings in Chicago) would: (1) honor ALA's binding contract with the Palmer House; (2) avoid an indirect boycott which could hurt workers in convention-related services; (3) use ALA's resources to develop constructive strategies for ERA support; (4) turn toward constructive efforts not punitive ones; (5) lessen the risk of an anti-trust suit and a breach of contract action; and (6) ensure the continuity of ALA's efforts on behalf of other human rights issues.

The ballot also contained a statement prepared by Fay Blake, Elizabeth Futas, and Eric Moon explaining that a "no" vote (to move meetings from Chicago) was important because the issue is "primarily a test of the strength of our principles and our conviction. To maintain principle only when there is no risk involved in doing so is not to uphold principle at all." The statement explained that the ERA is not a "women's issue" but a human rights issue in line with long-standing ALA traditions such as the Freedom to Read Statement and ALA Goals and Objectives.[35]

The results of the mail vote were against the boycott. A record response found 9,597 voting to hold the 1980 Midwinter Meeting in Chicago. The boycott was supported by 5,785 individuals.[36] The COALITION arguments that rested on legal contracts with the Palmer House and general response to the issue were reported heavily in the literature.

One victory at the 1979 Midwinter Meeting was approval of a resolution on an ERA Task Force supported by ALA to work with chapters and states which had not ratified the Equal Rights Amendment. Executive Board approved this resolution brought by ten Illinois councilors[37] and allotted funds as requested by Alice Ihrig at its May 1979 meeting.[38] Kay Cassell and Alice Ihrig were appointed co-chairs of the Task Force. Other members designated were: Anita Anker, Karen Jackson, Barbara Bryan, June Engle, Norma Royal, Jim Nelson, and Kathleen Heim.

The 1979 Dallas Conference gained financial support for ERA from ALA. A Drexel Student Library Association ERA Resolution called for $1.00 of each individual and institutional member's dues to be contributed to ERAmerica.[39] Membership approved and Executive Board reported to Council that $10,000 would be set aside for ERA action in a manner to be recommended by the ERA Task Force. Additional funds ($667) were collected from Council. A dues checkoff for membership renewal forms was also approved, allowing members to contribute directly to ERAmerica or the ERA Task Force.[40]

The ERA Task Force, with ALA staff liaison Peggy O'Donnell, held only one meeting outside regular Conference time--a two-day marathon in Pittsburgh on August 10 and 11, 1979. Suone Cotner, executive director of ERAmerica, suggested tactics for ALA's work to gain ERA ratification. The Task Force developed a detailed "Plan of Action" which included Association activity (meetings at Midwinter Meeting and Annual Conference with fundraising through donations and the sale of buttons); mailing a status report/survey to all chapters, with a special letter to states which had not ratified ERA; development of a brochure explaining why ALA was for ERA [1980-01]; development of services (speakers, strategy kits, financial support, exhibits); reports to Executive Board; research; and case studies.[41]

After the August meeting surveys were sent to chapters, and requests for literature, speakers, and financial support for ERA work were channeled through the Task Force. In some cases the Task Force effort generated commitment from state chapters which had not yet gone on record as supporting ERA. In her essays on ERA and ALA, Kay Cassell has documented efforts by various state chapters (notably Illinois, Florida, Missouri, Oklahoma, North Carolina, and Utah) whose work was catalyzed by the Task Force.[42] Amid the Task Force activity many ALA members made one last stand against Illinois by sponsoring a "Boycott Chicago" campaign for the 1980 Midwinter Meeting. The Women in Libraries Caucus of the Florida Library Association issued a statement requesting ALA members either to boycott the 1980 Midwinter Meeting or to spend as little money in Illinois as possible.[43] Many members who did attend wore "Goodbye Chicago" buttons and commuted to the meeting from states which had ratified the Equal Rights Amendment.

Following Midwinter 1980, ALA members were active on the national scene. Task Force co-chair Kay Cassell attended a briefing on ERA at the White House on February 12. A coalition of business, labor, civil rights, and religious groups was addressed by President Carter, Polly Bergen, Dorothy Hecht, and Liz Carpenter.[44] ALA president Peggy Sullivan led a group of librarians carrying an ALA banner at the Mother's Day March [1980-90] held in Chicago, May 1980. At that demonstration librarians joined thousands of women in solidarity to show their support for ERA passage.

The 1980 Annual Conference in New York included a program on ERA featuring Sharon Percy Rockefeller, co-chair of ERAmerica. An ERA booth, backed by a traveling exhibit developed by Cora Thomassen, was an active meeting place for ERA supporters. "ALA's for ERA" buttons were sold and brochures and other information were passed out.[45]

Task Force meetings were held at the 1980 and 1981 Annual Conferences and the 1981 Midwinter Meeting. At these sessions requests for more money from chapters, reviews of chapter actions, and progress planning took place. The Task Force participated in a national petition drive for ERA. The newly designated ALA staff liaison, Patricia Scarry, collected petitions from members to be delivered to Washington, D.C., in April 1981 by the National Organization for Women.[46]

By Midwinter 1982 the Task Force realized that contingency plans had to be made in the event that ERA was not ratified. Repeated questions on the part of the ALA Executive Office and Headquarters staff as to the end of the boycott period were held in abeyance as Task Force members waited to learn of national policy. In a positive move the Task Force submitted a proposal for a Carnegie Reading List Fund grant to prepare and distribute an annotated bibliography and accompanying essay about ERA as a first step to a national dialogue and study of the overall issue.[47]

The 1982 Annual Meeting in Philadelphia marked the end of ERA Task Force responsibility. A resolution discontinuing the boycott and affirming "ALA's continued support of the principle of equal rights for women," sponsored by COSWL member Cynthia Johanson, was passed unanimously by the ALA Council and ERA-monitoring responsibility devolved to the ALA Committee on the Status of Women in Librarianship.[48] A final program, "The ERA: Where Do We Go from Here?" with a speaker from the National Education Association, ended the period of Task Force action on a note of hope. Though this round of effort for the ERA was defeated, the American Library Association stood ready to fight for a new series of ratification efforts. The Association's work not only demonstrated its commitment to human rights but also gained new allies for ALA on a national level.[49]

Special Libraries Association

The Women's Caucus of Special Libraries Association (SLA) met for the first time in New York at the Catalyst conference room in December 1979 to hear Elizabeth Futas and Rachael Goldstein speak and to discuss future strategies. In February 1980, Kathleen Weibel spoke to the group on the status of women in special libraries and on current research designed to identify the barriers confronted by working women. Five concerns of the caucus were identified: (1) professional isolation; (2) changes in economics, politics, and technology which affect women; (3) comparable worth; (4) sex stratification in librarianship; and (5) the need for new work patterns. A mailing list for the proposed newsletter [1980-71] was developed and some long-range goals to "encourage and assist women in other chapters to form local caucuses and eventually establish a national committee on the status of women in the National SLA" were identified.[50]

At the 1983 Midwinter Meeting of SLA in Newport Beach, California, the Board of Directors and Social Science Division rejected the motion of the Women's Caucus to create a provisional division on women's interests. A standing committee within a division was suggested as more appropriate.[51]

Society of American Archivists

In the fall of 1980, the Women's Caucus of the Society of American Archivists (SAA) met to reassess their position within SAA and to review the status of women in the profession. The Caucus had been in existence since the SAA Council established an Ad Hoc Committee on the Status of Women in 1972, as a direct result of one of four papers given at a panel discussion in Columbus, Ohio. At that meeting, Miriam Crawford's speech "Women in Archives: A Program for Action" proposed a standing committee, a women's caucus, and other long-term actions. In Ms Archivist, a short-lived publication of the Ohio Historical Society, Lynn Bonfield Donovan listed thirteen purposes which the Women's Caucus might identify. In 1975, the Ad Hoc Committee was replaced by a Status of Women Committee and the Women's Caucus was appointed to be the "spontaneous arm of the Women's Committee which has definite responsibilities, but which anyone is free to attend."[52] The first issue of the SAA Women's Caucus Newsletter was published in December of that year [1975-102].

On March 7, 1980, the Status of Women Committee developed a concise statement of its position: "The purpose of the Committee is to monitor the status of women in the profession. The Committee strives for equitable participation of women in the archival field."[53]

At the September 29, 1980, meeting of the SAA Women's Caucus, it was proposed that the two groups merge, since the overlapping membership and common goals of the groups often caused confusion for members of the Society at large. The proposal was rejected, however, and the groups have remained separate.

Other activities of both SAA groups during this period included the development of a women's roster, "designed as a means to increase the participation of women at national and regional meetings,"[54] and lobbying for SAA commitment to ratification of the Equal Rights Amendment [1980-125]. They have continued to press for salary and placement analysis [1980-112] and for the monitoring of affirmative action commitment on the part of employers [1981-125].

Association of American Library Schools

The national association of library educators, Association of American Library Schools (AALS), formed a Women's Interest Group at its 1977 annual conference [1977-46]. The group is a forum for research on the position of women in librarianship, investigation of curricular aspects of library education impinging on service to women and career development of practitioners, and a mechanism for the exchange of information among members. This group may be the most unusual of the association-based groups explored in this essay for it has consistently counted among its members a small number of male educators. Since library education's positions of power continue to be dominated by men who hold the majority of deanships, directorates, and professor posts, the recognition of issues and consistent exploration of the problem at national meetings of AALS is especially important.

The initiation of the AALS <u>Library Education Statistical Report</u> [1980-04; 1980-21; 1981-06; 1981-25], with data on faculty and students broken out by sex, provides the basis of a longitudinal set of data with which to investigate changing patterns of faculty composition and enrollment in degree programs at all levels.[55]

Library of Congress Women's Program Office

The Library of Congress, though not an association, is an organization of importance to U.S. librarianship that has proved its concern for women's status in a number of ways. In November 1976, five years after the Women's Program at the Library of Congress was developed, the Women's Program Office acquired a full-time coordinator and a 16-member committee called the Women's Program Advisory Committee to assist her.[56] The committee is composed of representatives from each of the seven departments of the Library and the Office of the Librarian. There are four standing committees: Program and Publicity, Training Programs, Statistics, and Information Resources. Volunteers send written memoranda to their department directors if they want to be appointed. Candidates should be "men and women who are actively interested in improving the status of women at the library" [1977-70].

Early accomplishments of the committee included the removal of marital status information from personnel files, revision of maternity leave policy, liberalization of policies on employment of relatives, and increased opportunities for part-time work [1977-69]. The committee also wrote and published a survey of the Library of Congress recruitment and internship program [1977-61]. In 1978 it completed a 255-page report, "Women's Program Statistical Study," which analyzed the position of women at the Library of Congress over the last decade. Other responsibilities include assistance in developing, negotiating, and implementing the annual affirmative action plan.[57]

During the five-year period from 1977 to 1981, the Women's Program Office sponsored numerous programs, panels, workshops, and exhibits. Their program "Bringing Dead Ends Back to Life" received White House recognition.

Women Library Workers

Women Library Workers (WLW) has emerged in the movement for equality in librarianship as an organization which transcends associational and institutional boundaries. From 1977 through 1981 national, chapter, and regional actions took place.

National Activity

WLW had already shown itself to be a visible, cohesive, and energetic force in many battles for equal rights for women in libraries before 1977. The group was formed in 1975, late in the week of the 94th ALA Annual Conference, in San Francisco, with the goal "to combine the energies of credentialed and non-credentialed women to change the existing distribution of power in libraries."[58] In 1976, Carole Leita and Nancy Schimmel took a seven-month, 2000-mile trip across the country to meet with over 1000 people to organize local chapters. Before the journey Leita participated in a two-week intensive workshop on organizing sponsored by the Midwest Academy in Chicago, an organization dedicated to teaching women skills for recruitment and leadership development and how to select political issues and execute campaign strategies.[59] During that time, the Bay Area Chapter of Women Library Workers (later renamed the Ina Coolbrith Brigade) brought pressure on the Oakland (California) City Council to appoint a woman to the directorship of the Oakland Public Library. As a result a woman was hired to hold the position for the first time in 102 years.

Late in 1976 seven local chapters were involved in a campaign to send letters to Edward Blume, chief of subject cataloging at the Library of Congress, requesting that LC reform its application of sexist occupational subject headings. Less than a year later, WLW member Pat Schuman published WLW member Joan Marshall's On Equal Terms: A Thesaurus for Nonsexist Indexing and Cataloging.

By mid-1977, WLW had a complete set of operational by-laws. Article 1.1 states "the purposes of Women Library Workers ... are to advance the career and educational interests of women working in the field of library and information science."[60] National members met at the 1977 ALA Midwinter Meeting hosted by the Washington, D.C., Chapter and feminist publishers. The second national conference for women library workers was held during the 1977 ALA Annual Conference in Detroit, where chapter councilors met to set down policy for the third edition of the Share Directory, to appoint the WLW Newsletter staff, and to develop a mechanism for WLW's chapter action funds. The fund was meant "to create positive change and to be shared in the spirit of sisterhood."[61] Money was to be made available: (1) to individual women whose jobs were endangered by sex discrimination; (2) to particular causes; (3) as loans for continuing education and/or consciousness-raising projects; (4) as seed money for new chapters; and (5) for projects with money-making potential. Most of the money for the fund was generated by the Bay Area Chapter, which held a benefit concert featuring Malvina Reynolds, Margie Adam, and Janet Smith.

WLW members held a third national conference in Kenosha, Wisconsin, in August 1978 [1978-124] where they made decisions regarding distribution of chapter action funds, addressed the issue of the role of the national WLW as a support system for local chapters, and discussed the SHARE Directory.

WLW's fourth national meeting was held on June 26, 1979, in Dallas, where members again addressed the role of the national organization in relation to its local chapters and new policy in relation to the newsletter was determined. Susan C. Griffith was asked to take over the organization as coordinator-elect. Her reports in the organization's journal show the directions for 1980 during which the fourth edition of SHARE was published, and the WLW Journal revised its format [1980-54]. In 1981 WLW was "on hold" as responsibility for national coordination was transferred. Members who met at the 1981 ALA Annual Conference in San Francisco reaffirmed commitment to the national journal and reallocated organizing responsibilities.

Chapter Action

From 1977 to 1981, WLW's greatest impact was felt at the local level. Over 21 chapters were formed in California, Wisconsin, New Jersey, Illinois, New York, Minnesota, Georgia, Florida, Hawaii, Missouri, Oregon, Massachusetts, Pennsylvania, Ohio, Texas, North Carolina, South Carolina, Washington, D.C., and Toronto, demonstrating WLW's evolution into a decentralized, action-oriented network of chapters.

Throughout the years covered in this book, the Ina Coolbrith Brigade observed and influenced hiring practices in several Bay Area libraries, rallied behind efforts by support staff to take library-related courses, and launched comparable-worth studies. The Boston Chapter worked to bring women into responsible positions within the Massachusetts Library Association and held a one-day retreat. In Eugene-Springfield, Oregon, WLW activity included preparing power-flow charts, lists of WLW objectives, and letters to the president of the University of Oregon when the School of Librarianship was threatened with closure. Minneapolis-St. Paul Women Library Workers, founded to develop the organizational and personal skills of women working in libraries, worked with public libraries in their area and targeted support staff and unions as special topics of concern. In New Jersey, WLW presented "assertiveness training" workshops at state association meetings, and published a local SHARE Directory. In Illinois and St. Louis, WLW members struggled for ERA ratification.

Wisconsin WLW members first became visible at the Wisconsin Library Association annual meeting on October 27-29, 1976, with a booth and a panel discussion on the implications of librarians with degrees taking paraprofessional positions in libraries. Since then Wisconsin WLW has continued to participate actively at WLA conferences and to publish an informative regional newsletter [1976-14]. They have developed a Muriel L. Fuller memorial postcard series of women librarians, which is available through Helaine-Victoria Press of Bloomington, Indiana; packaged slide-tape presentations on working women and other resource media; and created several feminist quilts to raise funds.

For coverage of chapter action, see their reports in Women Library Workers and the WLW Journal.

A Regional Show of Solidarity

The greatest show of WLW solidarity occurred in 1979. Year-long planning by Wisconsin Women Library Workers brought forth "programs, feasts and celebrations"[61] at the Midwest Federation of Library Associations (MFLA) conference held October 31-November 3, 1979, in Milwaukee, Wisconsin. Women Library Workers from the six affiliated states (Illinois, Indiana, Ohio, Minnesota, Wisconsin, and Michigan) were a strong presence at the conference and demonstrated their diversity by staffing a booth, producing women's resource notebooks for each state (see [1980-50] as an example), and participating in a multimedia theater presentation written by Donna Barkman called "Who Is This Woman?" Kathleen Weibel came from New York to speak on the topic, and addressed concepts of youth, isolation, working, violence, and old age as they affect women who work in libraries and women who use them.[62]

Women Library Workers also offered a "Celebrate Motherhood" lunch as an alternative to attending the Muriel Fuller Memorial Day brunch;[63] a "Celebrate Ourselves" dinner, in the place of the MFLA banquet; and a "Where Do We Go from Here?" breakfast, "so that those who feel we can offer as much or more insight into women's thoughts and feelings as Joyce Brothers and Nancy Friday will be able to get together, and so that those who cannot afford or cannot be accommodated by MFLA meals will have an option."[64] MFLA activities generated a tremendous amount of energy among midwestern women librarians and resulted in a number of feminist publications.[65]

THE FUTURE FOR WOMEN IN LIBRARIES

The depressed economic status of women librarians has been meticulously documented by a variety of sources.[66] The difficulty in making broad generalizations derives from the fact that different statistical universes are used in different studies and data gathering is not comparable from study to study.[67] However, at the end of 1981 it is possible to assert on the basis of all the evidence that, for the most part, a dual career structure still exists in the library profession. Four association-based studies released in 1980 found that the salary differential for members of the ALA, SLA, ASIS, and SAA ranged from 19 to 25 percent in favor of men.[68] Key positions--those of "power and might"--such as administrative posts in Association of Research Libraries institutions, directorships of large public libraries, and top posts in library education programs, continue to be disproportionately held by men.[69]

With these facts recognized and irrefutably documented with precision and consistency for over a decade, future directions to remedy the status quo are in order. The profession is attacking the problem on two major fronts: career development and comparable worth.

Career Development

The COSWL study data reported a divergence in career activities for women and men members of the American Library Association. Men publish more, receive more support for research and continuing education activities, and participate more extensively in Association activities than women [1980-132].[70] Martin's study, "Salary and Position Levels of Females and Males in Academic Libraries," found that professional development activities were an important variable in career success.[71] If there are specific traits or characteristics which lead to success in the library profession, attention to career development variables may be one strategy for women desiring promotion.

During the period from 1977 to 1983 a major project was launched intended to enable women to develop as managers. The W. K. Kellogg Foundation funded the first application of assessment center technology to individual career development and to a feminized profession at the University of Washington School of Librarianship. The Career Development and Assessment Center for Librarians (CDACL), co-sponsored by the Washington State Library and the School of Librarianship, was intended to improve the relative positions of women in the library profession by providing them with an assessment of management skills and potential and by providing career development assistance. In an analysis of the CDACL's impact and implications for management practice, Peter Hiatt noted:

> Women librarians who were assessed were generally unaware of their management potential; and their management skills typically exceeded their own expectations. It seems likely that the director who works on confidence building, particularly for women librarians, offers opportunities for women librarians to exercise greater managerial responsibilities, and, in general, makes more effective use of feminine resources, will benefit from an increase in managerial leadership in her/his library.[72]

The CDACL team is continuing to work to obtain funding for regional centers which will use assessment techniques. Career development is viewed as a positive action to gain women entrance to the power positions in the profession.

Comparable Worth

The broadest attack against status inequities within the library profession comes with the alliance of librarians in the growing movement for comparable worth. This movement requires a societal shift in attitudes and a major deployment of resources in new areas. It does not single out men or women for advancement within a profession but seeks to gain recognition for the entire profession on the basis of job evaluation.

xxviii The Women's Movement

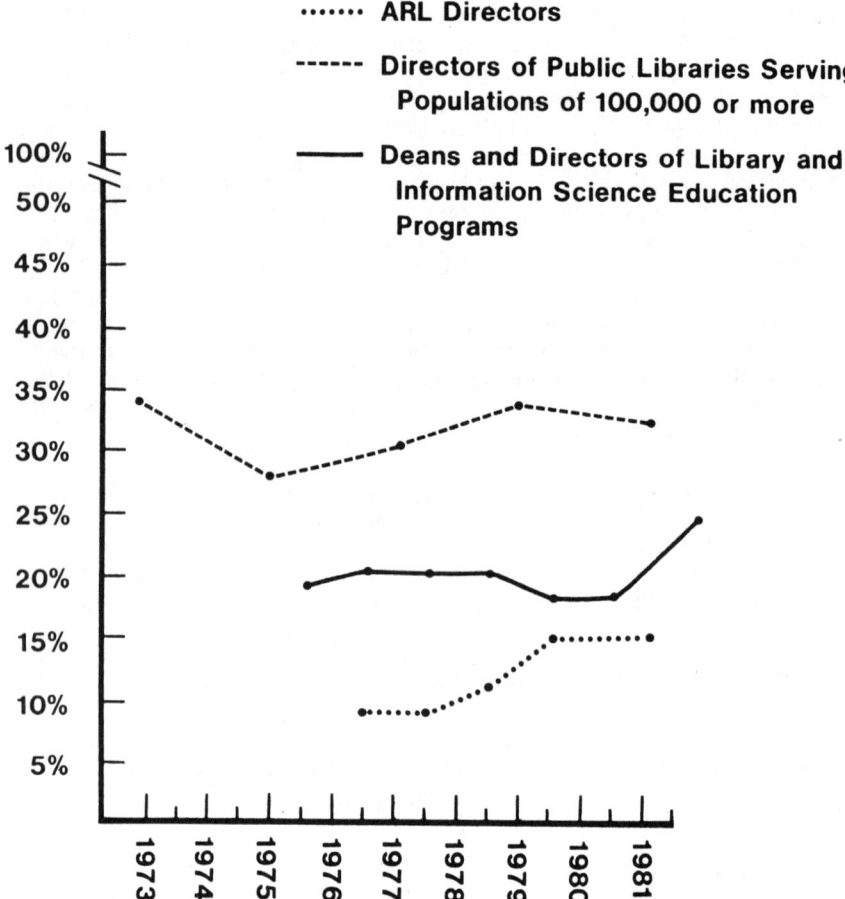

Power and Might Index

······· ARL Directors

----- Directors of Public Libraries Serving Populations of 100,000 or more

——— Deans and Directors of Library and Information Science Education Programs

Percentage of Women in Library Positions
Perceived as Powerful
1973 - 1981

Selected Comparative Median Salaries for Women and Men in the Library and Information Science Professions

	FEMALE	MALE
Associations		
ALA Members, 1980	$14,700	$19,500
ASIS Members, 1980	23,600	29,700
SLA Members, 1979	17,400	21,100
Academic Libraries		
Directors, 1980 (all)	$24,999	$32,999
Branch & Dept. Heads, 1980 (all)	18,307	20,396
ARL Directors, FY 1982	49,111 (avg.)	52,438 (avg.)
ARL librarians employed less than five years, FY 1982	15,897 (avg.)	16,445 (avg.)
Public Libraries		
Directors, 1980 (all)	$19,908	$30,241
Branch & Dept. Heads, 1980 (all)	17,139	19,495
Directors serving populations of 100,000 or more, 1981	29,220	34,505
Entry-level positions, 1981	$15,000	$15,500

Librarians have been involved in comparable worth issues for over a decade. Helen Josephine has been a central figure in documenting these efforts. In her 1978 "Pay Equity" issue of <u>Women Library Workers</u>, Josephine summarized the legal actions involving librarians at the University of California--Berkeley, San Diego Public Library, and Temple University.[73] Josephine later wrote a successful proposal for a "Pay Equity" project jointly sponsored by the ALA Committee on the Status of Women in Librarianship and the Office for Library Personnel Resources. The project resulted in <u>Pay Equity: Comparable Worth Action Guide</u>[74] and a series of open sessions on the problem at ALA meetings and Conferences.

Margaret Myers, director of the ALA Office for Library Personnel Resources and staff liaison to COSWL, reported on the National Conference on Pay Equity held in 1979.[75] Her succinct report indicates that a coalition of women from all professions is necessary to close the wage gap between women and men. Such efforts as ALA past-president Elizabeth Stone's testimony before Congressional committees in 1982,[76] Myers's testimony before the Equal Employment Opportunity Commission in 1980 on behalf of librarians,[77] and the enrollment of COSWL as a founding member of the National Committee on Pay Equity ensure that the library profession will be represented as the comparable worth struggle escalates.

Women in the Community

The main focus here has been on women who work in libraries. Feminist library workers have also been active on other fronts, most notably, services to women in the community. Few reports of this kind of activity are within the purview of this bibliography; however, one project deserves mention. Early in 1981 the Arthur and Elizabeth Schlesinger Library on the History of Women in America at Radcliffe College, supported by a National Endowment for the Humanities grant of $250,000, began assisting seven communities in Washington, Colorado, Tennessee, Georgia, Illinois, Wisconsin and New Jersey (selected in a national competition) with library projects for women. Women's music, art, political participation, health, and history are only a few of the topics chosen by Women in the Community planning teams and presented through 1982. Themes such as "Milwaukee Women Working for Change," "Yankee Women at Work," "Women at the Crossroads," "Atlanta Women: Speak Up! Speak Out!" and "Women Emerging"[78] generated active library support in many communities. The president of one New Jersey library Board of Trustees was quoted as saying, "I can think of no other activity in the history of the library that has created as much interest or brought as many new people to the library."[79] Perhaps more importantly, another community participant has written, "The whole project has been by and about women from the start. I guess an unwritten strategy I have is to involve more and more women in the process of affirmation of themselves through the goals of the project."[80]

CONCLUSION

From 1977 to 1981 library women joined in coalitions to fight for ERA, pay equity, and expanded human services for women. They also attacked professional issues such as the need for better advertising of positions, enhanced women's involvement in professional activities, and documentation of inequities. The convergence of national concerns with profession-specific problems promises to move library women in closer alignment with national efforts to improve the status of women in general as well as within the library and information professions.

Whether library women choose to focus on their own career development or the enhancement of the profession in general through comparable worth action, the central fact that emerges from an analysis of the five-year period is that women have cogently identified the various facets of the problem and are energetically working to solve it on all fronts.

Notes

1. Although this essay focuses on ERA struggles within the American Library Association, other associations have also taken strong stands. See "Equal Rights Amendment" in the subject index. For articles on the work of women elsewhere, see appropriate entries in the Subject Index for Africa, Australia, Canada, Great Britain, Japan, the Netherlands, New Zealand, Norway, the Soviet Union, and Sweden.

2. Kay Ann Cassell, "Librarians, Politics, and the ERA." Wilson Library Bulletin 57 (December 1982): 294.

3. Kay Ann Cassell, "ALA/SRRT Task Force on Women--A Brief History." Women in Libraries 6 (September 1976): 3-5.

4. "Index to Women in Libraries Available." Women in Libraries 8 (October 1978): 3.

5. "SRRT Task Force on Women--A Statement." Women in Libraries 6 (March 1977): 2.

6. "Feminist Task Force Meetings at ALA Midwinter." Women in Libraries 10 (November 1980): 1.

7. "Women in Librarianship, Status of." ALA Handbook of Organization 1982/1983. Chicago: ALA, 1982: 20-21.

8. Margaret Myers, "Conference on Pay Equity: A Focus on Equal Pay for Work of Equal Value." Women Library Workers 22 (November/December 1979): 8-10.

9. American Library Association, Committee on the Status of Women in Librarianship. "Annual Report: 1976-77."

xxxii The Women's Movement

10. American Library Association, Committee on the Status of Women in Librarianship, "Annual Report: 1977-78."

11. COALITION was the name given to the organizations and individuals who banded together in February 1979 to support ALA's commitment to ERA.

12. American Library Association, Committee on the Status of Women in Librarianship. "Annual Report: 1978-79."

13. Leigh S. Estabrook and Kathleen M. Heim, "A Profile of ALA Personal Members." American Libraries 11 (December 1980): 654-659.

14. American Library Association, Committee on the Status of Women in Librarianship. "Annual Report to ALA Council" (1980), p. 1.

15. Kathleen M. Heim, "Fighting for Social Change: Library Women Enter the Eighties." Wilson Library Bulletin 57 (December 1982): 311.

16. Kathleen Weibel, "ALA Midwinter Reports: Reference and Adult Services Division." Wisconsin Women Library Workers Newsletter 1 (March 1977): 8.

17. Conference coverage for the group is in [1977-64; 1979-88; 1981-99]. More detailed reports of conference programs can be found in the following: "Women's History Sources and WEECN." Women in Libraries 7 (May 1978): 3; "Women's Collections: Where Are They Going?" Women in Libraries 8 (June 1979): 2; "Information Services to Women." Women in Libraries 9 (March 1980): 7.

18. For additional information, see reports submitted to the RASD Board of Directors.

19. "LAD Women Administrators Discussion Group Annual Report," submitted by Sherrie S. Bergman and Kay Cassell, June 28, 1978.

20. "ALA Midwinter Reports: Women in Administration." Wisconsin Women Library Workers Newsletter 1 (March 1977) (8).

21. "Women Administrator's Discussion Group." Women in Libraries 7 (September 1977): 4.

22. "LAD Women Administrators Discussion Group." Women in Libraries 7 (March 1978): 7.

23. Marge Loch-Wouters, "LAD Women Administrators Discussion Group." Women in Libraries 7 (October 1978): 3.

24. "Resolution on Racism and Sexism Awareness," ALA Council Document #83, July 23, 1976. See also "Resolution on Prejudice, Stereotyping and Discrimination," ALA Council Document #55, June 22, 1977, which extends the mandate of the 1976 resolution.

25. Maurice P. Marchant and Lynn Lebare, "Library School Instruction in Discrimination Awareness." American Libraries 10 (January 1979): 42-43.

26. Mary A. Hall. "Final Report" [of the Library Administration and management Association, Personnel Administration Section, Racism and Sexism Awareness Training Committee, ad hoc] to LAMA Executive Board, December 20, 1979.

27. "ALA Policy on Combating Prejudice, Stereotyping and Discrimination: Summary Report on Implementation Steps," ALA Council Document #8, 1981-82.
28. "ALA Report." *Women in Libraries* 4 (September 1974): 3.
29. Helen Josephine, "ALA & ERA." *Women Library Workers* 10 (August 1977): 16.
30. "Resolutions Passed at ALA." *Women in Libraries* 7 (September 1977): 3.
31. "The ERA Is the Issue." *Women in Libraries* 8 (January 1979): 2-3.
32. "ALA Supported the ERA Extension." *Women in Libraries* 8 (November 1978): 2; also Helen B. Josephine, "ALA 1978: Victories for Women." *Women Library Workers* 16 (August 1978): 2-3.
33. Letter from COALITION to ERA supporters signed by Kay Cassell and Kathleen Weibel, February, 1979.
34. Letter from COALITION to members signed by Kathleen Weibel, March 1979.
35. Statements accompanying mail ballot sent to members March 1979.
36. Helen B. Josephine, "ERA & ALA." *Women in Libraries* 19 (April/June, 1979): 4-5.
37. Illinois Councilors included Elaine M. Albright, Herbert Biblo, Mary Biblo, Linda Crowe, Valerie Jean Downes, Elizabeth Ohm, Amanda Rudd, Peggy Sullivan, Donald Wright, and Alice Ihrig.
38. Alice B. Ihrig, "Implementation and Costs on the Resolution on ALA Assistance to States Which Have Not Ratified ERA." 1978-79 ALA Executive Board Document #58, April 1, 1979.
39. "Drexel Student Library Association ERA Resolution," Membership Document #2, June 24, 1979.
40. Kay Ann Cassell, "ALA and the ERA." *American Libraries* 13 (December 1982): 691.
41. American Library Association, ERA Task Force. "Minutes of the First Meeting of the Task Force Held August 10 and 11, 1979 in Pittsburgh, Pa."
42. Cassell, "ALA and ERA," pp. 691-692, 694, 695.
43. "Florida Women in Libraries Caucus Encourages Chicago Boycott." *Women in Libraries* 9 (November 1979): 1.
44. Memo to ALA/ERA Task Force, from Kay Cassell, February 19, 1980.
45. For a photograph of the exhibit as well as photographs of other ERA-related events, see Cassell, "ALA and the ERA."
46. "ERA Petition." *Women in Libraries* 10 (March 1981): 2.
47. "Notes from Denver." *Women in Libraries* 11 (March 1982): 1.
48. "Report from Philadelphia." *Women in Libraries* 12 (September 1982): 1.
49. Cassell, "ALA and the ERA," p. 696. Also her essay, "Librarians, Politics, and the ERA." *Wilson Library Bulletin* 57 (December 1982): 292-294.

50. "New York: Women's Caucus in SLA." Women Library Workers Journal 5 (March/April 1980): 3-4.

51. "Information Access, Copyright and Women's Issues at SLA Meeting." Library Journal 108 (April 1983): 624.

52. Nancy V. Menen. "The Way We Were: A Review of the Women's Caucus," paper given at a SAA Session on the status of women in the profession, October 3, 1980. Excerpts are reprinted in the SAA Women's Caucus Newsletter. An example can be found in the vol. 6, September 1982 issue.

53. Letter from Nancy Sahli, Chair, Committee on the Status of Women, to members of the Committee, April 15, 1980.

54. "The Women's Roster" form distributed to SAA Women in the SAA Women's Caucus Newsletter. An example can be found in the vol. 6, September 1982 issue.

55. The Library Education Statistical Report series which began in 1980 is published annually by AALS. Earlier data on the status and salaries of faculty by Russell E. Bidlack appeared annually in the Association's Journal of Education for Librarianship and have been distributed by the ERIC system.

56. Morrigene Holcomb. "Library of Congress Women's Program." Women Library Workers Newsletter 4 (April 1978): 10-11.

57. "Women's Program Office Fiscal Year 1978 Annual Report," submitted by Morrigene Holcomb, October 16, 1978.

58. "Many library workers are no longer content with the lip service that ALA and other library associations pay to the needs and demands of women library workers." Women Library Workers 1 (January 1976): 1.

59. See [1977-32C]; Carole Leita, "Movin' On." Women Library Workers 3 (June 1976): 8-9; and Carole Leita, "Trek Tales." Women Library Workers 4 (August 1976): 6-7.

60. A by-laws draft was mailed with Women Library Workers 7 (February 1977); a copy of the approved document was included with Women Library Workers 8 (April 1977).

61. "Chapter Action Fund," Women Library Workers 10 (August 1977): 4; see also "WLW in Detroit" (p. 1) and "WLW Council Decisions" (pp. 2-3) in the same issue.

62. Kathleen Weibel, "Women at the MFLA Conference." Women in Libraries 9 (November 1979): 2.

63. Wisconsin Women Library Workers had strong objections to the choice of Nancy Friday as a speaker at the brunch. For a full history, see their open letter to the Muriel L. Fuller Memorial Lecture Committee and the reply from Charles Bunge, the chair of the committee: "WLW Protests Choice of Lecturer: Nancy Friday," Wisconsin Women Library Workers Newsletter 3 (May 1979): 1-2 (also reprinted in the Women Library Workers Newsletter 20/21 (July/October 1979): 10-11). Other articles include Donna Barkman's "Say No to Friday

on Wednesday" Wisconsin Women Library Workers Newsletter 3 (July 1979): 1 and "Celebrate Motherhood Lunch." Wisconsin Women Library Workers Newsletter 3 (September 1979): 1-2.

64. Letter from Donna Barkman and Susan Griffith to MFLA Women participants, August 29, 1979.

65. Conference planning is reported by Ceci Chapple in the Wisconsin Women Library Workers Newsletter 3 (May 1979); 7 and 3 (July 1979): 4. It is also reported in the "Wisconsin WLW Chapter" column in the Women Library Workers Newsletter 20/21 (July/October, 1979): 13 and in "Multi-State Cooperation: Process and Planning" Women Library Workers Journal 5 (January/February 1980): 4. Aftermath of the conference is documented in the December 1979 issue of the WLW Newsletter (vol. 3) in "MFLA Lies Behind: The Lunch" by Julie Chase (p. 1); "The Dinner" by Christine Jenkins (p. 6); "The Breakfast" and "The Booth" by Marge Loch-Wouters (p. 7); and "The Buttons" by Kathy Leide (p. 7). Further reporting appeared in "MFLA Report" WLW Newsletter 22 (November/December 1979): 4; Jan Behn, "The Program (A Participant's View)"; and Miriam Pollack, "The Program (An Onlooker's View)," in WWLW Newsletter. (Both are reprinted in the WLW Journal 5 (January/February 1980): 2-3.) More reports were published in the WWLW Newsletter: Kathleen M. Heim, "Illinois, Post MFLA" 4 (January 1980): 8; Kathleen Weibel, "Conference Critique: MFLA" 4 (May 1980): 1-2; Deborah Elkins, "Ohio, Post-MFLA" 4 (May 1980): 6; in the WLW Journal "Multi-State Cooperation: Results" 5 (January/February 1980): 4 and by Peggy Daub, "Women's Action at the University of Illinois at Urbana-Champaign Graduate School of Library Science," 5 (July/August 1980): 3. See also [1980-50].

66. For a summary of sources and comparison of variables, see Kathleen M. Heim, "The Demographic and Economic Status of Librarians in the 1970s, with Special Reference to Women." In Advances in Librarianship, volume 12. Edited by Wesley Simonton (New York: Academic Press, 1982): 1-45.

67. Ibid., p. 2.

68. Ibid., p. 21, table 13.

69. Kathleen M. Heim, "Fighting for Social Change: Library Women Enter the Eighties." Wilson Library Bulletin 57 (December 1982): 308-309.

70. Kathleen M. Heim and Leigh S. Estabrook, Career Profiles and Sex Discrimination in the Library Profession (Chicago: ALA, 1983).

71. Jean K. Martin, "Salary and Position Levels of Females and Males in Academic Libraries." In The Status of Women in Librarianship: Historical, Sociological, and Economic Issues, edited by Kathleen M. Heim (New York: Neal-Schuman, 1983): 243-285.

72. Peter Hiatt, "Should Professionals Be Managers?" Journal of Library Administration 4 (Spring 1983): 21-39.

73. Helen Josephine, "Comparable Pay for Comparable Work." Women Library Workers 13 (February 1978): 12-15.

74. American Library Association Committee on the Status of Women in Librarianship and Office for Library Personnel Resources, <u>Pay Equity: Comparable Worth Action Guide</u>. Written and compiled by Helen Josephine. Topics in Personnel no. 2. Chicago: ALA/OLPR, 1982.

75. Margaret Myers, "Conference on Pay Equity: A Focus on Equal Pay for Work of Equal Value." <u>Women Library Workers</u> 22 (November/December 1979): 8-10.

76. Margaret Myers, "EEOC Hearing: A Focus on Equal Pay for Work of Equal Value." <u>WLW Journal</u> 5 (May/June 1980): 12-13.

77. Helen Josephine, "All Things Being Equal: Pay Equity for Library Workers." <u>Wilson Library Bulletin</u> 57 (December 1982): 303.

78. <u>Women in the Community, Newsletter of the Arthur and Elizabeth Schlesinger Library on the History of Women in America, Radcliffe College</u> 1 (August 1982). Three issues of this newsletter were published to report on the activities of the community projects. This last and final issue is a collection of the reports written by the community organizers.

79. <u>Women in the Community</u> 1 (Fall 1982): 3.

80. <u>Ibid</u>.

Introduction

The dominant theme of the years from 1977 to 1981 for library women was the same theme that powered the women's movement at all levels: the struggle for a constitutional amendment for equal rights. The late but nevertheless intrepid entry of library associations into the battle to ratify the Equal Rights Amendment provides a central focus for this five-year period. Efforts to combat sexism, to document salary and status inequities, to develop career path models, and to achieve pay parity begun in the early seventies continued with steady intensity, but the fight to ratify the ERA dominated the period.

On Account of Sex is a bibliographic record of the continuing efforts of women in the library and information professions to gain equality both within the professions and in society at large. In the preceding essay major events in the ongoing struggle are summarized. Citations to items in the annotated bibliography which follows, as well as primary source material from committees, task forces, and discussion groups, document various events and activities which took place in the five-year period.

On Account of Sex supplements the earlier volume prepared by Kathleen Weibel and Kathleen M. Heim with assistance from Dianne J. Ellsworth, The Role of Women in Librarianship 1876-1976: The Entry, Advancement, and Struggle for Equalization in One Profession (Phoenix, Arizona: Oryx Press, A Neal-Schuman Professional Book, 1979). It includes earlier items omitted from The Role of Women and is comprehensive in coverage from 1977 through 1981.

Materials listed contribute to an understanding of women's evolving status and position in the library and information science professions. Individual biographies of women are not included unless they contain discussion of women in a larger context than their own careers.

xxxvii

xxxviii   Introduction

The bibliography was compiled by searching <u>Library Literature</u>, <u>Library and Information Science Abstracts</u>, <u>Dissertation Abstracts</u>, ERIC, and <u>American Statistics Index</u>. To ensure comprehensiveness, especially for news items which are indexed with less care by the indexing and abstracting services, a page-by-page search was conducted of major periodicals. All bibliographies included in articles and essays on the topic were perused. Many volumes on women's issues, occupations, and sociology were examined for reference to the library profession.

The bibliography does <u>not</u> contain references to newspaper articles, with a few exceptions. The <u>Chronicle of Higher Education</u> regularly includes statistics on academic librarians in its various reports on faculty salaries which are derived from reports included in the bibliography. Since these did not add new information, they are not included.

A number of journals and newsletters devoted to women in librarianship (such as <u>WLW Journal</u> [1980-54], <u>SAA Women's Caucus Newsletter</u> [1975-102], <u>Women in Libraries</u> [1974-51] or <u>Wisconsin Women Library Workers Newsletter</u> [1976-14]) are cited only once. These are major sources of information and must be read in their totality for a comprehensive understanding of the women's movement in librarianship. Archival collections of associations also contain important material including annual reports of committees and task forces devoted to the concerns of women. Since these are unpublished they are not listed.

A by-product of this bibliographical effort has been the collection of many of the items cited both in this volume and <u>The Role of Women</u>. Materials keyed to the numeric coding scheme used in both bibliographies have been deposited at the ALA Headquarters Library to facilitate future research on the topic. A list of items available may be obtained by writing to:

American Library Association
Office for Library Personnel Resources
COSWL Bibliography Collection
50 East Huron Street
Chicago, Illinois 60611.

Organization of the Bibliography

The bibliography includes items from 1918 through 1976 omitted in the earlier volume. The standard numbering sequence of year and item number has been continued. Thus, while the last item in <u>The Role of Women</u> for 1918 was 1918-07, new items identified for that year and listed for the first time in this volume continue that sequence: 1918-08 and 1918-09. This practice ties the two volumes together closely. A scholar desiring comprehensive access must consult the indexes to both volumes.

Introduction   xxxix

The arrangement of this volume is the same as for The Role of Women. Material is cited in chronological order by publication date. Citations with the same date are arranged alphabetically by author. Within each year those publications with the year as the only date precede those dated by month. Items with seasonal publication dates are arranged in this order: Spring before March; Summer before June; Fall before September; and Winter before December. Materials with a publication date of more than one month (e.g., January/February) are found after the first month of that date.

Identification Numbers and Letters

An identification number composed of the year of publication and sequence within that year has been assigned to each item with the exception of letters in response to articles, reviews, and editorial comment. These are indented and entered below the item to which they pertain, first by date then alphabetically by author. If letters generate other letters, additional sequences are identified by further identation and entered below the letters to which they refer, for example:

1981-63 "For Men Only." Incite 2 (March 6, 1981): 4.

Reprints a letter by W. H. Ifould from the Library Record of Australia 2 (1902) for readers of Incite. Ifould referred readers to Chennell's attack on women in public libraries [1902-03] and pointed out that Australia would soon have the same problem.

Letters: "For Gentlewomen." Incite 2 (April 3, 1981): 2.

Prompted by the reprint of the 1902 Ifould letter, another librarian submits a quote from an 1880 publication, Occupations Accessible to Women, in which it is suggested that a single woman might enjoy the work of a librarian since she would be capable of living on a pittance which a married man with a family would not.

Whyte, J. P. "Cheap Labour." Incite 2 (April 17, 1981).

Notes that Ifould did employ women when he became a librarian since they worked more cheaply than men.

Gawler, Kathleen. "Women Librarians." Incite 2 (May 1981): 5.

Tells that 1880 and 1902 acts and deeds of discrimination against women have nothing on 1947. On writing to the public library at Perth in that year the author was told categorically, "we do not employ women librarians in our library."

Letter: Lukis, Mollie. "Unsafe for Women." Incite 2 (July 17, 1981): 8.

Responds to Gawler's letter. Notes that the principal librarian at that time, Dr. J. S. Battye, believed it unsafe for women to

xl   Introduction

leave the library late at night due to the dangerous neighborhood. Author relates lower salaries paid to women at that time.

Entire Issue or Volume Devoted to Women

Entire issues of journals, complete volumes, or proceedings devoted to women in the library and information professions have an identification number shared by all articles or papers. Articles or papers are further distinguished by a capital letter notation which also shows this relationship, as in:

1977-32A   Gerhardt, L. N. "Before--and Since--Angie." School Library Journal 23 (January 1977): 6-8.

1977-32B   Josephine, Helen B. "Beyond Awareness: Women in Libraries Organize for Change." School Library Journal 23 (January 1977): 31.

1977-32C   Josephine, Helen B. and Leita, Carole. "Women Library Workers." School Library Journal 23 (January 1977): 32-33.

Other Symbols and Devices

1. Asterisk (*) citations refer to items identified but not obtainable for annotation.
2. Numbers followed by a lower-case letter (1981-16a, for example) were inadvertently left out until after the bibliography was indexed. They have been inserted at their appropriate place in the chronology and are included in the index with the lower-case notation.
3. Imbedded citations are used to call attention to relationships between items within the two volumes. For example:

1981-26   Lynch, Mary Jo. "Research on Libraries and Librarianship in 1980: An Overview." In Bowker Annual 26th ed. New York: Bowker, 1981: 263-267.

Reports personnel-related studies including ALA/OLPR The Racial, Ethnic, and Sexual Composition of Library Staff in Academic and Public Libraries [1981-02] and the COSWL Study to investigate careers of librarians [1980-132].

Indexes

Author, title, and subject indexes keyed to the citation number follow the bibliography. NB: Those wishing to do a comprehensive search for the period 1876-1981 should consult the indexes both in this volume and in The Role of Women.

Annotated Bibliography

1918-08 "Library Union Organized in Boston." <u>Library Journal</u> 43 (June 1918): 411.

Report of a meeting of 50 Boston Public Library employees includes a review of coverage in the <u>Boston Herald</u>, which focused on the issue of high school versus college educated "girls" working in the library. A letter by Charles K. Bolton, librarian of the Boston Athenaeum, also published in the <u>Boston Herald</u> is included. He writes, "if these young women are to be taken at their own estimation in fixing salaries and assigning tasks and not on the judgment of the librarian, have we not reached a Russian standard of 'self-determination' in the Boston Public Library?"

1918-09 "Papers and Proceedings 40th Annual ALA Conference at Saratoga Springs, New York, July 1-6, 1918." <u>ALA Bulletin</u> 12 (January/November 1918): 283-287.

Coverage of War Library Service session at the Conference includes: report of the policy on employment of women; a roster of women; objections to their employment as chief librarians; protests from women that they are "excessively weary of being protected, shielded from hard work"; and general statements about women's status.

1932-03 Zimmerman, Lee Frank, "The Academic and Professional Education of College and University Librarians." Thesis, University of Illinois, 1932. p. 78-79.

A survey of the academic and professional head librarians using catalogs of 260 institutions in relation to class, size and type of institution. Extensive tables break down data by type of institution, and sex of librarian is specified in most tables. Findings and conclusions state that there are more women than men who are head librarians, and men hold the more responsible positions (which are found chiefly in the men's, large, complex institutions). Men have a higher level of education, while women have more professional training.

1939-06 Herbert, Clara W. Personnel Administration in Public Libraries. Chicago: ALA, 1939.

Urges recruitment of men possessed of vigor and personality since they bring to the library a career attitude and fewer personal reactions than women. Notes it is wiser not to complicate staffing by hiring married women and "it is certainly desirable not to appoint mothers of young children" (pp. 50-51).

1950-05 Kraus, Joe W., "The Qualifications of University Librarians, 1948 and 1953." College and Research Libraries 11 (January 1950): 17-21.

Compares the actual qualifications of 29 chief librarians in 1933 with those of 32 chief librarians in university libraries in 1948. Only one of these librarians was a woman. Findings indicated four trends: post-graduate study was more likely to be considered necessary; the value of library school training was fairly well established; increased mobility; and less movement from publishing firms and from public, special, and other types of librarianship to university libraries.

1950-06 Schick, Frank L. "Meet the College Librarian." Library Journal 75 (June 15, 1950): 1017-1019.

Report of a survey of 170 libraries, of which 155 replied, aimed to "describe librarians collectively." Of the chief librarians 84 percent were male; in large institutions five out of six chief librarians were male. Notes that this may be because of different educational backgrounds. One-fifth of the women had no academic degrees or a B.A. only, compared to only 5 percent of the men. One-third of the men held Ph.D.'s, while only one woman did so.

1957-07 Blades, William. "Blades on Enemies of Books." In Classics of Librarianship. Edited by John L. Thornton. London: Library Association, 1957: 55-59.

Reprint from Blades' 1881 volume, The Enemies of Books, which was reprinted in 1882, 1887, 1888, and 1896, includes criticism of women who enter men's studies pretending to dust. Notes, "Why need women-folk . . . bother themselves about the insides of a man's library?"

1957-08 James, Minnie Stewart Rhodes. "Women Librarians." In Classics of Librarianship. Edited by John L. Thornton. London: Library Association, 1957: 119-126.

Reprint of [1892-01].

1957-09 Reagan, Agnes Lytton. "A Study of Certain Factors in Institutions of Higher Education Which Influence Students to Become Librarians." Ph.D. thesis, University of Illinois, 1957.

Includes some comments on librarianship's appeal to women.

1957-10 Tedder, Henry Richard. "Librarianship as a Profession." In <u>Classics of Librarianship</u>. Edited by John L. Thornton. London: Library Association, 1957: 92-104.

Includes reprint of [1882-01].

1957-11 Thornton, John L. "Minnie Stewart Rhodes James." In <u>Classics of Librarianship</u>. London: Library Association, 1957: 119.

Biographical note on a "fitting advocate for the employment of women librarians" who accounted for a number of items [1890-01, 1892-01, 1892-03, 1892-04, 1893-02, 1893-03, 1893-04, 1894-05, 1895-02, 1899-17, 1900-01C, 1900-03, 1902-02] in the earlier bibliography [1979-28] which this volume supplements. Since biographical data on James were scarce (see [1979-28], p. xxxiii) we are glad to direct readers to this source.

1958-04 McAnally, Arthur M. "The Dynamics of Securing Academic Status." In <u>The Status of American College and University Librarians</u>. Edited by Robert Bingham Downs. Chicago: ALA, 1958: 28-41.

Discussion notes that the predominance of women does not seem to alter the University's decision to grant faculty status but that women are discriminated against in salary and rank. Reprinted from <u>College and Research Libraries</u> 18 (September, 1957): 386-395.

1958-05 Reagan, Agnes L. <u>A Study of Factors Influencing College Students to Become Librarians</u>. Chicago: ALA, 1958.

Study based on dissertation [1957-09] contains some comments on librarianship's appeal to women.

1963-09 Williamson, William Landram. <u>William Frederick Poole and the Modern Library Movement</u>. New York: Columbia University Press, 1963.

Notes that Poole took a brave step in employing Mrs. A. B. Harnden, who may have been the first woman employed in an American library--an action which flew in the face of a warning by Poole's predecessor that the presence of women in a library containing examples of "the corrupter portions of the polite literature" would cause "frequent embarrassment to modest men." Notes that Harnden was first in a long series of female employees at the Boston Athenaeum (pp. 28-29).

4   1966-11 Annotated Bibliography

1966-11   Blades, William. "Blades on <u>Enemies of Books</u>." In <u>Selected Readings in the History of Librarianship</u>, 2nd ed. Edited by John L. Thornton. London: Library Association, 1966: 123-127.
   Reprint of [1957-07].

1966-12   Ginzberg, Eli. <u>Life Styles of Educated Women</u>. New York: Columbia University Press, 1966.
   Study of women college graduates includes some observations on those who became librarians.

1966-13.   James, Minnie Stewart Rhodes. "Women Librarians." In <u>Selected Readings in the History of Librarianship</u>, 2nd ed. Edited by John L. Thornton. London: Library Association, 1966: 244-251.
   Reprint of [1892-01]; earlier reprint appeared in [1957-08].

1966-14.   Tedder, Henry Richard. "Librarianship as a Profession." In <u>Selected Readings in the History of Librarianship</u>, 2nd ed. Edited by John L. Thornton. London: Library Association, 1966: 212-224.
   Includes reprint of [1882-01]; earlier reprint appeared in [1957-10].

1966-15   Thornton, John L. "Minnie Stewart Rhodes James." In <u>Selected Readings in the History of Librarianship</u>, 2nd ed. Edited by John L. Thornton. London: Library Association, 1966: 243-244.
   Reprint of [1957-11].

1968-17   Library Association. <u>A Report on the Supply and Training of Librarians</u>. London: Library Association, 1968.
   Report concludes, "Because of their longer professional lives men fill the majority of the senior posts, and it is therefore important that sufficient men should be recruited to fill these posts."

1968-18   Bolino, August C. "Trends in Library Manpower." <u>Wilson Library Bulletin</u> 43 (November 1968): 269-278.
   Summarizes [1970-02; 1970-13; 1970-25; 1972-01] human resources data in five general areas of the library and information fields: employment trends, expenditures, salaries, placements and supply factors. Women librarians are specifically mentioned in the section on salary comparisons. Low librarian salaries are "explained" by the predominance of women in the field, "many of whom have second incomes, a higher turnover, less mobility, and fewer alternatives for employment of their MSLS degrees."

1969-22   Filter, Nancy H. "Selected Characteristics of Members of the Music Library Association." (A research paper submitted to the Kent State University Library School in partial fulfillment of the requirements for the degree of Master of Library Science. May 11, 1969).

Reports the results of a survey of music librarians returned by 426 librarians. Discusses personal characteristics of MLA members, education, employment, publishing, continuing education and memberships. Includes 19 tables, most of them broken down by sex. Conclusions are published in <u>MLA Notes</u> [1970-34].

1969-23 U.S. Department of Labor. Women's Bureau. <u>1969 Handbook on Women Workers.</u> (Bulletin 294). Washington, D.C.: GPO, 1969.

Women college graduates of the class of 1957 were surveyed in 1963. Lowest average earnings were reported by secretaries, clerical workers, and librarians (p. 175). Degree information is also included.

1969-24 Bolino, August C. <u>Supply and Demand Analysis of Manpower Trends in the Library and Information Field.</u> Final Report (July 1969). Bethesda, Md.: ERIC Document Reproduction Service, 1969: ED 038 986.

Analyzes library manpower data under five headings: (1) employment trends, (2) expenditures, (3) salaries, (4) placement, and (5) conditions of supply. Notes that men earn more than women and the gap between the two widens with experience (p. 1). Suggests that women's "geographical mobility tends to be limited relative to men" as a reason for salary differential (p. 5). Provides table displaying library science degrees by sex (p. 62). None of the other data reported are broken down by sex.

1969-25 Lillard, R. S. "On Principal University Librarians." <u>Southeastern Librarian</u> 19 (Fall 1969): 133-140.

Compares "exterior" credentials of twenty chief administrators at the largest U.S. research libraries. All the librarians were male, "indicating a marked prejudice against qualified female librarians." Notes aspirants should be male.

1970-33 Levitt, Eleanor Sosnow. "A Study of Four Career Patterns and Associated Life History Characteristics among Female Professional Librarians." Ph.D. dissertation, New York University, 1970.

Study of 118 female professional librarians from U.S. metropolitan areas. Life history characteristics were contrasted among four distinct "female career patterns": stable working (49 percent of sample); double track (31 percent); interrupted (10 percent); and delayed (10 percent). Only three of seven background variables differentiated among the career pattern groups: family constellation, mother's level of education, and stage in married life when graduate degree granted. Of the ten current life-situation variables investigated, only three discriminated among the double track, interrupted and delayed entrance patterns: number of children, age of youngest child and annual income of husband. The "delayed entrance" group had older children and husbands earning higher incomes.

1970-34 Filter, Nancy H. and Marco, Guy A. "MLA: A Membership Profile." MLA Notes 26 (March 1970): 487-490.

Reports surveys of members of the Music Library Association based on [1969-22]. A questionnaire mailed to 1,076 personal members found 59 percent are male. Men earned more money than women, even in comparable job situations, with slight regard for educational attainment. The authors offer short, composite sketches of the typical male music librarian and the typical female music librarian.

1970-35 Frarey, Carlyle J., moderator. "Law Library Salaries." Law Library Journal 63 (November 1970): 471-504.

Discussion at American Association of Law Libraries 63rd annual meeting. Moderator - Carlyle J. Frarey; Panelists - Dan F. Henke; Lindsey Cowen; and Morris Cohen. Panel begins with a discussion of a survey of the membership of the American Association of Law Libraries in May 1970 which reported replies from 742 respondents or 54 percent of the membership. Findings show that 53 percent of law librarians are women (11 percent did not respond to the question)--a ratio that is "higher than that observed in librarianship as a whole." In general, women are found in smaller libraries, are less likely to have law degrees, are more likely to be in technical services, and have lower salaries, even when their employment, education and experience are comparable. Later discussion by Dan F. Henke on other factors bearing upon salary, blames women, "the deadliest of the species," for undercutting salaries, since they are supposedly less mobile, are "unwilling or unable to resist a low bid," will work hard when no other help is hired, and, like some men, lack the courage to apply for better jobs.

1971-42 Blankenship, W. C. "Head Librarians: How Many Men? How Many Women?" In The Professional Woman. Edited by Athena Theodore. Cambridge, Mass.: Schenkman, 1971: 93-102.

Reprint of [1967-04].

1971-43 Index of Opportunity in the Library and Information Sciences, 1971: A Directory of Career Opportunities for Qualified Librarians and Information Science Specialists with Public, Private, University and Special Libraries and Information Centers. Princeton, N.J.: W.T. G-W Resource Publications, 1971.

Introduction notes 80 percent of librarians are women, with men more frequently employed in technical libraries, and in executive and administrative positions in large libraries. [Similar statement appeared in earlier editions]

1971-44 Lipow, Ann et al. "A Report on the Status of Women Employed in the Library of the University of California, Berkeley, with Recommendations For Affirmative Action." December 1971. Arlington, Va.: ERIC Document Reproduction Service, 1971: ED 066 163.

Report written by the Library Affirmative Action Program for Women Committee (AAPWC) describes the origin of the committee, women in the work force, in libraries, and at the University of California, Berkeley. Chapters deal with salaries, classification, promotion, hiring, recruitment, in-service training, parental leave, child care, and other affirmative action issues. Includes recommendations to help eliminate sex discrimination in libraries. Tables display salaries for librarians as compared with other occupations.

1971-45 McAnally, Arthur M. "Status of the University Librarian in the Academic Community." In Research Librarianship: Essays in Honor of Robert B. Downs. Edited by Jerrold Orne. New York: Bowker, 1971: 19-50.

Describes the predominance of women in libraries as having had a serious effect on the attitudes of the academic community towards librarianship, partly because in the 1870-1890's librarians were considered housekeepers and there was little differentiation between professional and clerical tasks (p. 20). Under the heading "The Problems and Captives of Sex," the current position of women in libraries is mentioned (p. 44-45).

1973-72 Campbell, Jean W. "Women Drop Back In: Educational Innovation in the Sixties." In Academic Women on the Move. Edited by Alice S. Rossi and Ann Calderwood. New York: Russell Sage, 1973: 93-124.

Of 500 women who sought career counseling at the University of Michigan from 1964 to 1965, most were apt to consider some phase of education in social work or a library career.

1973-74 Graham, Patricia Albjerg. "Status Transitions of Women Students, Faculty, and Administrators." In Academic Women on the Move. Edited by Alice S. Rossi and Ann Calderwood. New York: Russell Sage, 1973: 163-172.

When women are found on college faculties, they are most likely to be found in areas considered suitable for them: social work, education, home economics, nursing and library service.

1973-75 Klotzburger, Kay. "Political Action by Academic Women." In Academic Women on the Move. Edited by Alice C. Rossi and Ann Calderwood. New York: Russell Sage, 1973: 359-392.

Notes that women librarians were spurred to political action when the profession tried to "upgrade" its status by enticing men into the field. The origin of the ALA SRRT Task Force on Women is noted.

1973-76 Loeb, Jane W. and Ferber, Marianne A. "Representation, Performance and Status of Women on the Faculty at the Urbana-Champaign Campus of the University of Illinois." In <u>Academic Women on the Move</u>. Edited by Alice C. Rossi and Ann Calderwood. New York: Russell Sage, 1973: 239-254.

Provides tables which demonstrate the position of women on various faculties, including librarians at the University of Illinois at Urbana-Champaign.

1973-77 Morlock, Laura. "Discipline Variation in the Status of Academic Women." In <u>Academic Women on the Move</u>. Edited by Alice C. Rossi and Ann Calderwood. New York: Russell Sage, 1973: 255-309.

In a table, "Selected References by Discipline," divided into 18 disciplines, Blankenship [1967-04]; Kronus and Grimm [1971-37A]; Manchak [1971-20]; and Schiller [1970-11] are listed. Master's degree recipients in library science were 83 percent women. Another table shows proportion of Ph.D.'s, Master's and B.A.'s awarded from 1969 to 1970 by sex. Article states that although men are only 33 percent of academic librarians, they constitute 79 percent of all deans of library schools (1971) and 95 percent of the chief librarians in 74 large college and university libraries (1969). Only 18.8 percent of the 85 past presidents of ALA were women, and only 30 percent of journal editors were women.

1973-78 Rossi, Alice S. "Summary and Prospects." In <u>Academic Women on the Move</u>. Edited by Alice S. Rossi and Ann Calderwood. New York: Russell Sage, 1973: 505-529.

Discusses how organized political efforts by women have surfaced in professional fields such as law, medicine, education and library science.

1973-79 U.S. Department of Health, Education, and Welfare. <u>The Education Professions 1971-72, Part IV: A Manpower Survey of the School Library Media Field</u>. Washington, D.C.: GPO, 1973: p. 21.

The differences between library and audiovisual fields are described. Traditionally, women chose the library field over the more technological media centers. One study reported 95 percent of the librarians in elementary and secondary schools in 1962 were women, with a median age of 50.2 years and 10 percent were under 34 years of age [1966-01].

1973-80 Sandler, Rhoda with Judith Platt. "Job Sharing at Montgomery County." Library Journal 98 (November 1973): 3234-3235.

Describes job sharing experience and explains advantages. Notes that "job sharing is liberation."

1974-69 "Report on Pilot Study of Woman Graduates in the Library Service Field." New York: Columbia University School of Library Service, n.d. (1974?) (mimeographed).

Study of 1967 and 1971 female graduates of the Columbia University School of Library Service, conducted in 1973, was undertaken to understand problems of late entrants.

1974-70 Bergmann, Martha. "Job Sharing." Booklegger Magazine 1 (March/April/May/June, 1974): 44-46.

Describes job sharing (as opposed to part-time work) at San Francisco Public Library. Notes that a married woman with children is the usually cited candidate.

1974-71 Peterson, Gary T. "Graduates of Media Programs in 1972-73." Audiovisual Instruction 19 (March 1974): 26-28.

Second annual survey of instructional media graduates completing their media degrees. The first year that degree recipients were identified by sex, survey reports that 449 were men and 295 were women.

1974-72 Kahl, Anne. "What's Happening to Jobs in the Library Field?" Occupational Outlook Quarterly 18 (Winter 1974): 20-25.

Report notes highlights of Bureau of Labor Statistics Bulletin, Library Manpower--A Study of Demand and Supply [1975-13]. Persons in librarianship are described by gender, age, education, mobility and employment opportunity.

1975-92 "Librarians." In New Women's Survival Sourcebook. New York: Knopf, 1975:12.

One-page history of women in libraries includes an essay by Elizabeth Futas of the ALA/SRRT Task Force on Women, statistics on salary distribution by sex from ALA Salary Survey [1971-20], and ads for SHARE: A Directory of Feminist Librarians, the TFW Bulletin Board, Women in Libraries Newsletter, and Margaret Myers' Women in Librarianship: A Bibliography [1975-09].

1975-93 U.S. Department of Health, Education, and Welfare. National Center for Education Statistics. Survey of Federal Libraries 1972. Washington, D.C.: GPO, 1975.

Statistical survey of all federal libraries in the continental United States and overseas includes as "Highlights" (back cover) that 64 percent of all federal library employees are female; 71 percent of all professional librarians are female; but 71 percent of librarians in Grades GS-13 and above are male. Data broken out by sex include: percent of female employees (pp. 10-11; Table 6); percent of females in the three national libraries--Library of Congress, National Library of Medicine, National Agricultural Library (p. 22; Table 13); commentary on sex differential in grade level at national Libraries (p. 26); commentary on employment of women at libraries reporting individually (p. 40, 42); percent female at federal libraries worldwide by type of library and government organization by education (p. 55; Table 30); in filled positions by fund and classification (pp. 56-57; Table 30); and by grade level (pp. 57-60; Table 30).

1975-94 U.S. Department of Labor. Women's Bureau. Handbook on Women Workers, 1975. (Bulletin 297). Washington, D.C.: GPO, 1975.

Librarians employed in 1973 are reported by sex (p. 89). Influx of men into the profession is noted (p. 94).

1975-95 Josey, E. J. "Can Library Affirmative Action Succeed? The Black Caucus of ALA Surveys Minority Librarians in 22 Leading Libraries." Library Journal 100 (January 1, 1975): 28-31.

The Black Caucus of ALA surveyed minority librarians in 22 leading libraries. Findings showed inequality with respect to racial and ethnic minorities in libraries.

1975-96 Wood, Frances E. "Scientists in Librarianship and Information Work: A Survey of Former Information Studies Students of the Postgraduate School of Librarianship and Information Science, University of Sheffield,1964-1973." Journal of Librarianship 7 (January 1975): 31-48.

Surveys the careers of former students of the Post Graduate School of Librarianship and Information Science. Questionnaires were sent to graduates from the years 1965 to 1973. An 83 percent response rate generated 95 usable returns. Table 1 "Career Choice--on Entering University" and "On Graduating," the only table broken out by sex, reports that one-third of the female respondents had left the field temporarily by the beginning of 1972. At the time the questionnaires were completed, 12 women were not presently working. Previous surveys had found that 44 percent of the women had left the field.

1975-97 Robertson, S. E. "The Institute's Remuneration Survey." Information Scientist 9 (June 1975): 71-74.

Reports the Institute of Information Scientists salary survey results from 706 members, with a 72 percent response rate. Results are broken down with tables demonstrating salary inequalities between women and men. Discussion of results, however, is only in terms of age, qualifications, type of employer and staff responsibility. Median total pay in 1975 for women was £3,710 and £4,280 for men.

1975-98 Garland, Henry Walter, III. "The M.L.S., Affirmative Action, Equal Employment Opportunity, and Equivalency: A Report to the Board of Directors of the California Society of Librarians." California Librarian 36 (October 1975): 40-58.

Outlines the issues of equal employment opportunity and affirmative action which affect librarianship, with emphasis on minorities. Includes an annotated chronology of legislation and the text of a policy statement approved by the Council of the California Library Association.

1975-99 Ballard, Bob et al. "Salary Discrimination Program Packet Available." Special Libraries 66 (November 1975): 545.

Announces program materials on salary discrimination designed by the Special Committee on the Pilot Education Project (Salary Discrimination), chaired by Laura Gasaway. Packet includes a bibliography, quiz, and tapes. Chapters and divisions are urged to use these materials for a program on salary discrimination in special libraries.

1975-100 Collins, Judith. "Guest Editorial." The Information Scientists 9 (December 1975): 125-126.

Notes that total personal membership of Britain's Library Association includes 67 percent women, but the proportion of women in senior posts is "not high." Also notes that in the Institute of Information Science, women are paid £500 less per annum. Asks whether librarianship is downgraded because it is a female profession.

1975-101 Reed, Sarah R. "Library Manpower Planning in the USA." Libri 25 (December 1975): 332-347.

In a paper originally presented at the International Federation of Library Associations in Washington, D.C. in 1974, the author discusses librarian employment projections. She notes the rise of men in the field, salary differentials for men and women, and the success of affirmative action programs.

1975-102 Society of American Archivists. Women's Caucus. SAA Women's Caucus Newsletter 1, no. 1 (December, 1975).

Newsletter of the Women's Caucus of the Society of American Archivists (SAA) informs the SAA membership about women's status in the archival profession, reprints minutes of SAA's Status of Women Committee, analyzes participants in the annual meeting by sex, and carries general information of interest to women archivists.

1976-78 Baker, Curtis O. and Well, Agnes Q. <u>Earned Degrees Conferred 1972-73 and 1973-74: Summary Data.</u> Washington, D.C.: GPO, 1976. (NCES 76-105).

Companion piece to [1976-79] provides summary information, by sex, on bachelor's, master's and doctoral degrees awarded in library science. (Note to researchers: earlier reports in this series were <u>not</u> included in the 1876-1976 bibliography; <u>The Role of Women in Librarianship</u> [1979-28]. Earlier reports issued by the National Center for Education Statistics should be checked by those researchers needing complete longitudinal information for degrees granted in library science.)

1976-79 Baker, Curtis O. and Wells, Agnes Q. <u>Earned Degrees Conferred, 1973-74: Institutional Data.</u> Washington, D.C.: GPO, 1976. (NCES 76-106).

Summary data include degrees received, by sex, in library science in the bachelor's, master's, and doctoral degree categories for the aggregate United States, from 1970-71 to 1973-74. Data are also provided for each institution. (Note to researchers: earlier reports in this series were <u>not</u> included in the 1876-1976 bibliography, <u>The Role of Women in Librarianship</u> [1979-28]. Earlier reports issued by the National Center for Education Statistics should be checked by those needing complete longitudinal information for degrees granted in library science.)

1976-80 Cheatham, Bertha M. "SLJ News Roundup 1975." In <u>Bowker Annual</u>, 21st ed. New York: Bowker, 1976: 83-89.

Adaptation of [1975-87].

1976-81 Dickinson, Elizabeth. "Personnel and Employment: Affirmative Action." In <u>ALA Yearbook 1976.</u> Edited by Robert Wedgeworth. Chicago: ALA, 1976: 257-260.

Review of the year's events includes summary observation that "Women and minority librarians continued to be underpaid, underutilized, and underrepresented within the power structure of the profession." Section on the status of women includes review of incoming personnel based on ALA data and information from recent surveys which show pay differentials exist between men and women at every level.

1976-82 Eldridge, Marie D. "NCES 1974 Survey of School Library/Media Center." In <u>Bowker Annual</u>, 21st ed. New York: Bowker, 1976: 250-251.

Data from early release of National Center for Educational Statistics survey report certified staff by sex.

1976-83 "Federal Libraries." In <u>ALA Yearbook 1976</u>. Edited by Robert Wedgeworth. Chicago: ALA, 1976: 158-160.

Summary of government survey of federal libraries [1975-93] has special section, "Women in the Study" (pp. 159-160) which notes 71 percent of all professionals were women. No women were in grades GS 15 or above.

1976-84 Grant, W. Vance and Lind, C. George. <u>Digest of Education Statistics: 1975 Edition</u>. Washington, D.C.: GPO, 1976. (NCES 76-211).

Includes statistics on libraries and librarians in scattered tables. Table 167 (p. 180) reports numbers of men and women in elementary and secondary, college and university, public, and special libraries for 1960 and 1970 with projections for 1980 and 1985. Enrollment for advanced degrees in library science by sex (Table 86, p. 85) and degrees conferred at bachelor's, master's, and doctoral level by sex (Table 104, p. 106) are also included. It should be noted that much of the data herein are derived from other National Center for Education Statistics publications and that there is, for example, a time lag on degrees conferred. (Note to researchers: earlier reports in this series were <u>not</u> included in the 1876-1976 bibliography, <u>The Role of Women in Librarianship</u> [1979-28]. Earlier reports issued by the National Center for Education Statistics should be checked by those needing complete longitudinal information.)

1976-85 Harris, Patricia R. "Council, ALA." In <u>ALA Yearbook 1976</u>. Edited by Robert Wedgeworth. Chicago: ALA, 1976: 147-148.

Coverage of "women's issues" faced by the 1975 ALA Council describes three resolutions: elimination of sexist language in ALA publications (approved); establishment of a Committee on the Status of Women in Librarianship (tabled); boycott of states which had failed to ratify the ERA (failed).

1976-86 Hess, Edward. "California." In <u>ALA Yearbook 1976</u>. Edited by Robert Wedgeworth. Chicago: ALA, 1976: 361-363.

In "Affirmative Action" section, adoption by the California Library Association of a statement on affirmative action is noted.

1976-87 Holley, Edward G. "<u>ALA at 100</u>." In <u>ALA Yearbook 1976</u>. Edited by Robert Wedgeworth. Chicago: ALA, 1976: 1-32.

Centennial review of the American Library Association includes observation that ALA preceded most organizations in electing women to leadership positions, with the selection of Theresa West Elmendorf as ALA president in 1911-1912 (p. 11). Photos of library leaders over the century show individual portraits of 20 men and 10 women (Sarah

C. N. Bogle, Theresa West Elmendorf, Mary Salome Cutler Fairchild, Caroline M. Hewins, Clara Stanton Jones, Allie Beth Martin, Mary Wright Plummer, Grace Stevenson, Ruth Warnecke, and Constance Winchell).

1976-88 Josey, E. J. "Social Responsibilities." In ALA Yearbook 1976. Edited by Robert Wedgeworth. Chicago: ALA, 1976: 322-324.

Reports publication of Women Library Workers Newsletter [1976-23].

1976-89 Kellum-Rose, Nancy. "Social Responsibilities Round Table." In ALA Yearbook 1976. Edited by Robert Wedgeworth. Chicago: ALA, 1976: 324-325.

Notes publication of the SRRT-Women's Task Force; an all-day Women's Festival held at the ALA San Francisco Conference; and the formation of Women Library Workers.

1976-90 Land, Brian. "Canadian Correspondent's Report." ALA Yearbook 1976. Edited by Robert Wedgeworth. Chicago: ALA, 1976: 440-443.

Section on "Status of Women" (p. 442) notes that theme of 1975 Canadian Library Association was "Women: The Four-Fifths Minority." The CLA Status of Women Committee successfully submitted eleven resolutions to the annual meeting. These included use of nonsexist language in CLA publications; day care at CLA conference; support of maternity and paternity leaves; and equality for women in pension and insurance plans.

1976-91 Mullins, Stephanie and Partington, Dorothy. "London Report." In ALA Yearbook 1976. Edited by Robert Wedgeworth. Chicago: ALA, 1976: 430-439.

Section "Women in Librarianship" (p. 439) notes that women remain subordinate to men and more married women are now employed.

1976-92 Savage, Noël. "LJ News Report 1975." In Bowker Annual, 21st ed. New York: Bowker, 1976: 63-82.

Adaptation of [1976-32].

1976-93 Sergean, R.; McKay, J. R.; and Corkill, Cynthia M. The Sheffield Manpower Project: A Survey of Staffing Requirements for Librarianship and Information Work. Sheffield, Eng.: Postgraduate School of Librarianship and Information Science, 1976.

Project on library staffing needs includes discussion (p. 261) and tables (19.1-19.4) on educational and professional qualifications by sex; discussion (pp. 261-262) and table (19.5-19.8) on job grades of men and women; discussion (pp. 262-263) and tables (19.9-19.12) on the nature of job involvement of men and women; discussion (p. 263) and tables (19.13-19.16) of salaries of men and women. Summary (p. 275) notes that women have more junior-graded posts, are less likely to be in planning/supervisory jobs, and are more poorly paid than men.

1976-94 Simon, Barry. "Personnel and Employment: Salaries." In ALA Yearbook 1976. Edited by Robert Wedgeworth. Chicago: ALA, 1976: 260-263.

Review of library salaries, in general, includes charts from U.S. Department of Labor Study, Library Manpower [1975-13], which compare employment and age of librarians by sex.

1976-95 Slanker, Barbara O. "Research." In ALA Yearbook 1976. Edited by Robert Wedgeworth. Chicago: ALA, 1976: 305-309.

ALA/OLPR study of degrees and certificates [1975-79] is summarized in "Surveys."

1976-96 Strable, Edward G. "Special Libraries." In ALA Yearbook 1976. Edited by Robert Wedgeworth. Chicago: ALA, 1976: 329-331.

Notes SLA's concern for women's low salaries, especially after the 1973 salary survey [1973-70], which resulted in the SLA's Special Committee on the Pilot Education Project development of program materials on salary discrimination. Among these was the pamphlet Equal Pay for Equal Work: Women in Special Libraries [1976-04].

1976-97 Women in Librarianship, 1892-1976. Chicago: ALA, 1976.

Bibliography of English-language articles and books on women in librarianship with author and subject indexes, arranged chronologically with short annotations. Originally compiled by the Women's Liberation Task Force of the Philadelphia Social Responsibilities Round Table, Connie Allsteller et al. (Nov. 1970); updated by ALA SRRT Task Force on Women, Margaret Myers (June 1973) and indexed by the "Women's Group" at the University of Wisconsin-Madison Library School as supervised by Kathleen Weibel (1975-1976).

1976-98 Young, Arthur Price. "The American Library Association and World War I." Ph.D. thesis, University of Illinois, 1976. (DAI 77-09246).

Camp librarians in the Library War Service were initially male. Women who did supervise camp library services were not given the title "camp librarian" and did not reside in camps until May, 1918. The bitter struggle of women librarians to perform full services for the war effort is recounted (pp. 85-92).

1976-99 Baker, Gladys L. "Women in the U.S. Department of Agriculture." Agricultural History 50 (January 1976): 190-201.

General discussion of the role of women at the USDA includes reference to librarian Ernestine Stevens, the highest paid woman of her time (1877) within the USDA. Throughout its history women librarians were prominent, but no woman has been director of the library since 1940.

1976-100 "Top Level Women's Professional Group Includes Library/Information Science Women." LJ/SLJ Hotline 5 (January 12, 1976): 1-2.

Reports new network of Women's Information Services.

1976-101 "Women Library Workers Announce Strategy to Take Power from Men." LJ/SLJ Hotline 5 (January 12, 1976): 1.

Reports formation and activities of Women Library Workers, which claims nine active chapters.

1976-102 "Affirmative Action/Reverse Bias." LJ/SLJ Hotline 5 (January 19, 1976): 4.

Library Journal requests that libraries report charges of reverse discrimination.

1976-103 "Women Gaining in French Libraries." LJ/SLJ Hotline 5 (July 26, 1976): 5.

Decline in the number of male French librarians worries Geneviève Boisard of the Bibliothèque Nationale, who feels that feminine professions are down-graded. Summary of [1975-83].

1976-104 "Library Clerks Seek Parity with Liquor Clerks." LJ/SLJ Hotline 5 (February 16, 1976): 5.

Disparity between salaries of library clerks ($12,500) and liquor clerks ($15,200) is the basis of a complaint by Maryland library clerks before the Equal Employment Opportunities Commission.

1976-105 Lockhart, Helen. "Report of the ALA Councilor." Tennessee Librarian 28 (Spring 1976): 76-77.

Notes the establishment of the ALA Standing Committee on the Status of Women in Librarianship and lists its charges.

1976-106 "Discrimination Charged in Oakland Recruitment." LJ/SLJ Hotline 5 (March 15, 1976): 1.

Reports Carole Leita's testimony before Oakland, California city council that women have been overlooked for the director position of the Oakland Public Library.

1976-107 "Maryland Library Clerks Seek Parity with Liquor Clerks." Library Journal 101 (March 15, 1976): 770.

News item notes that Montgomery County library clerks who earn less than liquor store clerks have filed with the Equal Employment Opportunity Commission on the basis of sex discrimination (74 out of 75 liquor store clerks are men; 53 out of 57 library clerks are women).

1976-108 "Oakland Job Goes to a Woman." LJ/SLJ Hotline 5 (March 22, 1976): 1.

Notes appointment of Lelia White--the first time in 108 years that Oakland Public Library has had a woman director.

1976-109 Parsons, Jerry L. "Characteristics of Research Library Directors, 1958 and 1973, How Have They Changed?" Wilson Library Bulletin 50 (April 1976): 613-617.

In 1958 all directors were men. By 1973 there were five women directors.

1976-110 Peterson, Gary T. "Job Picture Brighter for Graduates of Media Programs in 1974-75." Audiovisual Instruction 21 (April 1976): 9-11.

Data on graduates of media programs from 1974 to 1975, including some who work in libraries, show breakdown by sex. Nearly half (49.9 percent) are women.

1976-111 Shepard, M. L. "Fourth Annual Placement and Salary Survey." Feliciter 22 (April 1976): 6-7.

Reports data on new graduates in Canadian library education programs by sex.

1976-112 "SRRT Backs Eric Moon for ALA President." LJ/SLJ Hotline 5 (April 5, 1976): 4.

Notes that questions put to ALA presidential candidates on ALA's responsibilities toward women's rights will appear in Library Journal and School Library Journal.

1976-113 Nyren, K. E. "Affirmative Action and Charges of Reverse Bias." Library Journal 101 (April 15, 1976): 985-987.

Library administrators respond to the question of "reverse bias" due to affirmative action.

1976-114 "ALA Equal Employment Subcommittee Guidelines for Library Affirmative Action Plans." American Libraries 7 (July/August 1976): 451-453, 475.

Guidelines developed by Equal Employment Opportunity Subcommittee of the ALA Office for Library Personnel Resources, for their use in reviewing affirmative action plans of libraries. Main categories include "Affirmative Action Authority" (policy statements, implementation, level of staff input, dissemination, schedules for review and revision); "Identification of Problem Areas" (utilization analysis, personnel procedures and practices); "Goals and Timetables" (are goals related to problems, adequate and set at appropriate levels); "Internal Audit and Reporting System" (format and frequency, who evaluates, report dissemination); and "Action Program" (scope, relevant to problem areas). Libraries are asked to send plans to the OLPR/EEO Subcommittee for evaluation.

1976-115 "ALA Offers Checklist and Advisory Service for Affirmative Action Plans." American Libraries 7 (July/August 1976): 451.

Describes background of ALA Council Equal Employment Opportunity Policy and Guidelines [1976-116] adopted by the ALA Office for Library Personnel Resources Equal Employment Opportunity Subcommittee in preparation for review of library affirmative action plans. Announces that libraries submitting plans will be listed in American Libraries and that confidential commentary on the plans will be conveyed to those submitting them.

1976-116 "Equal Employment Opportunity: a Statement of Policy of the American Library Association." American Libraries 7 (July/August 1976): 450-451.

Policy statement (ALA Policy 106.11) passed by ALA Council January 25, 1974 is reproduced.

1976-117 "Recent ALA Action and Policy on the Employment of Library Workers." American Libraries 7 (July/August 1976): 446-453, 475.

Four-part report includes sections on equal employment opportunity and affirmative action.

1976-118 "SLA Salary Survey of 1976." Herald of Library Science 15 (July-October 1976): 405-406.

Summarizes fourth triennial Special Libraries Association salary survey (1976-75), which notes male/female disparities in salaries.

1976-119 Toth, George. "Amend Equal Opportunity--Or Abolish It." American Libraries 7 (July/August 1976): 453.

Author finds that affirmative action discriminates against new graduates and suggests adoption of equal opportunity in a strained job market.

1976-120 Gray, Robert. "Survey of Librarians' Salaries." New Zealand Libraries 39 (August 1976): 132-133.

Requests that librarians fill out survey on salaries mailed by the New Zealand Library Association Salary Committee. Sex-related variables will be investigated.

1976-121 Glasser, L. "Bibliotekaryrket--et feministyrke" ("Library Profession--a Feminist Profession?") Bok og Bibliotek 43 (September 1976): 397-398.

Responds to [1976-22] which discusses the role of women in U.S. librarianship. Similar staffing situation in Norway (i.e. 84 percent or more women). Men are preferred for top jobs. (LISA abstract #76/3384).

1976-122 *Kickbusch, I. "Abschied von der Eule der Minerva; Frauen--offentlicher Dienst--Bibliothek." Buch und Bibliothek 28 (September 1976): 637-644.

Adapted from a paper given at the 1975 Annual conference of the Verein der Bibliothekare an Offentlichen Buchereien. Kickbusch points out that women librarians are considered a "disposable workforce" and urges solidarity to fight for emancipation. (LISA abstract #76/2758).

*Comment: Wrose, I. Buch und Bibliothek 29 (January 1977): 27-28.

1976-123 Singh, Jennifer. "Library Technicians/Mysteries." Emergency Librarian 4 (September/October 1976): 3-8.

Discussion of the role of library technicians in Canada concludes that in a female-dominated profession seeds of animosity have been sown by insensitive structures and hierarchies. Urges technicians to broaden themselves by examining the politics which affect the profession. Feminism and joining Women Library Workers were among ideas presented for learning about broader issues.

1976-124 Vazhko, O. "Liudi odnoi professii." Bibliotekar' 9 (September 1976): 50.

A report of a regional Moscow conference on the work-related and professional problems of female librarians, and plans of a "commission on work among women" for improvements in various areas.

1976-125 "Salaries: Up in Library School Faculties." LJ/SLJ Hotline 5 (September 6, 1976): 2.

Reports of library school faculty salaries shows women beginning to catch up to men, as reported in Bidlack's study [1976-34].

1976-126 "Affirmative Action in Md.: Fairfax Updates AA Plan." Library Journal 101 (September 15, 1976): 1250.

News item notes that Maryland's Fairfax County Public Library has upgraded its affirmative action plan.

1976-127 Ellenberger, Jack S. "The Condition of the Law Librarian in 1976." Law Library Journal 69 (November 1976): 626-640.

American Association of Law Librarians 69th Annual Meeting includes discussion by: Moderator--Jack S. Ellenberger; and panelists--Michael L. Renshawe, Stanley G. Irvine, and James Matarazzo. Repeats Frarey's 1970 survey [1970-35] of law librarians which received a return of 70 percent or 1,400 questionnaires. Women comprise 68 percent of the profession, showing an increasing proportion of women to men in law librarianship. Women still outnumber men in the small library, making up 81 percent. Median salary for men is approximately $16,000; for women $10,620. Professors are 68 percent men, assistant professors are 58 percent men and associate professors are 65 percent men. Close examination reveals that there is still salary discrimination in law librarianship, and the differential is widening between men and women.

1976-128 "The Library of Congress Equal Employment Opportunity Plan of Affirmative Action for Fiscal Year 1977." Library of Congress Information Bulletin 35 (December 3, 1976): 748-751.

Describes plan to promote equal employment opportunity at the Library of Congress.

1976-129 "LC Minority Employment, November 1976." Library of Congress Information Bulletin 35 (December 31, 1976): 804.

Tables show ethnic employment at the Library of Congress by grade. Breakdown by sex shows only 11.1 percent of those in grades 16-18 are women.

1977-01 Baer, Mark. "Special Libraries Association." In Bowker Annual, 22nd ed. New York: Bowker, 1977: 62-64.

Summary of association year 1976-1977 notes that a prime goal of the association has been reduction of the inequities between salaries paid to men and women. The brochure, Equal Pay for Equal Work: Women in Special Libraries [1976-04], was designed to help women in special libraries to improve their situation.

1977-02 Baker, Curtis O. and Wells, Agnes Q. Earned Degrees Conferred 1974-75: Summary Data. Washington, D.C.: GPO, 1977. (NCES 77-328).

Summary data on earned degrees includes library science bachelor's, master's, and doctorates by sex (Table 5).

1977-03 Boisse, Josette Anne. "Vermont." ALA Yearbook 1977. Chicago: ALA, 1977: 411-413.

Notes that the Vermont Library Association held a preconference on women titled, "If We're So Smart, Why Ain't We Rich?"

1977-04 Brugh, Anne E. and Beede, Benjamin R. "American Librarianship." In Library Literature 7--the Best of 1976. Edited by W. A. Katz. Metuchen, N. J.: Scarecrow, 1977: 16-31.

Reprint of [1976-52].

1977-05 Cheda, Sherrill. "Women in Canadian Librarianship." In ALA Yearbook 1977. Edited by Robert Wedgeworth. Chicago: ALA, 1977: 341.

Reports the 1976 activities of the Canadian Library Association's Status of Women Committee, which included support of native women. CLA budget cuts drastically reduced committee effectiveness. The study of career paths of librarians [1977-35] is described, as well as some data on non-professional library workers. Canadian library school curricula are criticized for not including material on the status of women in the field. Some Statistics Canada data for Canadian public libraries are cited.

1977-06 Dickinson, Elizabeth. "Personnel and Employment: Affirmative Action." In ALA Yearbook 1977. Edited by Robert Wedgeworth. Chicago: ALA, 1977: 237-239.

Published salary surveys for public and academic librarians are reviewed, as well as affirmative action programs for recruitment of women and minorities.

1977-07 Frankie, Suzanne, comp. ARL Annual Salary Survey 1976-1977. Washington, D.C.: Association of Research Libraries, 1977.

First Association of Research Library salary surveys to include sex as a variable. Highlights imbalance in the distribution of staff by sex and position with a special table (p. 4), and notes that men hold 72 percent of the top posts. In 16 of the 19 categories reported, men earned a higher average salary than women.

1977-08 Genova, B. K. L. et al. A Study of Salary Determinants Within the SUNY Librarians Association Between 1973 and 1974. Arlington, Va.: ERIC Document Reproduction Service, 1977: ED 134 189.

Contains 56 tables of data derived from a survey of 758 librarians employed at the State Universities of New York. Details salary rank, sex, education, and years of experience. Average earnings of women were lower than men's. Men moved up through the ranks more quickly.

Rank, years of experience and sex were found to be predictor variables for salary.

1977-09 Grant, W. Vance and Lind, C. George. Digest of Education Statistics, 1976 Ed. Washington, D.C.: GPO, 1977. (NCES 77-401).

Repeats information from the 1975 Bureau of Labor Statistics report on librarians by sex [1975-13], for elementary and secondary, college and university, public and special libraries (Table 180,, p. 198) as well as information on degrees conferred and enrollment for advanced degrees.

1977-10 Harris, Patricia R. "Council, ALA." In ALA Yearbook 1977. Edited by Robert Wedgeworth. Chicago: ALA, 1977: 104-106.

Section on "Race and Sexism Issues" includes the institution of a standing ALA Committee on the Status of Women in Librarianship, and a directive to ALA publishing to eliminate sexist language.

1977-11 Johnson, Richard D. "Academic Libraries." In ALA Yearbook 1977. Edited by Robert Wedgeworth. Chicago: ALA, 1977: 1-7.

Subsection "Salaries" (p. 5) includes summary of ACRL report by Talbot and von der Lippe on salaries [1976-59], which found that in academic libraries women earned less than men for every position and category.

1977-12 Josey, E. J. "Social Responsibilities." In ALA Yearbook 1977. Edited by Robert Wedgeworth. Chicago: ALA, 1977: 303-307.

Reports attention given to improving women's status in the profession in the form of comments by Women Library Workers (WLW) on hiring new directors for Oakland Public Library and San Francisco Public Library and establishment of an ALA Standing Council Committee on the Status of Women in Librarianship (p. 305). Additional information on women and ALA appears in the section "The American Library Association" (p. 306).

1977-13 Lawson, A. Venable. "Education, Library." In ALA Yearbook 1977. Edited by Robert Wedgeworth. Chicago: ALA, 1977: 112-116.

Report includes summary of faculty salary data (p. 114) as analyzed in [1976-34].

1977-14 Learmont, Carol L. and Darling, Richard D. "Placements and Salaries 1975: A Difficult Year." In Bowker Annual, 22nd ed. New York, Bowker, 1977: 345-360.

Reprint of [1976-56].

1977-15 Luethe, Marie. "The Status of Women and Ethnic Minorities Employed in the Libraries of the California State University and College System." Arlington, Va.: ERIC Document Reproduction Service, 1977: ED 127 984.

Master's research paper at California State University, Hayward, investigates possible discrimination at the California State University and Colleges System. Major findings: some discrimination within the system; less mobility for women; more men librarians were likely to be involved in professional associations; more women librarians belonged to unions.

1977-16 Lynch, Beverly P. "Association of College and Research Libraries." In ALA Yearbook 1977. Edited by Robert Wedgeworth. Chicago: ALA, 1977: 30-32.

Reprints tables (p. 30) from ACRL Talbot and von der Lippe report [1976-59] showing male salary advantage and includes brief discussion (p. 31).

1977-17 Lynch, Beverly P. "Women and Employment in Academic Librarianship." In Academic Libraries by the Year 2000. Edited by Herbert Poole. New York: Bowker, 1977: 119-127.

Considers sex discrimination in hiring, promotion, and compensation of women in libraries. Possible explanations of salary differentials are: fewer employment opportunities, interrupted careers, child care considerations, women's professional objectives, mobility, skills, publications activity. Notes a paucity of salary data that would create a clearer picture of the salary differentials between women and men in librarianship.

1977-18 Marchant, Maurice P., Smith, Nathan M. and Stirling, Keith H. SPSS as a Library Research Tool (School of Library and Information Sciences--Occasional Research Paper Number 1). Provo, Utah: Brigham Young University, 1977.

Authors use data appropriate for the study of sex discrimination in libraries to demonstrate the capabilities of SPSS. The origin of the data is not identified.

1977-19 Molenda, Michael. "AECT Member Opinion Survey: 1975-1976." In Educational Media Yearbook 1977. New York: Bowker, 1977: 52-56.

Summary of Association for Educational Communications and Technology member opinion survey [1977-42; 1977-49] notes that 73 percent of the membership is male.

1977-20 Nyren, Karl and Savage, Noël. "News Report 1976." In Bowker Annual, 22nd ed. New York: Bowker, 1977: 3-13.

Coverage of the year's events notes that several women have moved into top positions (p. 3), and a visible advance in receptivity to women's promotion (p. 6).

1977-21 Osso, Nicholas. *Statistics of Public School Library/Media Centers, 1974.* Washington, D.C.: GPO, 1977. (NCES 77-203).

Includes data on staff with and without certificates, by sex and highest degree (p. 29). Data on part-time staff by sex are also included (pp. 34-36).

1977-22 Ott, Mary Diederich. *Analysis of Doctor's Degrees Awarded to Men and to Women, 1970-1971 through 1974-75.* Washington, D.C.: GPO, 1977. (NCES 77-333).

Library science is categorized as a discipline with "high" female representation (39.9 percent) among doctoral recipients. Tables show degrees by sex for the years studied.

1977-23 Peterson, Gary T. "Media Manpower and the Future: Survey Results." In *Educational Media Yearbook 1977.* New York: Bowker, 1977: 52-56.

Includes degree production data on women and men.

1977-24 Pierce, Sydney. *Public Libraries and Affirmative Action; Exploiting the Resources of ALA.* Arlington, Va.: ERIC Document Reproduction Service, 1977: ED 127 963.

In a paper presented at ALA, Chicago, June 1976, the urgent need for more accurate statistics describing the ethnic and sexual composition of ALA is noted. Reveals that the Office for Library Personnel Resources seeks funding for such a survey.

1977-25 Ritzer, George. *Working: Conflict and Change*, 2nd ed. Englewood Cliffs, N.J.: Prentice-Hall, 1977: 179-188.

In the chapter, "Conflict in the Marginal Professions," librarianship is placed in the semi-professional category because it is dominated by women, and the power of the semi-professional is insufficient to overcome the power of those forces which oppose their efforts to professionalize.

1977-26 Sergean, R. *Librarianship and Information Work: Job Characteristics and Staffing Needs* (British Library Research and Development Reports. Report No. 5321 HC) London: British Library, 1977.

Part of the Sheffield Manpower Project [1976-93]. Section 10, "Staffing and the Roles of Men and Women," analyzes education and professional attainment of men and women and their relative positions. Only 56 percent of qualified women hold senior posts compared to 73 percent of the men. Men have more planning responsibilities and are paid better than women at all levels.

1977-27 Shearer, Kenneth D. and Carpenter, Ray L. "Public Library Support and Salaries in the Seventies." Bowker Annual, 22nd ed. New York: Bowker, 1977: 360-370.

[Reprint of 1976-43].

1977-28 Smith, Stanley V. Library Statistics of Colleges and Universities Fall 1975 Institutional Data. Washington, D.C.: GPO, 1977. (NCES 77-206).

This report is part of the NCES 10th annual Higher Education General Information Survey (HEGIS) and part of the first Library General Information Survey (LIBGIS). Data are reported for 2,922 public and private universities, four-year institutions with and without graduate programs, and two-year institutions. Table 5 (pp. 221-278) provides data for full-time professional staff by sex and highest degree and part-time professional staff by sex for each reporting library.

1977-29 Tees, Miriam. "Special Libraries." In ALA Yearbook 1977. Edited by Robert Wedgeworth. Chicago: ALA, 1977: 308-311.

Summarizes SLA triennial salary survey [1976-75] showing median women's salary is 19 percent below median men's.

1977-30 Weibel, Kathleen. "Women in Librarianship, Status of." ALA Yearbook 1977. Edited by Robert Wedgeworth. Chicago: ALA 1977: 328-329.

Reviews surveys and notes gains in the organizational spheres of librarianship (especially establishment of the Standing Committee on the Status of Women in Librarianship within ALA).

1977-31 "Womenpower and Librarianship: The Changing Career Pattern of Female Qualified Librarians Since 1945." In Report of the Commission on the Supply of and Demand for Qualified Librarians. London: Library Association, 1977: Appendix 4, xii-xviii.

Tables demonstrate the decline in the number of male chartered librarians from 1947 (45 percent) - 1976 (26 percent); the percentage of married women qualified but not practicing; the percentage of men and women in full-time posts by age; and women returning to their careers by 1976 who were not gainfully employed in 1963 and 1968. Discussion of future career prospects includes the observation that women wishing to return to their careers will have a very limited choice of posts.

1977-32 "Beyond Awareness: Women in Libraries Organize for Change." School Library Journal 23 (January 1977).

Major portion of this issue is devoted to women in libraries working to change sex discrimination. Focus is on three organizations: Women Library Workers, the ALA SRRT Task Force on Women and the ALA Standing Committee on the Status of Women in Librarianship.

1977-32A Gerhardt, L. N. "Before--and Since--Angie." School Library Journal 23 (January 1977): 6-8.

Editorial by Gerhardt introducing issue on women's organizations in librarianship reproduces a letter from C. Folsom (Librarian at the Boston Athenaeum from 1847 to 1856) written in 1856 which provides reasons why a woman should not be employed to charge books, relieve the Librarian when he goes to dinner and be generally useful. Folsom's objections included the occasion for indecent display of a woman's person as she ascended staircases; disarrangement of her clothing as she carried dusty books; lack of a suitable retiring room for females with sudden indisposition; the possibility of encountering the public as they issue from the urinal; and embarrassment caused modest men who might need to request a corrupt book. In spite of the fact that the introduction of female service might reduce expense, Folsom dissuades the Library Committee from such action. Gerhardt then observes that upon Folsom's retirement, his successor, W. F. Poole, hired Mrs. A. B. Harnden (perhaps the first woman to be employed in am American library). In search of more information on Harnden Gerhardt contacted the Athenaeum staff who confirmed that Harnden was the first woman employed and earned $260 a year. Unable to locate a photograph of Harnden, Gerhardt uses her case and Folsom's letter to introduce the issue on women's activism in the profession.

1977-32B Josephine, Helen B. "Beyond Awareness: Women in Libraries Organize for Change." School Library Journal 23 (January 1977): 31.

Introduces articles on three library women's groups: Women Library Workers, the ALA SRRT Task Force on Women, and the ALA Status of Women in Librarianship Committee.

1977-32C Josephine, Helen B. and Leita, Carole. "Women Library Workers." School Library Journal 23 (January 1977): 32-33.

Describes Women Library Workers as organized around issues rather than jobs. Efforts of Carole Leita, national organizer, who journeyed 2000 miles setting up 14 chapters, are outlined. Focal discussion points include realization that to give better service women require more decision-making power in libraries and need to know more about the politics of power.

1977-32D Kadanoff, Diane Gordon. "SRRT Task Force on Women." School Library Journal 23 (January 1977): 33-34.

A short history of the ALA SRRT Task Force on Women. Describes publications, conference activities, and political actions.

1977-32E Dickinson, Elizabeth. "ALA's Committee on Women in Librarianship." School Library Journal 23 (January 1977): 35-36.

A descriptive history of the formation of the ALA Standing Committee on the Status of Women in Librarianship. Describes the background of the committee's formation, the purpose of the committee, and its areas of concern.

1977-33 "California Librarians Tell Employers: Equal Pay for Equal Work!" Wilson Library Bulletin 51 (January 1977): 393-394.

Reports that Stanford University women librarians were awarded $50,000 in back pay and benefits as settlement of a grievance filed by Lise Giraud; success at San Diego Public Library is also reported.

1977-34 "San Diego Librarians Charge Sex Bias in Wages." Library Journal 102 (January 15, 1977): 152.

Describes San Diego Public Library Concerned Librarians' filing of a complaint of sex bias against the city. Data collected which document the charges show that librarians make less money than such city workers as buyers, assistant park designers, guidance counselors and recreation specialists. While salaries for beginning librarians fall in the "lower" range their educational requirements are in the "middle upper" range; most women (69 percent) in this classification are librarians.

1977-35 Fischer, Linda, Wasylycia-Coe, Mary Ann, Cheda, Sherrill, and Yaffe, Phyllis. The Career Paths of Male and Female Librarians in Canada: Report to the Canada Council. Supported by Canada Council Grant 574-1740. Submitted January 26, 1977.

Report of national study conducted in 1975. Although several articles [1978-37; 1981-96] were based on findings, the full report has never been released to the public. Examines the interrelationship between motivational and structural factors in career paths. Describes findings in 48 tables. Background data are also provided. A study of major importance.

1977-36 Bidlack, Russell E. "Faculty Salaries of 62 Library Schools, 1976-77." Journal of Education for Librarianship 17 (Spring 1977): 199-213.

Results of fourth survey of ALA accredited library schools reports salaries by sex and rank. Possession of doctorate and tenure status are also required. Seventy-seven percent of the deans and 89 percent of the directors are male. Data are reported for academic and fiscal year appointments.

1977-37 Kenney, Brigitte L. "AALS Conference Summary." Journal of Education for Librarianship 17 (Spring 1977): 254-273.

Report on new AALS interest group on "Women in Librarianship" in conference program coverage.

1977-38 Milden, James W. "Women, Public Libraries, and Library Unions: The Formative Years." <u>Journal of Library History</u> 12 (Spring 1977): 150-158.

Summarizes an "important and unwritten chapter in the history of female librarianship"--the story of early library unionism. Focus is on the New York Public Library Employees Union (formed 1917) with an exclusively female executive board and other early efforts in Washington, D.C. and Boston. Heated debate at the 1919 ALA conference is outlined including remarks by the "firebrand of early library unionists," Maude Malone, and the 121 to 1 vote against a resolution denouncing sexual inequality.

1977-39 American Library Association. Office for Library Personnel Resources. <u>Degrees and Certificates Awarded by U.S. Library Education Programs 1974-1975</u>. Chicago: ALA, March 1977 (mimeographed).

Continues [1975-79]. Reports numbers and types of degrees and certificates awarded by U.S. library education programs by sex and ethnicity.

1977-40 "Editors' Midwinter Notebook." <u>American Libraries</u> 8 (March 1977): 108; 138-146.

Coverage of 1977 Washington, D.C. ALA Midwinter Meeting includes recognition that the Intellectual Freedom Committee should develop a set of policies reflecting a clear consensus against sexism and racism (p. 140); a report on the LAD ad hoc committee to develop a model in-service program providing racism and sexism awareness training for personnel (p. 140); and a focus on women's groups at ALA, especially the Women Administrator's discussion group which called for an Old Girls Club (p. 145).

1977-41 Gerhardt, Lillian N., Cheatham, Bertha M., and Pollack, Pamela D. "ALA Midwinter Meeting '77." <u>School Library Journal</u> 23 (March 1977): 110-119.

Midwinter Meeting coverage notes that the ALA Council Committee on Committees brought in a white, four-man slate for two Executive Board seats, since geographic rather than sexual or racial balance was sought. Although four women were nominated from the floor, two men won (p. 110). Problems with the Intellectual Freedom Committee's Resolution on Racism and Sexism Awareness are outlined.

1977-42 Molenda, Michael and Cambre, Marjorie. "The 1976 AECT Member Opinion Survey: Income Comparisons." <u>Audiovisual Instruction</u> 22 (March 1977): 65-69.

First two parts of a four-part report on the Association for Educational Communications and Technology membership which report results by sex [1977-49]. Nearly three-quarters of the membership is male, in spite of the fact that new graduates in the field are evenly split between the sexes.

1977-43 Shepard, M. L. "Mobility and Flexibility Key Factors for U of T Grads." Feliciter 23 (March 1977): 6-7.

Provides data on graduates of the University of Toronto library education program. Sex of graduates is reported but salary by sex is not.

1977-44 "Continuing Reports on the Midwinter Meeting of the American Library Association, Washington D.C., January 30 - February 5, 1977." Library of Congress Information Bulletin 36 (March 11, 1977): 173-180.

Includes a report of a meeting of the ALA SRRT Task Force on Women (p. 180). Discussion about the TFW job roster, career counseling, newsletter subscription rates and a promotional brochures are reported.

1977-45 Christofferson, Rea. "The High Cost of Hiring." Library Journal 102 (March 15, 1977): 677-681.

In a general description of hiring procedures at the University of Georgia Libraries, several procedures related to affirmative action policies are described. Faculty appointments and the attendant procedures are sometimes avoided by hiring paraprofessionals instead. This hiring procedure is seen as counter-productive because it removes existing opportunities for women and minorities for professional employment.

Letter: Lansman, Jeanne, "Letter." Library Journal 102 (July 1977): 1432.

Protests implication that fair hiring practices are expensive and time consuming as a new excuse on the part of administrators for not hiring qualified women and minority persons into high paying and responsible positions.

1977-46 Horrocks, Norman. "A Few New Projects ... The Annual Meeting of the Association of American Library Schools January 26-30, 1977. Shoreham Hotel, Washington, D.C." Library Journal 102 (March 15, 1977): 688-689.

Notes foundation of a new interest group on Women in Librarianship and the report which supported the group, presented by Sydney Pierce and Kathleen Weibel. Its purposes will be to provide a forum for research on the position of women in librarianship; to foster greater awareness in library education of the present and potential impact of library education of women in the profession; and to identify means of encouraging broader career aspirations in women as students, practitioners, and library educators. Ellen Gay Detlefsen was named chair of the group.

1977-47 "It All Boiled Down To." Library Journal 102 (March 15, 1977): 682-691.

Coverage of 1977 ALA Midwinter Meeting in Washington, D.C. Includes reports on Racism/Sexism and the Intellectual Freedom Committee (p. 687), and the Women Administrator's Discussion Group's call for an "old girls network" (p. 690).

1977-48 Kellum-Rose, Nancy. "Affirmative Action in Libraries." Catholic Library World 48 (April 1977): 389-392.

Reports that although ALA has accepted affirmative action as official policy, it has so far failed to create equal employment opportunities for women and minorities. ALA SRRT surveys of Northern California libraries are cited which show the position of women and minorities in 1972 and 1974. No official ALA unit has addressed the issue of women in libraries; however, the SRRT Task Force on Women, the ALA Standing Committee on the Status of Women in Librarianship, and Women Library Workers are responding in various ways.

Comments: Casey, Philip. "Affirmative Action Can Be like the Boy with His Finger in the Dyke." Catholic Library World 48 (April 1977): 392.

Affirmative action means a fair deal for Spanish surnamed and black people. Proper attitude and skills may be substitutes for a degree in library science.

Field, Carolyn W. "Nancy Kellum-Rose Has Provided Many Facts." Catholic Library World 49 (April 1977): 390-391.

Identifies the fact that libraries have problems locating librarians from minority groups when positions and money are available. Questions the number of women who are interested in administrative positions.

Kelly, Gloria A. "Although the Author Presents a Bleak Enough Picture." Catholic Library World 48 (April 1977): 392.

Foresees positions of women in libraries worsening because of economic crisis. Instead of urging affirmative action policies, librarians should promote librarianship as an important community service.

Shapiro, Lillian L. "On The Whole I Find Little to Argue with in Ms. Kellum-Rose's Statement." Catholic Library World 48 (April 1977): 391-392.

Notes that affirmative action involves both recruiting women and minorities and promoting them once in the field. Advocates that advancement within the profession should be equal, but asks whether the librarian population will ever reflect the sexual and ethnic composition of the population as a whole.

Letters: Myers, Margaret and Salazar, Marilyn. "More on Affirmative Action in Libraries." Catholic Library World 49 (September 1977): 50.

Clarifies the position of ALA on affirmative action. Describes the establishment of the Equal Employment Opportunity Subcommittee of the Office for Library Personnel Resources and its activities.

Pierce, Sydney. "More on Affirmative Action in Libraries." Catholic Library World 49 (September 1977): 51.

Points out that guidelines for review of affirmative action plans have been written. They are available from the Equal Employment Opportunity Subcommittee of the ALA Office for Library Personnel Resources.

1977-49 Molenda, Michael and Cambre, Marjorie. "The 1976 Member Opinion Survey." Audiovisual Instruction 22 (April 1977): 47-51.

Second part of the membership survey of the Association for Educational Communications and Technology reveals a significant difference between women's and men's salaries. Women's income is nearly $3000 less than men's. It is suggested that this disparity occurs because 40 percent of the women members are found in library/joint media service positions. There are proportionately fewer women in the higher paying positions in education administration and commercial job categories. Survey results did not determine whether women received equal pay for equal work. See also part one [1977-42].

1977-50 Peterson, Gary T. "Graduates of Media Programs 1975-76: An Optimistic Study." Audiovisual Instruction 22 (April 1977): 19-21.

Includes degree production data on women and men.

1977-51 "Preliminary Report on Salary Survey." MLA News 89 (April 1977): 10-12.

Summarizes [1977-53]. Notes that 60 percent of directors in U.S. and Canadian medical school libraries are male and that they earn significantly more than women. Tables include mean basic salaries of librarians (excluding directors), directors, by NLM region and by years of professional experience.

1977-52 *"Besoldungs--and Vergutungsgruppen von Depl.--Bibliothekaren mach der Schnellstatistik 1976/77." (Salary and pay scales of certified librarians from the quick statistics 1976/77) Buch und Bibliothek 29 (May 1977): 354-355.

1977-53 Stangl, Peter and Hoke, William Neff. A Survey of Salaries of Medical School Librarians in the United States and Canada 1976-77.

Stanford, Calif.: Lane Library, Stanford University Medical Center, May 1977.

Report of an in-depth salary survey of medical school librarians in the United States and Canada, undertaken on behalf of the Medical Library Association Survey and Statistics Committee. Found that men earn consistently more than women in most subsets of the population, especially for positions of the greatest administrative responsibility. Includes 65 tables displaying cross-tabulated data.

1977-54 Walker, Susan. "Status of Women Committee C.L.A." Emergency Librarian 4 (May 1977): 3-5.

Traces the history of the Canadian Library Association's Status of Women Committee from its inception in 1975 as it grew out of the 1973 Task Force on the Status of Women. Emphasis is on the 1975 CLA conference [1976-46] which was focused on women in librarianship. In 1976 the committee organized a workshop on the rights of native women. An all-day conference on assertiveness training for women librarians planned for 1977 is described. Suggests that the future of the Status of Women Committee is in doubt, and questions the commitment of the CLA executive to the original goals of the Task Force. Many references are made to the Canada Council Study [1977-35].

Letter: Haycock, Ken. "Letter." Emergency Librarian 4 (July/August 1977): 2.

CLA president refutes report that he said the group had outlived its mandate.

1977-55 Hurst, Lannie. "Ina Coolbrith: Forgotten As Poet . . . Remembered As Librarian." PNLA Quarterly 41 (Summer 1977): 4-13.

A short biography of Ina Coolbrith describes her work with libraries in California. She was not the first public librarian in California, but among the first, and wished to be remembered as a librarian rather than as an author.

1977-56 Perkins, Stephanie and Brown, Gretchen Davidson. "Job Sharing and the Woman Librarian with Family Responsibilities." PNLA Quarterly 4 (Summer 1977): 14-17.

Explores the social and economic issues surrounding women who wish to enter the job market on a part-time basis. Describes the attitudes which prevent greater opportunities for this, such as Jesse Shera's [1965-10], but predicts a greater acceptance of half-time work. Carefully describing the difference between part-time work (which is repetitive and generally non-professional) and job sharing, the authors support job sharing because it has advantages in a competitive market, provides for specialization and allows women to meet family demands as well as career responsibilities.

1977-57 Van Alystyne, Carol et al. <u>Women and Minorities in Administration of Higher Education Institutions: Employment Patterns and Salary Comparisons</u>. Washington, D.C.: College and University Personnel Association, June 1977.

Survey of administrative positions in higher education for: white coeducational institutions; white women's institutions; white men's institutions; and minority institutions. Data on head librarians include employment shares, job concentration, salary comparisons, and median salaries broken out by sex and ethnicity.

1977-58 "Semiannual Report on Developments at the Library of Congress June 1977." <u>Library of Congress Information Bulletin</u> 36 (June 10, 1977): 379-412.

Programs held by the Women's Program are reported. Among them is a request to prepare a four-year comparison of the status of women at the Library by division and department.

1977-59 Learmont, Carol L. and Darling, Richard L. "Placements & Salaries 1976: A Year of Adjustment." <u>Library Journal</u> 102 (June 15, 1977): 1345-1351.

New women graduates from ALA accredited programs lagged $400 behind men in starting salaries.

1977-60 "Attacking the 'Woman's Profession' Barrier." <u>LJ/SLJ Hotline</u> 6 (June 20, 1977): 6.

Announces workshop at California Library Association meeting to spur the movement to end sex discrimination in libraries.

1977-61 Holcomb, Morrigene. "Women's Program Survey of the Special Recruit/Intern Program." <u>Library of Congress Information Bulletin</u> 36 (June 24, 1977): 445-447.

Describes a study done by the Library Women's Program Advisory Committee which shows the difference between the careers of men and women recruits. There are seven tables broken down by sex.

1977-62 Freedwoman, Janet. "Sheehy's Passages and Ours." <u>Emergency Librarian</u> 4 (July 1977): 9-10.

The myriad activities of women librarian support groups at ALA's annual conference in Detroit are reported. The Task Force on Women sponsored Gail Sheehy, who discussed her book, <u>Passages</u>. The Library Administration Division provided a forum for women aspiring to administrative positions. Some concern over the divisiveness of the many women's groups is expressed. The Women Library Workers meeting at the Detroit Feminist Women's City Club is described and the success of the ALA Committee on the Status of Women motion to boycott states that have not ratified the ERA is documented.

1977-63 Goldstein, Rachael K. "Women and Health Sciences Librarianship: An Overview." Bulletin of the Medical Library Association 65 (July 1977): 321-329.

Discusses implications of underrepresentation of women in the administration of health science libraries and suggests courses of action.

Letter: Teich, Steve. "Women and Health Sciences Librarianship." Bulletin of the Medical Library Association 65 (October 1977): 458.

Percentages of women heading health sciences libraries in 1950 are misleading because veterans of World War II were just entering the job market.

Ambrose, Karen S. "Power, Women and MLA." Bulletin of the Medical Library Association 66 (January 1978): 66-67.

Offers a table (p. 67) of "Percentage of men and women in elected and appointed positions in MLA" which shows that 35 percent of the positions are filled by men (who make up 15 percent of the membership). Suggests that women rule the membership by virtue of sheer numbers, but do not appear to seek control of power because they willingly vote for men for office.

1977-64 "ALA Steps Lively Through Detroit." American Libraries 8 (August 1977): 370-390.

Reports ALA's resolution not to schedule conference in states that have not passed ERA (p. 377); SRRT Task Force on Women meetings; and formation of two new discussion groups: LAD's for Women Library Administrators and RASD's on Women's Materials and Women Library Users.

1977-65 Berry, John. "The Key Word Was Access." Library Journal 102 (August 1977): 1555-1572.

ALA Annual Conference coverage notes Council extension of the resolution on sexism and racism awareness to include in a survey of library schools a question to discover the extent to which the schools include awareness training against "prejudices, stereotyping, and discrimination because of race, sex, and creed, color, and national origin" in their curricula; and instruction to LAD's Personnel Administration Section to develop a model in-service training for the same purpose.

1977-66 "LC Minority Employment, May 1977." Library of Congress Information Bulletin 36 (August 5, 1977): 525.

Table shows pay systems, number of full-time employees, breakdown by sex and percent change since 1976. Categories GS 16-18 are 87 percent male and 13 percent female. Women gained only 1.9 percent since 1976.

1977-67 "Announcements." Library of Congress Information Bulletin 36 (August 12, 1977): 548.

Announces an open meeting of the Women's Program Advisory Committee scheduled for August 26. Notes that this date is also Women's Equality Day.

1977-68 "Continuing Reports on the Annual Conference of the American Library Association, Detroit, Michigan, June 17-23, 1977." <u>Library of Congress Information Bulletin</u> 36 (August 12, 1977): 551-560.

Report on the ALA Committee on the Status of Women in Librarianship includes ERA activity; a recommended resolution deleting sexist language from the Library Bill of Rights; the possibility of developing a profile of ALA members; report on the Women's Advisory Committee of the Library of Congress; and liaisons with other women's interest groups.

1977-69 Wolfskill, Mary. "Women's Equality Day Observed." <u>Library of Congress Information Bulletin</u> 36 (August 19, 1977): 561-564.

Recounts the genesis of the Women's Program Office, renamed the Women's Program Advisory Committee, and describes its concerns.

1977-70 "New Members Sought for Women's Program Advisory Committee." <u>Library of Congress Information Bulletin</u> 36 (August 26, 1977): 579-580.

Outlines the requirements for Committee membership and describes Committee concerns.

1977-71 "ALA/ERA--Where Do You Stand?" <u>Louisiana Library Association Bulletin</u> 40 (Fall 1977): 38.

Opening paragraph describes ALA Council vote to boycott states that had not ratified ERA. Considering that Louisiana is one such state and that New Orleans is a possible ALA conference site, LLA members are asked to vote yes or no on the resolution. Pro-ERA statements are offered by Bonita Brown; con-ERA by Meb Norton.

1977-72 Frye, Larry. "Survey of Salaries in West Virginia Academic Libraries." <u>West Virginia Libraries</u> 30 (Fall/Winter 1977): 34-41.

Notes that women are paid 15 percent less than men when all institutions are compared. Men hold most director posts and earn 35 percent more than women. Tables provide comparative data for directors, and public and technical services librarians, by sex and type of institution.

1977-73 Rudy, Michelle. "Equity and Patterns of Library Governance." <u>Library Trends</u> 26 (Fall 1977): 181-193.

Examines methods of effecting social change in library governance by identifying the effect of legislating equity. Offers insight into why it is difficult for women and minorities to achieve equity by working within the system.

1977-74 Collins, Carol. "Carefully Prepared Campaign." Wyoming Library Roundup 33 (September 1977): 16-17.

Describes how women on the staff of the George Amos Memorial Library used their experience at a Wyoming Library Association workshop, "Teamwork Produces Results" to work on a problem defined as "inadequacy of wages for female staff." The women developed charts showing the discrepancy between take-home pay and cost of living, and presented their results to the county commission, which earned them an eventual 25 percent increase for full-time female staff.

1977-75 Gerhardt, Lillian N., Cheatham, Bertha M. and Pollack, Pamela D. "Issues, Arguments, Actions: ALA in Detroit." School Library Journal 24 (September 1977): 27-37.

Coverage of ALA's 96th Annual Conference includes Council's agreement to meet no longer in states that have failed to ratify the Equal Rights Amendment.

1977-76 "The Month in Review." Wilson Library Bulletin 52 (September 1977): 16-20.

Includes discussion in section, "ALA's Resolution on ERA Making Waves," of ALA's ERA boycott as reported in the New York Times of August 1, 1977. Reports that ALA Executive Director, Robert Wedgeworth, sent letters to governors and mayors in affected states with copies to Chambers of Commerce and presidents of state library associations notifying them of ALA's position. Chris Hoy, ALA conference coordinator, notified states which had not ratified ERA with options for conferences of the decision to boycott. Since the average conference-goer spends $375 during a five-day meeting and ALA's conferences attract 10,000, the loss to these cities is significant.

1977-77 "Professional Librarians of Temple University Have Filed a Class Action Sex Discrimination Complaint with the Equal Employment Opportunity Commission against the University Administration on the Basis of the Low Salaries Paid to Those Who Work in a Woman's Occupation." College and Research Libraries News 8 (September 1977): 246-247.

Describes class action complaint filed with EEOC.

1977-78 "Temple Librarians File Sex Bias Complaint." Library Journal 102 (September 1, 1977): 1707-1708.

Describes the failure of a second attempt to align librarian salaries with other faculty salaries at Temple University in Philadelphia. With backing of 51 of 53 librarians, a class action suit was filed with the EEOC by the AAUP.

Annotated Bibliography 1977-85   37

1977-79 "Reports on the 66th Annual Conference of the Special Libraries Association, New York, N.Y. June 5-9, 1977." <u>Library of Congress Information Bulletin</u> 36 (September 16, 1977): 633-660.

Summary of the second general session includes major points by Pat Carbine of <u>Ms.</u> magazine in her speech " . . . But Can He Type."

1977-80 "Alabama First Non-Era State to Squawk at ALA Boycott Plans." <u>LJ/SLJ Hotline</u> 6 (September 15, 1977): 1.

Alabama State Librarian, Tony Miele, condemns ALA for its stand on ERA.

1977-81 <u>Information Management in the 1980's</u> (Conference Program of 1977 American Society for Information Science 40th Annual Meeting held September 26-October 1, 1977). Washington, D.C.: ASIS, 1977.

The only documentation of a short-lived ASIS women's caucus appears in this program.

1977-82 "Library of Congress Equal Employment Opportunity Plan of Affirmative Action for Fiscal Year 1978." <u>Library of Congress Information Bulletin</u> 36 (September 30, 1977): 679-690.

Section VI, "Women and Minorities in Management" outlines the problem, the remedy sought, and objectives for fiscal year 1978. Other sections on career counseling target women as well.

1977-83 "Library Schools Present Statistical Reports for 1975-76." <u>Feliciter</u> 23 (October 1977): 4-6.

Statistics are generally reported as of October 1, 1976. Tables include "Degrees Awarded, Placements," "Geographic Placements," "Type of Library Placement," "Salaries," and "Number of Applicants." No analyses are presented. However, the small numbers of men would make generalizations meaningless.

1977-84 "Sex Discrimination Complaint: Professional Librarians at Temple University Have Filed a Class Action Complaint." <u>Herald of Library Science</u> 16 (October 1977): 448.

"Notes and News" section briefly describes Temple University librarians' class action sex discrimination complaint.

1977-85 "Sex Bias Charged in Milwaukee Firing." <u>Library Journal</u> 102 (October 1, 1977): 1977.

Library staff member, Nancy W. Boone, charged sex bias as a factor in her dismissal as coordinator of fine arts at Milwaukee Public Library. She was backed by the EEOC, which investigated the case and recommended that the Department of Justice bring suit against the library.

1977-86 "More on ALA's Equal Rights Amendment Stand." LJ/SLJ Hotline 6 (October 10, 1977): 1.

Notes response of COSWL Chair, Ellen Gay Detlefsen, to Tony Miele (Alabama State Librarian) who protested ALA's boycott of states which had not ratified ERA. Louisiana also complained.

1977-87 "ALA Women's Rights Stand: Alabama Warns of Impact." Library Journal 102 (October 15, 1977): 2105-2106.

Reports response of Anthony Miele, head of the Alabama Public Library Service, to the ERA boycott. Told by Governor George Wallace that the boycott might affect libraries, Miele wrote ALA Executive Director, Robert Wedgeworth, that he was appalled that ALA would be foolish enough to become embroiled in social and political issues.

Letters: Schwebke, Ruth N. "Supporting Equality." Library Journal 103 (February 15, 1978): 410.

Finds Alabama response highly ironic in light of the impact inequality has had on women's lives and careers.

Sellen, Betty-Carol. "ALA, Ala., & ERA." Library Journal 103 (February 15, 1978): 410.

Responds to news item as "refreshing" but is disheartened by Miele's lack of understanding.

Parsons, Jerry L. "Ala., ALA, ERA." Library Journal 103 (August 1978): 1450.

Notes ALA is not dictating to anyone, but reminds readers that controversial actions beget consequences.

Rufe, Charles P. "Ala., ALA & ERA." Library Journal 103 (August 1978): 1450.

Responds to Sellen and ERA proponents that their "sometimes summary actions begin to resemble the behavior of which they accuse their 'oppressors.'"

1977-88 "Making More Money as a Librarian." American Libraries 8 (November 1977): 578-579.

In response to American Libraries query, "If your salary is greater than $35,000 would you offer a few words of wit, wisdom ... or inspiration to benefit those who despair of ever earning a decent income as a librarian?" editors note that of 25 library trained persons, most of the women answered, "Thanks for the compliment, but I'm very sorry to say I don't earn that much." Of the seven printed replies, several authors mention being white and male is helpful, as well as contact with the 'old boy' network. Letters are mostly tongue in cheek.

1977-89 "Career Development for Women Librarians." LJ/SLJ Hotline 6 (November 7, 1977): 4.

Reports a series of "needs assessment workshops" to be held at the University of Washington School of Librarianship to meet the needs of women.

1977-90 Wert, Lucille M. "1977 Conference-Editorial Viewpoint." Journal of Education for Librarianship 17 (Winter 1977): 179-181.

Includes report of new AALS interest on "Women in Librarianship."

1977-91 Cheatham, Bertha M. "SLJ's 1977 News Roundup." School Library Journal 24 (December 1977): 17-23.

Describes Status of Women Committee efforts to promote ALA involvement in women's issues; lists states that have not ratified the Equal Rights Amendment; reports ALA Council activity in favor of the ERA, and summarizes correspondence between Anthony Miele and Robert Wedgeworth about ALA's ERA boycott of states which have not ratified the ERA.

1977-92 "Head-on Collision: ALA in Motor City." Wilson Library Bulletin 51 (December 1977): 30-44.

Special section on "Women's Work: (pp. 38-39) in ALA Annual Conference coverage reports Council's passage of a resolution to hold conferences after 1981 only in cities that have ratified the ERA. Meetings of the Library Administration Division's Women's Discussion Group and RASD Women's Users Group are mentioned. Notes that Women Library Workers will hold a national meeting in 1978 and reports activities of the SRRT Task Force on Women.

1977-93 "ALA Equal Rights Stand Draws Louisiana Protest." Library Journal 102 (December 1, 1977): 2382-2383.

Reports Louisiana State Librarian has decried endorsement of the Equal Rights Amendment as a prerequisite to holding library conferences in his state. Alabama's protest is also noted.

1978-01 Almquist, Elizabeth M. and Wehrl-Einhorn, Juanita L. "The Doubly Disadvantaged: Minority Women in the Labor Force." In Women Working: Theories and Facts in Perspective. Edited by Ann H. Stromberg and Shirley Harkess. Palo Alto, Calif.: Mayfield Publishing, 1978: 71.

Notes that between 1960 and 1970, nearly one-fourth of employed black women moved into clerical occupations and female-dominated professions, including librarianship.

1978-02 American Library Association. Office for Library Personnel Resources. Degrees and Certificates Awarded by U.S. Library Education Programs 1973-1976. Compiled by Barbara O. Slanker. Chicago: ALA, 1978. (mimeographed).

Continues [1975-79] and [1977-39]. Reports numbers and types of degrees and certificates awarded by U.S. library education programs by sex and ethnicity.

1978-03 Blau, Francine D. "The Data on Women Workers, Past, Present, and Future." In Women Working: Theories and Facts in Perspective. Edited by Ann H. Stromberg and Shirley Harkess. Palo Alto, Calif.: Mayfield, 1978: 44.

Uses 1950 and 1970 census data to show that men had moved into female dominated professions such as librarianship.

1978-04 Brown, George H. Doctoral Degree Awards to Women. Washington, D.C.: National Center for Educational Statistics, 1978. (NCES).

Notes that the increase in women recipients of the doctorate has been steady from 1971 to 1976. Library science is the third highest field with 45 percent of degrees awarded to women in 1976--a 25.9 percent gain since 1971 (pp. 2-3). In terms of percentage gain over the period studied, library science ranked highest (p. 4). Discussion includes remarks that the highest gain has been in "women's fields." An appendix gives year-by-year breakdowns by sex and discipline.

1978-05 Brown, George H. Master's Degree Awards to Women. Washington, D.C.: GPO, 1978. (NCES 78-336C).

Table 1 (p. 2) gives 1971 and 1976 data for general awards of master's degrees by sex. Table 2 shows library science master's degrees awarded as a percentage of all master's degrees for men and women.

1978-06 Cheatham, Bertha M. "1977 News Roundup in Children's and Young Adult Services." In Bowker Annual, 23rd ed. New York: Bowker, 1978: 22-23.

Reprint of [1977-91].

1978-07 Cooper, Michael D. California's Demand for Librarians: Projecting Future Requirements. Berkeley: University of California, Institute of Governmental Studies, 1978.

Includes observations on women in chapter, "Replacement Demand." Observes a different replacement rate for men and women (p. 65).

1978-08 Dickinson, Elizabeth and Myers, Margaret. "Affirmative Action and American Librarianship." In Advances in Librarianship, v. 8. Edited by Michael H. Harris. New York: Academic, 1978: 81-133.

General overview of the legal and socioeconomic aspects of affirmative action, as well as the present commitment within librarianship to this concept. Includes discussion of women in programs of library education (pp. 89-90), the employment picture for women (pp. 90-94), prospects for the future, and research needs.

1978-09 Eckard, Helen M. Statistics of Public Libraries, 1974. Washington, D.C.: GPO, 1978. (NCES 77-200)

Data from the Library General Information Surveys (LIBGIS I) report include information on public library staff by sex and highest degree for full and part-time employees (pp. 37-40).

1978-10 Fennell, Janice Clinedinst. "A Career Profile of Women Directors of the Largest Academic Libraries in the United States: An Analysis and Description of Determinants." Ph.D. thesis. Florida State University, 1978. (DAI 7909754)

Develops a composite career profile of eleven women directors of the largest academic libraries in the United States using the interview research method. Fifteen conclusions describe the general characteristics of current (1978) women directors of large academic libraries.

1978-11 Frankie, Suzanne O. ARL Annual Salary Survey, 1976-1977. Arlington, Va.: ERIC Document Reproduction Service, 1978: ED 148 348.

Microreproduction of [1977-07].

1978-12 Frankie, Suzanne O. "Association of Research Libraries." In ALA Yearbook 1978. Edited by Robert Wedgeworth. Chicago: ALA, 1978: 38-41.

Includes table reporting 1976-77 salaries by sex (p. 39) and tables reporting minority salaries by sex (p. 40).

1978-13 Goldstein, Rachael. Women and Biomedical Library Administration. New York: Mount Sinai School of Medicine, Levy Library, 1978).

This book, part of an instructional package for a one-day workshop, is designed to meet six objectives, including examining factors that impede women's administrative career movement; coping with stereotypes; and analyzing conflicting career and home responsibilities. Tables include percentage of head librarians by sex from 1950 to 1972 (p. 3); and earnings by type of library (p. 5). Uses question-and-answer format and contains selected bibliographies.

1978-14 Grant, W. Vance and Lind, C. George. Digest of Education Statistics, 1977-78. Washington, D.C.: GPO, 1978 (NCES 78-402).

Reprints information from earlier reports in this series on librarians by sex for elementary and secondary, college and university, public and special libraries (Table 185, p. 189). Statistics on public librarians

42   1978-15 Annotated Bibliography

by population served (Table 184, p. 189) and public school media librarians (Table 186, p. 190) by sex are reported. Library science degrees conferred and enrollment for advanced degrees are also reported.

1978-15   Griffen, Agnes M. "Personnel and Employment: Affirmative Action." In ALA Yearbook 1978. Edited by Robert Wedgeworth. Chicago: ALA, 1978: 223-227.

Annual report on affirmative action includes a section on the status of women.

1978-16   Grimm, James W. "Women in Female-Dominated Professions." In Women Working: Theories and Facts in Perspective. Edited by Ann H. Stromberg and Shirley Harkess. Palo Alto, Calif.: Mayfield, 1978: 293-315.

Provides an overview of female-dominated professions, including librarianship. Describes the extent of female domination, characteristics of the profession, income differentials, and future prospects.

1978-16a   Grotzinger, Laurel. "Dewey's 'Splendid Women' and Their Impact on Library Education." In Milestones to the Present: Papers from Library History Seminar V. Edited by Harold Goldstein. Syracuse, N.Y.: Gaylord Professional Publications, 1978: 125-152.

Describes Melvil Dewey's efforts to develop library education and the women who worked with him.

1978-16b   Detlefsen, Ellen Gay. "Commentary." In Milestones to the Present: Papers from Library History Seminar V. Edited by Harold Goldstein. Syracuse, N.Y.: Gaylord Professional Publications, 1978: 152-154.

Notes that author should be commended for her assemblage of facts. Suggests that these women are interesting because of their "intellectual, emotional, and physical attachments to Melvil Dewey, and their being part of that extended family around him."

1978-16c   Holley, Edward G. "Scholars, Gentle Ladies, and Entrepreneurs: American Library Leaders, 1876-1976." In Milestones to the Present: Papers from Library History Seminar V. Edited by Harold Goldstein. Syracuse, N.Y.: Gaylord Professional Publications, 1978: 80-108.

Mentions that there are "major contributions as well as a good deal of nonsense in the re-examination of the role of women in the [library] profession." Notes Dee Garrison's article, "The Tender Technicians" [1972-73]. Offers short career biographies of several "gentle ladies" of library leadership (pp. 89-92).

1978-17   Johnson, Richard D. "Academic Libraries." In ALA Yearbook 1978. Edited by Robert Wedgeworth. Chicago: ALA, 1978: 4-13.

Includes notice of Temple University librarians class action sex discrimination complaint (p. 5) and salary information by sex (p. 13).

1978-18 Kato, Komei et al. "Woman Librarianship: Cases of Private College and University Libraries in Japan 1977." Library and Information Science 16 (1978): 253-280. (Abstracted in Library and Information Science Abstracts as item 79/3481).

"The 1977 statistics of the Japan Association of Private University and College Libraries show that the ratio of female to male library staff is 53.6 percent. About 60 percent of the women had left work within the five-year period 1973 to 1977 either to marry or have children and did not return. Social pressure forces women to devote themselves to their families and there is no system of reinstatement. As a result, a study group was established within the Mita Society for Library and Information Science and carried out a survey to assess awareness of female librarians about their roles. They expressed their dissatisfaction about management's failure to inform them of their library's line policy, and felt little confidence in their superiors. Other results are analyzed." (LISA)

1978-19 Learmont, Carol L. and Darling, Richard L. "Placements and Salaries, 1976: A Year of Adjustment." In Bowker Annual, 23rd ed. New York: Bowker, 1978.

Reprint of [1977-59].

1978-20 Little, Robert David. "Public Library Statistics. Analysis of NCES Survey." In Bowker Annual, 23rd ed. New York: Bowker, 1978: 248-256.

Summary of data frm LIBGIS I [1978-09] shows predominance of women. Of full-time public library staff, 83.2 percent were women (p. 249).

1978-21 Little, Robert David. "Public School Library Media Center Statistics: Analysis of NCES Survey." In Bowker Annual, 23rd ed. New York: Bowker, 1978: 256-265.

Summary of NCES data notes full-time certified library staff was composed of seven times as many women as men (p. 265).

1978-22 Martin, Jean Krieg. "Factors Related to the Representation of Women in Library Management." M.A. thesis, University of Georgia, 1978.

Study of a sample of university librarians employed at Association of Research Libraries institutions. Examines variables related to promotion and salary for male and female librarians.

1978-23 Muriuki, M. N. "The Role of Women in African Librarianship--the Next 25 years." In Libraries and Information Services as

44   1978-24 Annotated Bibliography

<u>Instruments of Transition to the 21st Century in Africa: Proceedings of SCECSAL (Standing Conferences of Eastern, Central and Southern African Librarians) 2, Lusaka, October 4-9, 1976.</u> Lusaka, Zambia Library Association, 1978: 79-82.

After a brief history of women in libraries throughout the world, writer exhorts librarians to face the future . . . and women's "attribute of receptiveness should come in handy."

1978-24   Patterson, Michelle and Engelberg, Laurie. "Women in Male-Dominated Professions." In <u>Women Working: Theories and Facts in Perspective</u>. Edited by Ann Stromberg and Shirley Harkess. Palo Alto, Calif.: Mayfield, 1978: 268.

Discusses sex-typing of professions, calling librarianship a subordinate profession.

1978-25   Peterson, Gary T. "Media Manpower: Trusting the Trends or Making Them?" In <u>Educational Media Yearbook 1978</u>. Edited by James W. Brown. New York: Bowker, 1978: 68-72.

Degree production data for media graduates are broken down by sex.

1978-26   Ritchie, Sheila. <u>Career Aspirations of Female Librarians in English Public Libraries</u>. London: Elm Publications, 1978.

Investigates aspirations of women librarians through surveys of public libraries, library schools, and public librarians, as well as through literature searching. Five factors are examined: career length, qualifications, desire for promotion, present status, and the climate of employment. Author concludes that women are not represented in top library positions, have lower career aspirations, do not intend to retire earlier than men, and receive lower salaries. Tables and charts occupy a large portion of the paper.

1978-27   Savage, Noel. "News Report 1977." In <u>Bowker Annual</u>, 23rd ed. New York: Bowker, 1978: 3-22.

Reprint of [1978-46].

1978-28   <u>SHARE: A Directory of Feminist Library Workers</u>, 3rd ed. Compiled by Carole Leita. Berkeley, Calif: Women Library Workers, 1978.

Directory of feminist women employed in libraries expands first and second editions [1975-18, 1976-58] by including non-members of Women Library Workers. Arranged by state with subject and name indexes.

1978-29   Slanker, Barbara O. "Research." In <u>ALA Yearbook 1977</u>. Edited by Robert Wedgeworth. Chicago: ALA, 1978: 285-289.

ACRL study by Talbot and von der Lippe [1976-59] is summarized in section on surveys (p. 288).

1978-30 Smith, Ralph E. "Prospects for Women in the Paid Labor Market." In <u>Changing Times: Changing Libraries</u>. Edited by George S. Bonn and Sylvia Faibisoff. Urbana: University of Illinois, Graduate School of Library Science, 1978: 59-69.

General discussion about women in the labor force and their future prospects. Notes occupational segregation in librarianship (p. 61).

Response: Cooney, Jane. In <u>Changing Times: Changing Libraries</u>. Edited by George S. Bonn and Sylvia Faibisoff. Urbana: University of Illinois, Graduate School of Library Science, 1978: 70-79.

Response to Smith includes a summary of the Bureau of Labor Statistics report, <u>Library Manpower</u> [1975-13]; general remarks on the status of women in libraries illustrated with tabular data; salary discussion of male and female inequities with a focus on Canadian data; and exploration of the equal value concept.

1978-31 Smith, Stanley V. and Wells, Agnes Q. <u>Earned Degrees Conferred 1975-76</u>. Washington, D.C.: GPO, 1978 (NCES 78-300).

Reports bachelor's, master's and doctoral degrees awarded in library science by sex.

1978-32 Stangl, Peter and Hoke, William Neff. <u>A Survey of Salaries of Medical School Librarians in the United States and Canada 1976-77</u>. Arlington, Va.: ERIC Document Reproduction Service, 1978: ED 143 365.

Microreproduction of [1977-53].

1978-33 Stromberg, Ann H. and Harkess, Shirley. "Editors' Introduction." In <u>Women Working: Theories and Facts in Perspective</u>. Palo Alto, Calif.: Mayfield, 1978: 259.

Views occupational hierarchies in professional positions. Librarianship and nursing are associated with women while law and medicine are linked to men.

1978-34 Weibel, Kathleen. "Women in Librarianship, Status of." In <u>ALA Yearbook 1978</u>. Edited by Robert Wedgeworth. Chicago: ALA, 1978: 321-324.

Reviews the status of women in the profession during 1977. Focus is on statistical data; placements for 1976; and library-education faculty information. Status actions and the activities of various ALA women's groups are emphasized. Canadian information is also reported as studied in a national research project [1977-35]. The growth of Women Library Workers as a national organization is described.

1978-35 Ambrose, Karen S. "Power, Women and MLA." <u>Bulletin of the Medical Library Association</u> 66 (January 1978): 67-68.

Suggests that the imbalance of women in positions of power in MLA was brought about by the women themselves. Women should have control of the association by virtue of their numbers, but they relinquish control by allowing men to have a greater representation in elected positions. Table on page 67 shows percentage of men and women in elected and appointed positions in MLA.

1978-36 "Board Approves Task Force on Women." <u>Focus on Indiana Libraries</u> 32 (January/February 1978): 1.

Describes formation, and objectives of an Indiana Library Association Task Force on the Status of Women. Names of Task Force members are listed.

1978-37 Cheda, Sherrill, Fischer, Linda, Wasylycia-Coe, Mary Ann and Yaffee, Phyllis. "Salary Differentials of Female and Male Librarians in Canada." <u>Emergency Librarian</u> 5 (January-February 1978): 3-13.

Reports salary data from major study of the career paths of librarians [1977-35]. Reasons for the differential between women and men are explored for variables of education, career interruptions, motivation and aspiration. Most myths about discrimination are dispelled and sex remains as the primary differentiating factor.

Letter: Cheda, Sherrill et al. "Omission." <u>Emergency Librarian</u> 5 (March 1978): 22.

Justification of the exclusion of data in the reporting of salary differentials is made, by the fact that some sub-categories of position levels were too small to be included.

1978-38 Coughlin, Caroline M. "Children's Librarians: Managing in the Midst of Myths." <u>School Library Journal</u> 24 (January 1978): 15-18.

Analyzes the historical role of woman as nurturer and its effect on the perceived role of the children's librarian. Explores the shift of emphasis from "dispensing goodness" to "dispensing ideas" on the part of all librarians and the impact this shift could create on children's librarians. Referring to Henning and Jardim's <u>The Managerial Women</u>, the article concludes with methods women children's librarians may use to "manage children's services wisely and avoid being trapped by myths."

1978-39 "Editorial." <u>Emergency Librarian</u> 5 (January-February 1978): 2.

Introduces the salary article [1978-37] on the study to investigate the status of women in Canadian libraries.

1978-40 "Expressing Disapproval of the Film, 'The Speaker.'" American Libraries 9 (January 1978): 4.

California Library Association goes on record supporting the concept of "comparable wages for comparable work" and backs San Diego public librarians in their salary dispute.

1978-41 Gerhardt, Lillian N. "Of Bottom Lines and Top Jobs." School Library Journal 24 (January 1978): 5.

Editorial discusses best selling books which offer women tips on career advancement. Notes that library service is not a "money-grubbing business," but suggests that similar obstacles block women in many occupations.

Letter: Boyd, Barbara Gray. "Step Right Up . . . " School Library Journal 24 (March 1978): 61.

Describes a job of assistant county librarian at Berkeley Public Library. Notes that it is administrative, vacant, and that few women have applied for it.

Orr, Nancy A. "Career Traps." School Library Journal 24 (May 1978): 3.

Finds that editorial is relevant to the role of the children's librarian.

1978-42 "Librarians among Women on the Move in Houston." Wilson Library Bulletin 52 (January 1978): 387.

Librarians and libraries were visible at the National Women's Conference. Twelve librarians attended and libraries were mentioned three times during the conference.

1978-43 Williamson, Jane. "Sexism Is the Root." Library Journal 103 (January 1, 1978): 3-4.

Letter in reaction to Ellis Hodgins's "Orphans Without a Home" (Library Journal 102, September 1, 1977: 1722). Explains that professionalism is called into question because the profession is dominated by women.

1978-44 "LC Minority Employment, November 1977." Library of Congress Information Bulletin 37 (January 13, 1978): 13.

A table of statistics on minority employment, November 1977, includes a breakdown by sex of GS levels 1-18 for full-time employees showing "percent change" since May 1977.

1978-45 "Semiannual Report on Developments at the Library of Congress January 1978." Library of Congress Information Bulletin 37 (January 13, 1978): 15-48.

Describes activities of the Women's Program Advisory Committee.

1978-46 Savage, Noël. "News Report 1977." Library Journal 103 (January 15, 1978): 131-141.

Describes sex discrimination battles by librarians at San Diego and Temple University, plus Library of Congress, University of Washington Library School, and San Francisco Public Library activities.

1978-47 "New Statistics." LJ/SLJ Hotline 7 (January 16, 1978): 1-2.

Summary of surveys includes HEGIS XI: Academic Libraries information which shows that male chief librarians earned a median salary $5,000 greater than females.

1978-48 "Medical Librarians Vote to Boycott Dade and Atlanta." LJ/SLJ Hotline 7 (January 30, 1978): 1.

The MLA Board of Directors voted not to meet in Florida's Dade County "until such time as anti-discriminatory laws are re-enacted," cancelled the 1982 Atlanta meeting, and rejected invitations from New Orleans and St. Louis--located in states which have not ratified ERA.

1978-49 Beasley, Clarence, Jr. "Boycott Boomerang." American Libraries 9 (February 1978): 74.

Suggests that ALA's boycott tactics against states which have not ratified the Equal Rights Amendment may alienate state legislators toward the ERA.

1978-50 "Library Wage Parity Suit Overcomes Latest Obstacle." American Libraries 9 (February 1978): 68.

Reports events of San Diego librarians' salary dispute.

1978-51 "Salaries to Buy Less for Academic Librarians." American Libraries 9 (February 1978): 70-71.

Report of ARL Annual Salary Survey [1977-07] mentions that the survey was expanded to include information on salaries by sex.

1978-52 Shediac, Margaret. "Greater Philadelphia Law Library Association 1977 Survey." Law Library Journal 71 (February 1978): 170-176.

Survey conducted for the period of August 31, 1976 through September 1, 1977 returned 85 questionnaires reporting salaries and benefits of law librarians who were members of the Association. Table 2, "Age and Sex" (p. 171), shows data from 55 women and 12 men. Both the median and mean salaries of men were higher than those of women.

1978-53 Berry, John N. "You Can't Eat Prestige." Library Journal 103 (February 1, 1978): 301.

Berry's editorial summarizes ARL Annual Salary Survey, 1976-1977 [1977-07].

1978-54 Genaway, David C. "Bar Coding and the Librarian Supermarket: An Analysis of Advertised Library Vacancies." Library Journal 103 (February 1, 1978): 322-325.

Includes information on affirmation action policies and women.

1978-55 "Recent Study Surveys Employment of Women at the Library." Library of Congress Information Bulletin 37 (February 17, 1978): 109-110.

Reports on in-house study undertaken to present a comprehensive picture of women in the Library of Congress in 1977. Statistical data show that although the Library does twice as well as the other agencies of the Federal Government in grades GS 7-12, advancement of women in grades GS 9-15 has been at a standstill since 1970.

1978-56 "St. Paul Library Jobs Upgraded." LJ/SLJ Hotline 7 (February 27, 1978): 4.

Reports successful drive to counter the discrimination exercised against librarianship because of its traditional female-image problem by St. Paul, Minnesota public library, which brought before the Civil Service Commission the suit to upgrade the librarian I-IV range, and a study for career ladders for library assistants. Concluded that the library jobs involved called for more responsibility and ability than did other civil service jobs paying similarly.

1978-57 Bidlack, Russell E. "Faculty Salaries of 62 Library Schools, 1977-78." Journal of Education for Librarianship 18 (Spring 1978): 251-267.

The fifth report of the annual faculty salary survey of ALA accredited library school reveals sex and salary differences for heads of library schools, full-time faculty, assistant professors and lecturers.

1978-58 Carter, Jane Robbins. "Multi-Cultural Graduate Library Education." Journal of Education for Librarianship 18 (Spring 1978): 295-314.

Opening statement notes that the stereotype of a librarian is a middle-aged, white woman; "two out of ten times she will be a man." Discusses this phenomenon in the context of minority education in librarianship. Suggests rejecting prediction of educational achievement based on racial identity, economic status or sex.

1978-59 Thorne, Barbara. "Women in Librarianship." Journal of Education for Librarianship 18 (Spring 1978): 348-349.

Program at the 1978 Association of American Library Schools annual conference by the Women in Librarianship discussion group is reported.

1978-60 "At a Midwinter Career Workshop." American Libraries 9 (March 1978): 159.

Photo of Nancy Deutsch and Luan Gilbert with caption, taken during ALA SRRT Task Force on Women assertiveness training workshop.

1978-61 "Four New Takes on 1978 Activity from ALA Midwinter Meeting." American Libraries 9 (March 1978): 132-140.

Reporting on the Tom and Jerry debates during their campaign for presidency of ALA, it is mentioned that the sharpest questions came from the SRRT Task Force session. The Task Force considered a straw vote but decided to withhold endorsement of either candidate. It is noted that they would like to see a woman on the list.

1978-62 Gerhardt, Lillian N., Cheatham, Bertha M., and Pollack, Pamela D. "Plowing through Chicago: SLJ's Report on ALA's Midwinter Meeting '78." School Library Journal 24 (March 1978): 85-92.

The election of Grace Slocum, Connie Dunlap and Ella Yates to the ALA Executive Board is reported in the light of the all-male slate of nominees from the previous year to which feminist Council members had objected.

1978-63 Smith, Karen F. SUNYLA Salary Survey 1977--First Report SUNYLA Personnel Policies Committee, March 1978. Arlington, Va.: ERIC Document Reproduction Service, 1978: ED 190 043.

Twenty-eight SUNY and ten community college libraries give salaries by rank, type of library, sex, etc.

1978-64 "Snow Job: ALA Midwinter Meeting 1978." Wilson Library Bulletin 52 (March 1978): 542.

Under the heading, "Women's Commmittees, Down to Basics," activities of the ALA Committee on the Status of Women, the SRRT Task Force on Women, and the Women Administrators Discussion group are reported. The Status of Women Committee sent representatives to the National Women's Conference in Houston, planned to apply for an ALA goals award for a profile of women in librarianship, and sent letters to ALA officers urging the appointment of women to committees. The SRRT Task Force sponsored two workshops on careers, sent a list of issues to be considered by the Status of Women Committee, and decided to co-sponsor the third SHARE Directory with Women Library Workers. The Women Administrators Discussion group held a meeting on the woman administrator's role in decision making.

1978-65 "ARL Salaries Not Rising Fast Enough, Says Study." Library Journal 103 (March 1, 1978): 497-498.

Report of the first ARL Survey [1977-07] which provides salary information by sex, finds that of the 5,714 professional staffers employed in 90 ARL libraries 62 percent (3,521) are women and 38 percent (2,193) are men. Men occupy 72 percent of top administrative level positions (directors, associate directors, assistant directors, and heads of law and medical libraries). There is a disproportionate number of female department heads (71 percent in reference, 80 percent in cataloging, 74 percent in serials).

1978-66 Library of Congress Leads Government Agencies in Advancement of Women." LJ/SLJ Hotline 7 (March 13, 1978): 2.

Library of Congress study indicates that women did twice as well as other government agencies in grades GS 7 through GS 12 and five times as well in GS 13 through GS 18. However, improvement in GS 9 through GS 15 was not made, and declines took place in GS 14 and GS 15.

1978-66a "Medical Librarians & ERA: Dade & Atlanta Boycott." Library Journal 103 (March 15, 1978): 603-604.

Notes Medical Library Association decision to meet only in states which have ratified the ERA.

1978-67 "Concluding Reports on the Midwinter Meeting of the American Library Association, Chicago, IL, January 22-28, 1978." Library of Congress Information Bulletin 37 (March 24, 1978): 195-204.

Coverage of the Social Responsibilities Round Table includes: Task Force on Women forum for ALA presidential candidates, discussion on library schools and sexism-racism, use of sexist materials by exhibitors, Women Library Workers SHARE directory, and future action items. The Committee on the Status of Women in Librarianship meetings are also reported in depth.

1978-68 "Women Managers to Speak." Library of Congress Information Bulletin 37 (March 31, 1978): 221.

Question, "What's it like to be a women in top-level Library of Congress management?" announces panel entitled "LC Managers Speak Out."

1978-69 "Affirmative Action." California Librarian 39 (April 1978): 7-27.

Panel discussion sponsored by the California Library Employees Association offers insight into affirmative action and equal employment, with some emphasis on library policies. Topics are upward mobility for women and minorities in paraprofessional positions, and the situation of women professionals in administrative jobs.

1978-70 Busbin, O. Mell, Jr. "A Survey of the Writings of the First Fifteen Women Presidents of the American Library Association." (A project report submitted to the faculty of the graduate college in partial fulfillment of the specialist in arts degree.) Kalamazoo, Mich.: Western Michigan University, April 1978.

Paper attempts to determine whether the publications of these women helped them attain their positions as ALA presidents, to discover what contribution they made to library literature, to reveal the extent to which they were "aware of librarianship in general," and to identify major professional concerns as reflected in their writing. Charts and bibliographies are included.

1978-71 Berry, John. "The Dominant Issue Was Race." Library Journal 103 (April 1, 1978): 716-720.

Description of a panel sponsored by the ALA Women Administrators Discussion Group. Game plans, tactics, assertiveness and a case history of paternalism on the Kenosha, Wisconsin, library board were discussed. Notes that the audience was 99 percent women who were "learning truths we all could use" (p. 720).

1978-72 "St. Paul Library Jobs Upgraded by Civil Service." Library Journal 103 (April 15, 1978): 811-812.

Short chronology of the two-year battle of librarians to upgrade civil service job titles in the librarian I-IV range and to study a possible career ladder for library assistants and library technicians. Notes the San Diego Municipal Employees' suit against the city for higher salaries to match those of other city professionals.

1978-73 "Women's Advancement at LC Has Come to a Standstill." Library Journal 103 (April 15, 1978): 811.

Summarizes findings of LC's Women's Program Statistical Study.

1978-74 "ARL Statistics and Salary Survey, 1976-1977." Wilson Library Bulletin 52 (May 1978): 717.

Summary report of the 1976-1977 ARL Salary Survey [1977-07] notes that 62 percent of libraries' professional staffs are women but 72 percent of the top administrative jobs are held by men. Conversely, women hold 81 percent of jobs at the department-head level.

1978-75 Bailey, Nancy P. "Honorable Terms." School Library Journal 24 (May 1978): 3.

Letter responds to Lillian Gerhardt's essay, "Teeth for the Professionally Nameless" (School Library Journal 24, December 1977, p. 7).

Discusses the issue of the numbers of men in the Association for Educational Communications and Technology in comparison to the women in school library media positions. She notes, "We ladies have been bulldozed again. We sit back and watch the media males push their wares with incredible enthusiasm and drive."

1978-76 Berger, Patricia W., Corth, Annette, Gottleib, Ann K., and Lester, Daniel W. "SLA Faces the Equal Rights Amendment." Special Libraries 69 (May-June 1978): 223-224.

Philosophical discussion of SLA's commitment to social and political issues urges boycott of states which have not ratified ERA. Full text of the Equal Rights Amendment is reprinted.

1978-77 Chapman, Liz. "Pay Equal But Not Opportunities." Library Association Record (May 1978): 232-233.

Abbreviated version of a paper given at the Polytechnic of North London traces the history of women working in libraries in Great Britain. The marriage bar, whereby women were forced to leave work when they married, is viewed as a major cause of the sex stratification in libraries.

1978-78 Echelman, Shirley. "Some Issues Relating to SLA and ERA." Special Libraries 69 (May-June 1978). 225-227.

Outlines major issues in opposition to a Special Libraries Association boycott of states which have not ratified the Equal Rights Amendment. A list of SLA meeting sites and the status of the ratification effort in each state is provided. This is followed by a complete list of states and their action on the ERA.

Letter: Coble, Gerald M. "Boycott Issue." Special Libraries 69 (August 1978): 6A.

Notes that he resigned from ALA office when ALA instituted an ERA boycott and complains that associations should stay out of non-library matters.

1978-79 Elkins, Deborah. "Plus Ça Change." Library Occurrent 26 (May 1978): 53-58.

Survey of salary data from 200 academic and special libraries in Indiana finds that women predominate in all categories with very few men in libraries serving population smaller than 25,000. While more men overall serve as directors or head librarians (Table 2, p. 55) salary data show men earning higher salaries than women at every level in each type of library (Table 3, p. 56). Authors charge that women should be aware of the possibility of sex discrimination, and conclude with a list of the objectives of the Indiana Library Association Task Force on the Status of Women in Indiana Libraries and names of Task Force Officers.

1978-80 Galloway, Sue and Archuleta, Alyce. "Sex and Salary: Equal Pay for Comparable Work." American Libraries 9 (May 1978): 281-285.

General discussion of pay equity focusing on the 1977 California Library Association (CLA) preconference on "Sex and Salary: Achieving Parity Among Professions." Includes text of CLA resolution supporting the practice of comparable wages for comparable work, and summarizes cases at the University of California at Berkeley and San Diego Municipal Employees Association. Suggestions are made for achieving equal pay for comparable work by library workers.

1978-81 Grotzinger, Laurel A. "Women Who Spoke for Themselves." College and Research Libraries 39 (May 1978): 175-190.

Points out that women were active in library history and discusses the contributions of six women "who spoke for themselves." These women are Katharine Lucinda Sharp, Isadore Gilbert Mudge, Margaret Mann, Adelaide Hasse, Flora Belle Ludington, and Genevieve Walton. Points out that women are represented in great numbers in the field, and that women have attained leadership roles despite "long-standing and oppressive social traditions."

1978-82 "Indiana Forms Task Force." American Libraries 9 (May 1978): 296.

Describes establishment of five member Task Force on the Status of Women in Indiana Libraries.

1978-83 "Library Workers To Meet." American Libraries 9 (May 1978): 296.

Announces registration deadline for Women Library Workers conference to be held June 30-July 2, 1978 in Waukesha, Wisconsin. Includes a general description of conference objectives.

1978-84 Maxwell, Margaret F. "The Lion and the Lady: The Firing of Miss Mary Jones." American Libraries 9 (May 1978): 268-272.

Prizewinning article describes the events of 1905 leading up to and subsequent to the decision of the Los Angeles Library Board to fire Mary Jones because, as she was informed, "it would be in the best interests of the library to place a man at the head." Even with the support of Melvil Dewey, Susan B. Anthony, and the 1000 women from the Friday Club of Los Angeles, Mary Jones did not win her job back. Essay concludes that while it may not be as blatant, sex discrimination in libraries still exists today.

1978-85 "Task Force Seeks Name Change." American Libraries 9 (May 1978): 9.

Reports that the ALA Social Responsibilities Round Table Task Force on Women is considering changing its name to the Feminist Task Force, Task Force of Feminist Women, or Feminist Librarians Task Force. Other suggestions are sought.

1978-86 "Sex Bias at Temple U.: EEOC Okays Court Fight." *Library Journal* 103 (May 1, 1978): 922.

Coverage notes that while EEOC ruled that there was no reasonable cause to believe the allegation of sex bias, Temple's AAUP chapter was given authorization to file an action in Federal District court. Mentions other sex bias battles in Minnesota and California.

1978-87 "Women's Work." *Bay State Librarian* 67 (June 1978): 4-5.

Boston Area Women in Libraries (BAWIL) sponsored a pre-conference on women in libraries which included speakers on women in management, free-lance librarians, female-controlled capital, and part-time work. Article includes a report of the conference as well as a short history of the BAWIL.

1978-88 "Women's Program Panel Features Top Managers." *Library of Congress Information Bulletin* 37 (June 2, 1978): 344-346.

Report of a program entitled "LC Women Managers Speak Out," which included Carol Nemeyer, Barbara Ringer, Elizabeth Stroup, and Patricia Hines as panelists. Speakers discussed the status of women at the Library of Congress and ways for individuals to improve their positions.

1978-89 "Hell No, They Won't Go." *LJ/SLJ Hotline* 7 (June 26, 1978): 3.

Reports that many librarians won't be attending the ALA conference in Chicago since Illinois has not ratified the ERA and some cities (such as Iowa City, Ann Arbor, Detroit, and Madison, Wis.) have forbidden any public money to be spent there.

1978-90 "SLA in Kansas City: ERA/Copyright/Continuing Education and Etc." *LJ/SLJ Hotline* 7 (June 26, 1978): 1-2.

SLA 69th conference found that members voted support "in principle" of the Equal Rights Amendment, but tabled a motion to eschew meeting in states that have not ratified ERA.

1978-91 Hook, Robert D. "Report from the ALA Councilor." *Idaho Librarian* 30 (July 1978): 120.

Detailed report of ALA Councils I and II debate on support of ERA. Also mentioned are the passage of the Committee on the Status of Women resolutions on comparable wages, ALA support of the National Plan of Action, and salary range advertisement.

1978-92 Learmont, Carol L. and Darling, Richard L. "Placements and Salaries 1977: The Picture Brightens." *Library Journal* 103 (July 1978): 1339-1345.

Results of 27th annual survey of ALA accredited library school placement of graduates. Median female beginning salary is $11,000; male is $11,311.

1978-93 "Midwinter Meeting Moves to Washington, D.C., January 5-12." American Libraries 9 (July-August 1978): 400.

"Page One" notes that to implement Council's decision to move ALA's 1979 Midwinter Meeting out of Chicago to a city favoring ERA, space has been found in Washington, D.C.

1978-94 "Off the Air Videotaping, Intellectual Freedom, and ERA." American Libraries 9 (July-August 1978): 443.

For the second year in a row, the Association for Educational Communications and Technology was unable to reach a consensus to declare itself for or against the Equal Rights Amendment.

1978-95 "Running to--and from Illinois--Annual Conference Report." American Libraries 9 (July-August 1978): 426-436.

Discussion of "heightened visibility" of women's groups within the American Library Association. Report includes ERA strategies, efforts of the Task Force on Women to remove sexism from the exhibit hall, Council resolutions, and future representation of women on Council. Special section, "The Women's Impact," is included (pp. 433-434).

1978-96 "Salary Study." American Libraries 9 (July-August 1978): 417.

Section, "Career Leads," summarizes study of library wage differentials in Canada [1977-35].

1978-97 "LC Minority Employment, May 1978." Library of Congress Information Bulletin 37 (July 28, 1978): 440.

A table of minority employment, May 1978, includes a breakdown by sex of GS levels 1-18 for full-time employees showing "percent change" since November 1977.

1978-98 Berry, John. "ALA, SLA & ERA." Library Journal 103 (August 1978): 1482-1484.

Compares contrasting reactions of American Library Association and Special Libraries Association to call for a boycott of states not ratifying the Equal Rights Amendment. ALA opted to "put its money where its mouth is"; SLA opted to avoid any risk that might cost money.

1978-99 Berry, John, Fletcher, Janet, Havens, Shirley, and Nyren, Karl. "Tax Revolt--The Library Defense." Library Journal 103 (August 1978): 1469-1481.

Two reports, entitled "Women Administrators" and "SRRT Women," describe the activities of ALA women's groups and Council actions on several women-related resolutions. One report summarizes a program which featured best-selling author, Rita Mae Brown.

1978-100 Clubb, Barbara. "Is CLA in Danger of Being Taken Over By Its Members?" Emergency Librarian 5 (July-August 1978): 13-14.

The theme of the 33rd conference and annual general meeting of the Canadian Library Association, "Strategies for Change--Developing Support for Growth," is seen as appropriate in the light of salary differentials between female and male librarians. However, the conference itself is reported as lacking anything related to the status of women librarians.

1978-101 "Continuing Reports on the Annual Conference of the American Library Association, Chicago, IL, June 24-30, 1978." Library of Congress Information Bulletin 37 (August 11, 1978): 475-484.

Describes meeting sponsored by the ALA Social Responsibilities Round Table Task Force on Women which featured feminist poet and novelist Rita Mae Brown.

1978-102 "Continuing Reports on the Annual Conference of the American Library Association, Chicago, Il. June 24-30, 1978." Library of Congress Information Bulletin 37 (August 25, 1978): 514.

Summarizes resolutions considered by Council, including those regarding the Equal Rights Amendment, support of the concept of comparable worth, and the listing of salary ranges.

1978-103 "New Members Sought for the Women's Advisory Committee." Library of Congress Information Bulletin 37 (August 25, 1978): 505-506.

A description of the Committee's activities, including a list of guidelines for committee selection.

1978-104 Grant, LaRue Tucker. "A Survey of the Perceptions of Librarians Attending the TLA/NMLA Convention, Concerning the Status and Need of Human Resources as Media in Field of Career Awareness." Texas Library Journal 54 (Fall 1978): 192-193.

Librarians questioned about interest in compiling a human resource file were found to be in favor of the project. Response from a group made up of 95 percent women and 5 percent men showed no differences in perception by sex.

1978-105 Hall, Hal W. "Report on the ALA Annual Conference, Chicago, June 1978." Texas Library Journal 54 (Fall 1978): 207.

Reports Council actions on the Equal Rights Amendment and comments that many Texas Library Association members will consider them to be the most significant activities of the ALA Council.

1978-106 Lowenthal, Helen. "1978 Update on Women in Libraries." Bay State Librarian 67 (Fall 1978): 21-23.

General discussion of library-related feminism as it affects comparable pay for comparable work, the ERA, and other association activities. Events in Massachusets include a Massachusetts Library Associa ion pre-conference on women's work and other workshops on library unions.

1978-107 Gerhardt, Lillan N., Cheatham, Bertha M. and Pollack, Pamela D. "Marking Time in Chicago: ALA's 97th Annual Conference." School Library Journal 25 (September 1978): 29-38.

Annual ALA Conference coverage includes Council action on a number of resolutions submitted by Ellen Gay Detlefsen of the Status of Women in Librarianship Committee: endorsement of comparable wages for women, ALA support of the time extension for the Equal Rights Amendment, salary listings in job vacancies to avoid sex discrimination, and the move of ALA headquarters to a state which has ratified ERA. The last item is discussed in some detail. Report also includes ERA-related news discussed at the American Association of School Librarians preconference institute on "Focus on Change: Sexism Awareness."

1978-108 "Highlights of the Annual Conference Meetings of the ACRL Board of Directors." College & Research Libraries News 8 (September 1978): 231-233.

Report of the Association of College and Research Libraries' Board of Directors Meetings at the 1978 ALA Annual Conference includes notice that while the ACRL Board voted to reject the resolution of the Committee on the Status of Women in Librarianship that salary ranges be required in ALA placement advertising, Council did approve the resolution. The ACRL Board voted that this policy be reconsidered at the ALA 1979 Midwinter Meeting. The ACRL Board also endorsed non-support of ALA's boycott of states which had not ratified the ERA, and presented a motion to that effect which was defeated by ALA membership.

1978-109 Metz, Paul. "Administrative Succession in the Academic Library." College and Research Libraries 39 (September 1978): 358-364.

Study of academic administrative succession shows female directors to be concentrated in private institutions and are more likely to be appointed from within the library. Potential explanations are explored.

1978-110 Miele, Tony. "From the Desk of Tony Miele." Alabama Librarian 29 (September-October 1978): 13.

Complains that ALA's decision to boycott Chicago for its 1979 Midwinter Meeting due to Illinois' failure to ratify the ERA was inappropriate since ALA should not take positions on "non-library related issues."

1978-111 "The Qualm Before the Storm." Wilson Library Bulletin 53 (September 1978): 54-55.

Under the heading, "Salve for the Conscience" (p. 54) five resolutions presented by the ALA Committee on the Status of Women in Librarianship are described, followed by a report of Council action taken on them (p. 54).

1978-112 "Report Recommends Center." American Libraries 9 (September 1978): 497.

Discusses a project report from the University of Washington's School of Librarianship and the Washington State Library which grew out of needs assessment workshops. Suggests that women librarians need a clearinghouse for continuing education opportunities.

1978-113 "Roll Call on E.R.A. Council Vote." American Libraries 9 (September 1978): 490.

The ALA Council roll call vote to move ALA Headquarters was defeated 87-46. Yeas and nays are listed by name.

1978-114 Rosenfeld, Harriet E. "SLA's 69th Annual Conference: Out of Date in Kansas City." Wilson Library Bulletin 53 (September 1978): 42-44.

Reviews discussion leading up to the SLA vote which tabled a motion to boycott states which have not ratified the ERA.

1978-115 "Sarah Rebecca Reed: 1914-1978--An Interview on June 8." American Libraries 9 (September 1978): 464.

Part of an interview taped before her death. On Equal Rights Reed observed, "It's important to do all we can to bring women's salaries up to those of men employed in the same type of work. I'm very sympathetic to the need to make sure women are treated fairly--I've seen plenty of cases where they haven't been."

1978-116 Sink, Darryl L. "Beginning the Second Five Years." Audiovisual Instruction 23 (September 1978): 44-45.

The sixth annual study of employment trends for media program graduates uses data reported from 13 schools. The number of women receiving degrees increased 19 percent, from 336 in 1975-1976 to 401 in 1976-1977. The number of men graduates decreased 6 percent, from 414 to 390.

1978-117 Williams, Janet. "Best of Both Worlds: Librarian/Working Mother." American Libraries 9 (September 1978): 469-470+.

Describes the Princeton-Trenton Special Libraries Association Subgroup of working mothers and their plan of action. Discusses conflict between roles of mother and working librarian and choices women have to make.

1978-118 "ALA Midwinter Meeting Change Torpedoes Alabama Governor Conference." LJ/SLJ Hotline 7 (September 4, 1978): 1.

Tony Miele, Director of the Alabama Public Library Service, issues a scathing criticism of ALA's decision to change place and date of ALA 1979 Midwinter meeting due to conflict with Alabama Governor Conference. Demands membership poll and charges that ALA has acted irresponsibly at the behest of a few pro-ERA members.

1978-119 "Racism/Sexism Training Contract Going Begging." LJ/SLJ Hotline 7 (September 4, 1978): 3.

Notes training sessions on racism-sexism slated for ALA in Dallas and need for someone to conduct them.

1978-120 "Women's Program Reported." Library of Congress Information Bulletin 37 (September 15, 1978): 566-567.

Reports a program on Title IX of the Education Amendments of 1972.

1978-121 "Administrative Detail Program Begun." Library of Congress Information Bulletin 37 (September 22, 1978): 581-583.

Announcement of Administrative Detail Program, "Women and Minorities in Management." The program was designed to provide management experience to women and minorities in a short-term employment position of responsibility. The nine participants are named, along with their current positions and supervisors, and the 90-day ADP supervisors (p. 583).

1978-122 "Women's Program to Offer Career Development Workshops." Library of Congress Information Bulletin 37 (September 22, 1978): 584-585.

Describes six workshops offered to library staff members by the Women's Program Advisory Committee in October 1978. Topics included: career decisions, career goals, placement opportunities at LC, interviewing techniques and others.

1978-123 "Attorney's Union Calls Librarians Nonprofessional." American Libraries 9 (October 1978): 523.

Librarians protested when the California State Bar Journal published an ad containing a stereotyped photo of a librarian stating that lawyers had nothing in common with librarians. Protest letters proclaimed that the ad "smacks of arrogance, self-righteousness and . . . sexism."

1978-124 Chase, Julie Ann. "Special Report: WLW Meets in Kenosha." Wilson Library Bulletin 53 (October 1978): 123.

At a meeting of the Women Library Workers Coordinating Council held July 1, 1978 in Kenosha, Wisconsin, participants refocused the goals of the national organization toward support of local chapters and creation of a nationwide network of women working in libraries. The newsletter underwent some structural changes, and new national officers were elected.

1978-125 Galloway, Sue, and Blackburn, Mary. "CPEC Report: The Last Word on Librarians' Salaries?" Librarians' Advocate 8 (October 1978): 3-4, 6.

Summarizes the report adopted by the California Post-secondary Education Committee in May 1978 and the objections librarians have raised to its basic approach. The heart of the controversy is that the report uses the prevailing wage approach, which the California Commission on the Status of Women found to be discriminatory in 1974. Librarian reactions to the report are noted, several suggestions of ways to protest the CPEC report are listed, and a selected bibliography is appended.

1978-126 "It's Not All Fun." American Libraries 9 (October 1978): 519.

Report of a simulation technique used at Case Western Reserve University libraries to teach supervisors how to comply with equal employment opportunity regulations.

1978-127 "Resolution to Hold Midwinter 1979 in Washington, D.C." American Libraries 9 (October 1978): 521.

Text of ALA Council resolution to boycott Chicago since Illinois has not ratified the ERA.

1978-128 Slater, Margaret. "Career Patterns and Mobility in the Library/Information Field." Aslib Proceedings 30 (October-November 1978): 344-351.

Report of a paper presented at Joint Annual Conference of the Aslib Midlands Branch and Northern Branch, Llandudno, May 4-6, 1978. Using Who's Who in Librarianship and "career tracking," women were described as having shorter and generally more mobile professional lives than men, and are less likely to move out of the library information fields.

1978-129 "Women Earn 45 Percent of Doctoral Library Degrees." American Libraries 9 (October 1978): 559.

News note on National Center for Education Statistics report [1978-04] that 45 percent of the 1976 doctoral degrees were awarded to women.

1978-130 Special Issue on Women in Public Libraries. Bibliotheek en Samenleving 10 (October 1978).

1978-130A Introduction and Table of Contents to Special Issue on Women. <u>Bibliotheek en Samenleving</u> 10 (October 1978): 274.

This issue is designed to give an overview of the women's movement in the Netherlands, as well as to pay particular attention to women in European public libraries.

1978-130B "Vrouwenemancipatie in Nederland: een historisch overzicht." (Women's Emancipation in the Netherlands: An Historical Overview) <u>Bibliotheek en Samenleving</u> 10 (October 1978): 275-277.

Social, historical overview of librarianship from 1890 to the present.

1978-130C Drabble-Versteeg, Atie. "Juffrouw Bits: Vrouwenwerk in de bibliotheek van vroeger." (History of Women in Libraries) <u>Bibliotheek en Samenleving</u> 10 (October 1978): 277-279.

Brief, historical overview of women in Dutch Libraries.

1978-130D "De Kommissie Vrouwenwerk in openbare bibliotheken." (Commission on Women Workers in Public Libraries) <u>Bibliotheek en Samenleving</u> 10 (October 1978): 279-280.

A brief report on the Commission's work.

1978-130E "De opkomst van de man in een vrowenberoep." (Men in a Women's Profession) <u>Bibliotheek en Samenleving</u> 10 (October 1978): 280-282.

Describes women's professions, including librarianship, and notes that men are present in small numbers in higher positions.

1978-130F Kickbusch, Ilona. "De vrouw in de duitse openbare bibliotheek." (Women in German Public Libraries) <u>Bibliotheek en Samenleving</u> 10 (October 1978): 286-289.

Describes the library work force of libraries in Germany, which is made up of women--part-time workers, and its recent association with feminist ideals.

1978-130G Ward, Patricia Layzell. "De vrouw in de britse openbare bibliotheek." (Women in British Public Libraries) <u>Bibliotheek en Samenleving</u> 10 (October 1978): 289-291.

Statistical essay on the education and status of women working in British libraries.

1978-130H "Interviews met bibliotheekvrouwen." (Interviews with Women Library Workers) <u>Bibliotheek en Samenleving</u> 10 (October 1978): 282-286.

Women librarians discuss their job and life situations--some mention long hours and low pay.

1978-130I Jensen, J. Eide. "De vrouw in de Zweedse openbare bibliotheek." (Women in Swedish Public Libraries) <u>Bibliotheek en Samenleving</u> 10 (October 1978): 295-296.

Notes that 70 percent of all Swedish librarians are women, while 50 percent of the library directors are men. Salaries are lower than in other comparable professions.

1978-130J Corts, Ans. "Literatuurlijst vrouwenwerk in openbare bibliotheken." (Bibliography of Women in Public Libraries) <u>Bibliotheek en Samenleving</u> 10 (October 1978): 296-299.

Bibliography of 72 publications in Dutch and English on women in libraries.

1978-131 "Job Sharing in Canadian Libraries." <u>LJ/SLJ Hotline</u> 7 (October 16, 1978): 5-6.

Report on job sharing in Canada describes how two women have found a way to manage careers and families.

1978-132 "New Members Named to Women's Program Advisory Committee." <u>Library of Congress Information Bulletin</u> 37 (October 20, 1978): 634.

Announces names and positions of seven new members and describes committee activities.

1978-133 Frankie, Suzanne. <u>ARL Annual Salary Survey 1977-1978</u>. Washington, D.C.: Association of Research Libraries, November 1978.

Second ARL salary survey to include sex of individuals highlights differential between men and women's status and compensation.

1978-134 "General Sessions, Women Library Workers, ILL Draw Conference Audiences." <u>Virginia Librarian Newsletter</u> 24 (November-December 1978): 3.

Organizational meeting of women librarians drew 40 people to discuss discrimination, pay parity, women in library administration, and other topics. A steering committee was established.

1978-135 "Affirmative Action in Tucson: Library Develops Written Plan." <u>Library Journal</u> 103 (November 15, 1978): 2286.

Plans at the Tucson Public Library include the formation of a Library Affirmative Action Committee, staff surveys, and updates of a "utilization analysis chart" which shows the number and percentage of minorities, women and the handicapped in various library departments.

1978-136 "ALA/ERA--Where Do You Stand?" Louisiana Library Association Bulletin 40 (Winter 1978): 58.

Of the 39 responses to an open challenge to Louisiana librarians to express their views on the American Library Association ERA boycott [1977-71], 30 voted against the ALA resolution because ERA is "not a professional issue," and 9 voted in favor because "it's time ALA got political." It is noted that the text of all the responses were sent to the LLA Executive Board and to ALA.

1978-137 Monroe, Hamilton. "The Texas Librarian as a Censor: Two Configural Psychological Profiles." Texas Library Journal 54 (Winter 1978): 13-16, 36.

Study seeks to determine whether psychological profile of Texas librarians provided by configural psychological patterns interpreted from the Minnesota Multiphasic Personality Inventory can identify possible personality types who passively avoid censorship concerns and escape adverse conditions. The sample of professional librarians included 31 men and 69 women. Discussion of findings is unobjectively presented, with women described as naive, insecure, rigid, repressive, stereotyped, unoriginal, angry, suspicious, argumentative, irritable, schizophrenic, and strongly suggestive of having major emotional disorders. Men are described as responding relevantly and truthfully (unlike women), but as being obviously deviant.

1978-138 Cheatham, Bertha M. "Library News of 1978." School Library Journal 25 (December 1978): 17-21.

Notes that ALA has joined a number of other national associations which have decided to boycott states which have not ratified the ERA. Describes Iowa City public librarians and others who find that some city governments would not allow any conference money to be spent in states which haven't ratified the amendment. Notes, "An untold number of librarians fulfilled professional commitments by paying their own expenses."

1978-139 Vincent, Ida. "Womanpower--Part-time Work and Job Sharing in Libraries." Australian Library Journal 27 (December 8, 1978): 330-333.

An examination of part-time work in general leads into reasons why part-time positions are especially suitable for librarians and libraries. Article lists four reasons for the suitability of part-time library work, eight benefits to libraries, and five problems of implementation. Arguments in favor of part-time positions in libraries are based primarily on the fact that the work force is dominated by women who favor alternative work styles and who feel they cannot work full-time because of family responsibilities.

1978-140 "Helen Wheeler Discrimination Suit Dismissed." LJ/SLJ Hotline 7 (December 11, 1978): 6.

Reports that the case against Louisiana State University brought by Helen Rippier Wheeler, which charges that LSU discriminates against women in hiring and promotion, was dismissed.

1979-01 Beazley, Richard M. Library Statistics of Colleges and Universities, 1976. Institutional Data. Prepared in coordination with the U.S. National Center for Education Statistics. (University of Illinois, Graduate School of Library Science Monograph 16) Urbana: University of Illinois, Graduate School of Library Science, 1979. (NCES-78-234)

Part of the 11th annual Higher Education General Information Survey (HEGIS) and part of the second annual Library General Information Survey (LIBGIS). Data are reported for 2,987 public and private college and university libraries. Summary data section (pp. 3-5) remarks that at all employment levels, women accounted for more full-time equivalents than did men; that men earn a higher mean salary ($17,240) than women ($14,188) at the professional level; and that men earn more ($8,439) than women ($7,697) at the nonprofessional level.

1979-02 Behn, Jan, Geidel, Patti, and Herman, Mary Lou. SHARE: Sisters Have Resources Everywhere: A Directory of Wisconsin Women Library Workers. n.p. (Madison, Wis.?), n.d. (1979?).

Directory, illustrated by Marge Loch-Wouters, lists home and work address, type of work, interests, skills, and resources of Wisconsin Women Library Workers.

1979-03 Biblo, Mary. "Social Responsibilities Round Table." In ALA Yearbook 1979. Edited by Robert Wedgeworth. Chicago: ALA, 1979: 267.

Article includes report of the activities of the ALA SRRT Task Force on Women.

1979-04 Brown, George H. Degree Awards to Women: An Update. Washington, D.C.: GPO, 1979. (NCES 79-16686).

Includes information on librarians. Bachelor's degrees for women declined from 1971 to 1977 (p. 4, 7), as did master's degrees (p. 10), and women's overall representation (p. 11, 13). Doctoral degrees for women increased (p. 16), the largest percentage gain in all fields examined (p. 17). Other library science data are reported on pp. 26, 28-31.

1979-05 Brown, George H. Master's Degree Awards to Women. Arlington, Va.: ERIC Document Reproduction Service, 1979: ED 162 565.

Microreproduction of [1978-05].

1979-06 Buck, Vernon E. "Toward Professionals Managing Professionals: A Case Study of Career Development for Women Librarians." In The Evaluation of Continuing Education for Professionals: a Systems View. Seattle: University of Washington, 1979.

Summarizes background of "Career Development for Women Librarians" project at the University of Washington Library School. Contributions of Charlotte Wood and Ruth Hamilton are indicated through Buck's description of the assessment center technique designed to assist women in gaining upward mobility by acquiring increased managerial expertise. Goals and objectives are listed, and the program is described.

1979-07 Cheatham, Bertha M. "SLJ News Report, 1978." In Bowker Annual, 24th ed. New York: Bowker, 1979: 28-36.

Reprint of [1978-138].

1979-08 Dempsey, Frank J. "Illinois." In ALA Yearbook 1979. Edited by Robert Wedgeworth. Chicago: ALA, 1979: 339-341.

In section, "Illinois Library Association," adoption of a resolution in support of the ERA is noted.

1979-09 Euster, Joanne R. "A Woman's Profession in Academia: Problem and Proposal." In New Horizons for Academic Libraries. Edited by Robert D. Stueart and Richard D. Johnson. New York: K. G. Saur, 1979: 370-374.

Discusses the effect of sex discrimination on academic librarianship.

1979-10 Frankie, Suzanne O. ARL Annual Salary Survey, 1977-1978. Arlington, Va.: ERIC Document Reproduction Service, 1979: ED 168 473.

[Microreproduction of 1978-133].

1979-11 Garrison, Dee. Apostles of Culture: The Public Librarian and American Society, 1887-1920. New York: Free Press, 1979.

In the fourth and final section of a history of public librarianship and its place in historical and social reform in the United States, "The Tender Technicians" describes the role of women in libraries and their cumulative effect on the "feminization of the profession." Offers a chronology of the entry of women into the profession, their perceived strengths, weaknesses, education and positions held in libraries. Suggests that the predominance of women in librarianship is a major factor contributing to the current depressed status of the profession as a whole.

Reviews: Gaver, Mary. The Bookwoman 43 (September 1979): 10.
Positive descriptive review.

Kirkus Reviews 47 (March 15, 1979): 364.
Descriptive review notes that central chapters are marred by stodgy psychologizing as well as the author's general inability to sustain a narrative.

Josephine, Helen B. Library Journal 104 (June 15, 1979): 325.
Sees the final section of the book, devoted to the role of women in public libraries, as exploding the myths that stunted libraries' development.

Booklist 75 (July 15, 1979): 1598.
A positive review which notes that Garrison feels women diminished the cultural ambience of the public library by accepting their assigned feminized role and lending that "homey" atmosphere to the public library.

Wiegand, Wayne. History: Reviews of New Books 8 (October 1979): 7.
Notes that the book provides fresh insights.

Bobinski, George S. College and Research Libraries 40 (November 1979): 561.
Positive descriptive review.

French, Mary Blake. Spokeswoman (November 1, 1979): 14.
Review finds the book "an important source for women's studies and a fascinating account of a quiet revolution in the midst of middle-class America."

Ladd, Jay L. Ohio Library Association Bulletin 50 (January 1980): 33-35.
Positive review includes quote: "The feminization of public librarianship did much to shape and stunt the development of an important American institution."

Gould, Lewis L. Journal of Library History, Philosophy, and Comparative Librarianship 15 (Spring 1980): 216-218.
Review calls the book "ambitious and provocative" but notes "the disparate parts . . . do not make up a unified whole."

Lemons, J. S. Journal of American History 66 (March 1980): 953.
Notes the book is substantial, stimulating, and rewarding but adds "one does find her characterization of the genteel founders of librarianship . . . to be jarring and unhelpful."

McFarland, C. K. Social Science Quarterly 61 (June 1980): 175.
Descriptive review notes that so much of the book is devoted to the role of women and the feminization of the library profession that the word "women" or feminization should appear somewhere in the title.

DiMattia, Ernest A. Journal of Academic Librarianship 6 (July 1980): 163.
A positive review which points out the readability of the book.

Davis, A. F. American Historical Review 85 (October 1980): 994.
Calls the book provocative and interesting and notes it may not please librarians.

Grotzinger, Laurel. Library Quarterly 50 (October 1980): 501-503.
Generally positive review notes that "the very brief concluding commentary ... attempts, somewhat unsuccessfully, to relate the many ideas set forth in the earlier pages to the present state of women in librarianship." Observes the "biographical study of Melvil Dewey is the best synthesis of that complex individual published to date." Problems with the final chapters which attempt to focus on feminization are noted as glossing over the effects of women on the field.

American Book Collector 1 (November 1980): 58.
Reviewer finds book utterly hilarious.

Byam, M. S. Science Books and Films 16 (November-December 1980): 60.
Finds the book solid but observes its failure "to describe in detail even one female library leader" or to touch on the tremendous impact of the recruitment of women to library school. Concludes, "As a study of the feminization of a profession, however, it is at best, weak."

Deveny, Mary Alice. American Reference Books Annual 12 (1981): 87.
Descriptive review with no evaluative remarks.

Casey, Marion. Journal of Social History 15 (Fall 1981): 142-144.
Notes that Garrison will be most remembered for treating feminization as a deciding factor in giving libraries secondary status.

1979-12 Grant, W. Vance and Lind, C. George. Digest of Education Statistics: 1979. Washington, D.C.: GPO, 1979. (NCES 79-401).
Data from earlier reports on librarians in public libraries (Table 183, p. 199), all libraries (Table 184, p. 199), and school library-media centers (Table 185, p. 200) are included, as well as information on

library science degrees conferred, and enrollment for advanced degrees.

1979-13 Griffen, Agnes M. "Personnel and Employment: Affirmative Action." In <u>ALA Yearbook 1979</u>. Edited by Robert Wedgeworth. Chicago: ALA, 1979: 198-201.

Reviews affirmative action efforts for women, minorities, and handicapped. Under the section, "Status of Women," class action suits and EEOC litigation are discussed.

1979-13a Heim, Kathleen M. "Professional Education: Some Comparisons." In <u>As Much to Learn as to Teach</u>. Edited by Joel M. Lee and Beth A. Hamilton. Hamden, Conn.: Linnet Books, 1979: 128-176.

Essay comparing professional preparation for librarianship, law, medicine, nursing and teaching includes a section on "The Semi-Professions" (pp. 137-139) which explores the concept of occupational segregation.

1979-14 Heim, Kathleen M. with the assistance of Pamela R. Broadley. "Women in Librarianship, Status of." In <u>ALA Yearbook 1979</u>. Edited by Robert Wedgeworth. Chicago: ALA, 1979: 294-299.

Featured as a "comprehensive special report," this essay discusses salaries (in the U.S. and Canada), degree distribution, status actions, ALA-related actions, other library organizations and activities. Includes five tables.

1979-15 Hinding, Andrea. <u>Women's History Sources: A Guide to Archives and Manuscript Collections in the United States</u>. 2 v. New York: Bowker, 1979.

The papers of 174 women librarians are included, as well as material generated by the American Library Association.

1979-15a Holley, Edward G. "Library Issues in the Seventies." In <u>As Much to Learn as to Teach</u>. Edited by Joel M. Lee and Beth A. Hamilton. Hamden, Conn.: Linnet Books, 1979.

Identifies affirmative action as an issue which will be a matter of concern to librarians throughout the eighties (p. 31).

1979-16 Ladenson, Alex. "Law and Legislation." In <u>ALA Yearbook 1979</u>. Edited by Robert Wedgeworth. Chicago: ALA, 1979: 150-152.

Under section, "Discrimination," results of the St. Paul Public Library staff's requests to upgrade job titles to conform with their responsibilities are reported. The City Civil Service Commission approved the demands, which were justified on the basis of sex discrimination.

1979-17 Land, Brian. "Canadian Correspondent's Report." In ALA Yearbook 1979. Edited by Robert Wedgeworth. Chicago: ALA, 1979: 308-313.

Canada Council study [1977-35] of career paths of men and women librarians is reported in section, "Status of Women in Librarianship" (p. 313).

1979-18 Learmont, Carol L. "Placements and Salaries, 1977: The Picture Brightens." In Bowker Annual, 24th ed. New York: Bowker, 1979: 231-241.

Reprint of [1978-92].

1979-19 Martinez, Anna, and Martinez, Julio. "The Comparable Worth Study." In Personnel in Libraries. Edited by Karl Nyren. (Library Journal Special Report #10) New York: Bowker, 1979: 43-57.

Comprehensive description of comparable worth studies attempts to reveal gender-based discrimination as the real reason for low wages in the library profession. Includes a selected, annotated bibliography.

1979-20 Mullins, Stephanie, and Partington, Dorothy M. "London Correspondent's Report." In ALA Yearbook 1979. Edited by Robert Wedgeworth. Chicago: ALA, 1979: 314-322.

Section "Women in Libraries" notes that women's status remained unsatisfactory in the late 1970s because women, 70 percent of the chartered librarians, held only 3 percent of the top jobs.

1979-21 Ray, Jean M. "The Future Role of the Academic Librarian As Viewed through a Perspective of Forty Years." In New Horizons for Academic Libraries. Edited by Robert D. Stueart and Richard D. Johnson. New York: K. G. Saur, 1979: 404-410.

Recalls that in 1938 Simmons accepted only women and had an all-female faculty (p. 404), and that more men entered the field during the late 1940s.

1979-22 Reinshagen, Bill. "The Coming Male Majority." In Personnel in Libraries. (Library Journal Special Report #10) Edited by Karl Nyren. New York: Bowker, 1979: 41-42.

Short, sexist history of library personnel concludes that men will enter the library profession as the job market tightens. Assumes that they will bring backgrounds in other fields which will "raise the level of professionalism in library science and enhance the prestige of librarians."

1979-23 Savage, Noël. "LJ News Report, 1978." In Bowker Annual, 24th ed. New York: Bowker, 1979: 3-28.

Reprint of [1979-36].

1979-24 Shank, Russell. "American Library Association." In Bowker Annual, 24th ed. New York: Bowker, 1979: 79-87.

"Women's Issues" (pp. 82-83) is a special section in ALA activity coverage. Background on the ERA and ALA is given.

1979-25 Shiflett, Orvin Lee. "The Origins of American Academic Librarianship." Ph.D. dissertation, Florida State University, 1979.

Contains many references to women, including a discussion of Dewey's proteges, Katharine Sharp (p. 256), and Mary Wright Plummer (pp. 256-257).

1979-26 Shubert, Joseph F. "New York." In ALA Yearbook 1979. Edited by Robert Wedgeworth. Chicago: ALA, 1979: 363-365.

In section, "New York Library Association," the creation of the Round Table on Concerns of Women to promote the interests of women within the Association is noted. The group plans to develop programs to improve library services in areas of women's concerns, and to heighten public awareness of materials and services of interest to women.

1979-27 Watson, Elbert L. "Indiana." In ALA Yearbook 1979. Edited by Robert Wedgeworth. Chicago: ALA, 1979: 341-342.

Under "Task Force on Women" it is noted that the Indiana Library Association approved a Task Force on Women, and that surveys showed a 32 percent decline in the number of women directors since 1950. Salary differentials in favor of men are also underscored.

1979-28 Weibel, Kathleen and Heim, Kathleen M., with assistance from Dianne J. Ellsworth. The Role of Women in Librarianship 1876-1976: The Entry; Advancement and Struggle for Equalization in One Profession. Phoenix, Ariz.: Oryx Press, A Neal-Schuman Professional Book, 1979.

The book for which this bibliography is a supplement. An anthology of articles on women in librarianship, a bibliography from 1876-1976, and an introductory essay comprise its three parts.

Reviews: Gaver, Mary. The Bookwoman 43 (September 1979): 10.
Descriptive review.

Biggs, M. National Library Association Newsletter (May 1979): 6-7.

Positive review provides a good description and notes that the book is necessary for library science and women's studies collections.

Information Hotline 11 (June 1979): 24.
Descriptive note.

Women Library Workers 20-21 (July-October 1979): 22.

Positive descriptive review of this "herstorical" overview of women's role in the development of library science over the last 100 years.

Josephine, Helen B. Journal of Academic Librarianship 5 (September 1979): 224.

Positive descriptive review notes, "The anthology will have a permanent place in the curriculum of library schools and the study of the development of the profession."

Osborn, Jeanne. College and Research Libraries 40 (November 1979): 570-571.

Comprehensive positive review notes several indexing errors. [Excerpts reprinted in Journal of Academic Librarianship 6 (March 1980): 45.]

Hills, Kate. New Library World 80 (December 1979): 249.

Short descriptive review.

Moon, Brenda E. Library History 5 (1980): 90.

Short review finds that the book's evocative tone has something of a processional banner about it.

Cherry, Susan Spaeth. "Women in Librarianship." American Libraries 11 (January 1980): 73.

Description summarizes book.

Stineman, Esther R. American Reference Books Annual, 1980, v. 11. Edited by Bohdan S. Wynar. Littleton, Colo.: Libraries Unlimited, 1980: 57.

Notes, "There is no doubt that this is the authoritative historical and sociological book on women in librarianship."

Minudri, R. School Library Journal 26 (January 1980): 44.

Descriptive review notes that this is a truly fascinating collection and a book for serious students, scholars, and writers.

Ratner, Jane. Library Journal 104 (January 1, 1980): 79.

Calls the volume a "good, solid sourcebook" but notes a failure to provide an adequate argumentative structure for the material. [Excerpts reprinted in Journal of Academic Librarianship 6 (May 1980): 103.]

Ward, Patricia Layzell. Library Review 29 (Spring 1980): 41-42.

A positive descriptive review.

Wert, L. Journal of Library History 15 (Spring 1980): 226-229.

Descriptive negative review includes incorrect percentages in relation to the book's composition.

1979-29 Wiegand, Wayne A. The History of a Hoax: Edmund Lester Pearson, John Cotton Dana, and The Old Librarian's Almanack. Pittsburgh, Pa.: Beta Phi Mu, 1979.

"September hath 30 Days" (p. 63) contains the following excerpt:
Matrimony, so maintain'd worthy Master Peleg Gudger, is no fit Diversion for the Librarian ... all these concomitants of the Married State so conspire and agree to harass the Librarian and woo him from his legitimate tasks ... he will find himself badger'd when he desires to read in Peace; led forth to Domestic Duties when he should be marshalling his Books; and at all times Distract'd & Annoy'd, to the detriment of his Profession.

Dr. Simon Baglesy writes: "I have not found Wives to be altogether a too heavy Encumbrance. They can dust Books, and at times, they may be trusted to arrange the volumes properly in their places. Beyond this, it would perchance, be rash to go with them."

Master Enoch Sneed's opinion: "Steer a straight course, he says, away from feminine Blandishments. These Females are as Leeches or Bloodsuckers, hardly to be torn off. They would make you take your Victuals at certain fix'd seasons to conform to their rules of Housekeeping, regarding not that you may wish to read at those Hours; while again they will Babble & Complain should it chance that after a hard night's reading you ask that a hot Supper be served at Daybreak. Shun them as you would the Devil."

1979-30 Yohalem, Alice M. The Careers of Professional Women: Commitment and Conflict. Montclair, N.J.: Allanheld Osmun, 1979.

Career commitments of professional women are analyzed with several references to librarians (pp. 59, 60, 71, 152, 163).

1979-31 "Current Activities ... ERA." Focus on Indiana Libraries 33 (January-February 1979): 4.

Announcement of the report of the Task Force on the Status of Women in Indiana Libraries 1978. Report includes staffing statistics, sex discrimination laws and a bibliography.

1979-32 Hunt, Sally. "Equal Rights & Libraries." Focus on Indiana Libraries 33 (January-February 1979): 3.

Thoughtful essay on the Equal Rights Amendment. Describes ALA resolutions, lists some of the 230 organizations which also boycott states which have not ratified the ERA, and offers names and addresses of prominent politicians to whom letters might be sent.

1979-33 Marchant, Maurice P. and Lebare, Lynn. "Library School Instruction in Discrimination Awareness." American Libraries 20 (January 1979): 42-43.

Summarizes a report submitted to the American Library Association Council by the Research Committee of the Library Education Division. In response to Council document 55, "Resolution on Prejudice, Stereotyping, and Discrimination," the Committee mailed a questionnaire to 64 deans and directors of library schools. Summary of responses identifies library school administration attitudes toward discrimination awareness and their perceived role in this context.

1979-34 "Special Librarians Vote ERA Boycott Action." LJ/SLJ Hotline 8 (January 8, 1979): 1.

Results of a mail vote of SLA members show 69 percent voted in favor of boycotting states that have not ratified the ERA.

1979-35 "Palmer House Threat of $$ Lawsuit Faces ALA." LJ/SLJ Hotline 8 (January 15, 1979): 1-2.

Outlines ramifications of the American Library Association boycott of states which have not ratified the ERA, and its effect on ALA-Palmer House relations.

1979-36 Savage, Noël. "News Report 1978." Library Journal 104 (January 15, 1979): 155-169.

Under the heading "Sex & Disparity," activity in support of the Equal Rights Amendment by ALA, MLA and SLA is reported. Sex bias battles at Minnesota's St. Paul Public Library, Temple University, San Diego Public, and Seattle libraries are mentioned. Efforts of the Equal Employment Opportunity Commission, library associations in California and Indiana, and National Women Library Workers are reported.

1979-37 "ALA Chicago Decision Faces Mail Vote." LJ/SLJ Hotline 8 (January 22, 1979): 1.

Describes ALA Council vote to take Midwinter 1980 out of Chicago because of Illinois' failure to ratify the ERA. Arguments against leaving Chicago are based on financial considerations. Mail vote of membership will decide.

1979-38 "The Pro/Con ERA Mail Vote." LJ/SLJ Hotline 8 (January 22, 1979): 1.

Announces that ALA members should receive ballots by March 1. Members must vote on the motion to boycott Chicago as Illinois has not ratified ERA. Informational materials summarizing pro and con arguments will be included with ballots.

1979-39 "The Vote in Chicago." LJ/SLJ Hotline 8 (January 22, 1979): 1-2.

Lists some ALA leaders who voted to avoid meeting in Chicago because of Illinois' refusal to ratify the Equal Rights Amendment.

1979-40 Bauer, Caroline Feller. "Fun Place at Any Cost." <u>American Libraries</u> 10 (February 1979): 64.

Letter expresses willingness to spend extra money to meet outside Chicago for Midwinter. To avoid blizzards, author suggests the Caribbean or Hawaii. She feels the stand will give notice of ALA's concern for ERA.

1979-41 Dickinson, Elizabeth. "Affirmative Action Plans in Review: A Report from Equal Employment Opportunity Subcommittee." <u>American Libraries</u> 10 (February 1979): 69-70.

Summarizes activities of the ALA/OLPR Equal Employment Opportunity Subcommittee, focusing on its review of library affirmative action plans.

1979-42 "Midwinter Notebook." <u>American Libraries</u> 10 (February 1979): 54-63.

Section entitled "Women at Work" (pp. 61-62) reports conflict between ALA Executive Director, Robert Wedgeworth, and the Committee on the Status of Women in Librarianship over possible headquarters relocation. ALA's investigation of ways to promote ERA without threatening ALA's tax-exempt status and SRRT Task Force on Women's activities are also summarized.

1979-43 Rosenfeld, Harriet E. "ERA vs. Chicago in '80--ALA Members to Decide in Mail Ballot." <u>Wilson Library Bulletin</u> 53 (February 1979): 434.

Describes the events leading up to the ALA mail ballot sent to members for a vote on boycott action against states which have not ratified the ERA.

1979-44 "SLA Joins Boycott." <u>Wilson Library Bulletin</u> 53 (February 1979): 436.

Results of Special Libraries Association membership vote, with half the membership returning ballots, show 69 percent in favor of boycotting states which have not ratified the Equal Rights Amendment.

1979-45 Snider, David. "Notes from a Cold, Cold Capitol." <u>ASLA Newsletter</u> (February 1979): 7.

Arizona State Library Association ALA Councilor's report on the 1979 Midwinter Meetings council and membership vote on the ERA.

1979-46 "ALA-Palmer House Flap over ERA Boycott Unlikely to Ever See Court." <u>LJ/SLJ Hotline</u> 8 (February 19, 1979): 6-7.

Renee Feinberg, chairperson of the NYLA Round Table on the Concerns of Women, reassures ALA members that no professional association had yet been sued over the ERA boycott.

1979-47 "Coalition of Library Groups Mount Major Effort to Keep ALA behind ERA." LJ/SLJ Hotline 8 (February 19, 1979): 2-3.

Mail vote of ALA membership will decide if ALA will boycott Chicago for the 1979 and 1980 Midwinter Meetings because of the failure of Illinois to ratify the ERA. A coalition of librarians is marshalling support for allegiance to the ERA. Some of the groups (such as ALA-SRRT, REFORMA, and Women Library Workers) backing the coalition are listed. History of the struggle is outlined.

1979-48 "Pro ERA Supporters Asked for $5 Donations." LJ/SLJ Hotline 8 (February 19, 1979): 2-3.

The coalition to support ERA and get ALA out of Chicago asks for donations.

1979-49 "Sexism & Inflation: New Setbacks for Large Public Libraries." LJ/SLJ Hotline 8 (February 19, 1979): 2.

Summary of data on sex and public library support [1979-70] shows that women directors earn less than men and generate less support for their libraries.

1979-50 Bidlack, Russell E. "A Statistical Survey of 67 Library Schools, 1978-79." Journal of Education for Librarianship 19 (Spring 1979): 318-336.

Male-female distribution for deans and directors of library schools in 1978-79 shows that the number of women deans has dropped by seven. The number of female assistant professors has dropped from 114 to 111. However, women have gained in professor, associate professor, instructor and lecturer positions (Table 3, p. 321).

1979-51 Courain, Margaret E. "Women in Library Management: Stop, Look, & Listen." Library Management Bulletin 2 (Spring 1979): 2-7.

Considers definitions of management (not necessarily library-management) positions and practical ways to deal with them.

1979-52 Drake, Miriam A. "Women in Librarianship: Jobs and Careers." Library Management Bulletin 2 (Spring 1979): 7-8.

Suggests that the different value structures of genders create the disparity between women's and men's salaries in libraries, and that if women change their behavior and attitudes they can close the salary gap.

1979-53 Euster, Joanne R. "The MBA in Library Land." Louisiana Library Association Bulletin 41 (Spring 1979): 80-82.

An MBA in management can provide the skills necessary for effective library administration. Management workshops, continuing education programs, and seminars are springing up, but MLS programs are generally overlooking practical management. The ideal would make library administration a specialty in itself. Meanwhile, the MLS/MBA combination is lucrative, especially for "women who seek to redress the sex imbalance among library executives."

1979-54 Martin, Jean K. "Academic Library Management: A Comparison of Females and Males." Library Management Bulletin 2 (Spring 1979): 9-11.

Reports results of author's MBA thesis [1978-22] which found no evidence that females and males are being treated differently insofar as salary and promotion are concerned.

1979-55 Norsworthy, James A., Jr. "ALA Midwinter--A Happening in Washington, D.C." KLA Bulletin 43 (Spring 1979): 21-22.

Report by Kentucky ALA Councilor describes ERA boycott actions taken by Council.

1979-56 Westenberger, Jane W. "Literature Review: Women in Management." Library Management Bulletin 2 (Spring 1979): 12-15.

Bibliography of books, articles and dissertations on women in management.

1979-57 Dougherty, Richard M. "Who Will Speak for the Library Profession?" Journal of Academic Librarianship 5 (March 1979): 3.

Editorial discusses the American Library Association policies regarding the ERA.

1979-58 "The Flight from Chicago: ALA Midwinter 1979." Wilson Library Bulletin 53 (March 1979): 507-513.

Reports that the ALA Executive Board voted 7 to 14 to "reaffirm ALA's contract with the Palmer House" and to meet in Chicago in 1980 despite the ERA boycott, and discusses legal issues involved (p. 507). Coverage of Council discussion is included (p. 509), as well as events leading up to the tie vote in Council and the petition to let the membership decide by a mail vote.

1979-59 Gerhardt, Lillian N. "How to Show the Queen." School Library Journal 25 (March 1979): 77.

Relates a story about Queen Elizabeth II who was declared an honorary man to facilitate a speaking engagement, in the context of arguments in support of returning ALA's Midwinter Meetings to Chicago before Illinois ratifies the Equal Rights Amendment. Suggests that ALA members will vote in favor of women's rights when they vote against returning to Chicago. Notes that 85 percent of the ALA membership are women and that they have experienced or witnessed pay discrimination. Reprints the text of the Equal Rights Amendment.

Letter: Gelshenen, Linda. "No to ERA." School Library Journal 25 (May 1979): 3.

Objects to "ridiculous stand." Suggests that a boycott oversteps ALA boundaries, and that the Equal Rights Amendment has nothing to do with librarianship. Notes that she is "tired of making concessions to a lot of feminist nonsense." Asks that School Library Journal editorials stop presenting "distorted views." Declares herself against the Equal Rights Amendment.

1979-60 Gerhardt, Lillian N., Cheatham, Bertha M., and Pollack, Pamela D. "Tied Up in Washington: SLJ's Report on ALA's Midwinter Meeting '79." School Library Journal 25 (March 1979): 99-104.

Provides history of ALA vote to boycott states which had not yet ratified the Equal Rights Amendment and describes current legal status. Special attention is given to the "coalition" formed to lobby ALA members on the issue and provide an action network to respond to similar issues. Event is important since it marked a switch of meeting location from Chicago to Washington D.C. as part of the boycott.

1979-61 Ihrig, Alice B. "ALA Chapter Councilor." Illinois Libraries 61 (March 1979): 208-209.

Report includes account of ALA's efforts to support the ERA boycott.

1979-62 "Legislative--Library Development Committee." Illinois Libraries 61 (March 1979): 218-219.

Legislation platform of the Illinois Library Association lists efforts to ratify the ERA as a top legislative concern.

1979-63 Ritchie, Sheila. "2000 to 1: a Sex Oddity." Assistant Librarian 72 (March 1979): 38-41.

Results of a small pilot study of librarians in English public libraries show 106 men in senior posts and only 2 women. Survey findings describe qualifications, career length, and aspirations of English librarians. Suggests that odds against a woman reaching level 1 are 2000 to 1.

Letters: Davis, Eileen. "Peter Principle." Assistant Librarian 72 (May 1979): 80.

Reply to Ritchie suggests that men are more likely to risk occupational maladjustments by accepting promotions in order to support their dependents. Concludes, "It's the men what get the money (and the wars); ain't it all a bleedin' shame?"

Ayers, Jill. "Sex Discrimination." Assistant Librarian 72 (June 1979): 92.

Views sex discrimination in libraries as partially the fault of women, who accept traditional roles and are forced to choose children over career goals.

Day, Virginia. "Women 1." Assistant Librarian 72 (September 1979): 124.

Agrees with Ayers but suggests that modern legislation enables women to have both children and career.

Cohen, Sylvia. "Women 2." Assistant Librarian 72 (September 1979): 124.

Suggests that many women purposely do not seek job advancement, that having children is not necessarily "copping out," and that there are practical difficulties in trying to cope with both job and family.

Holbourn, Cheryl. "Women 3." Assistant Librarian 72 (September 1979): 124.

Considers her own views to be that of the "strong, silent majority" and announces that after five years in libraries she now "joyfully awaits" the birth of a baby. Having children is a fundamental part of life, she says, and concludes that she has never encountered any discrimination.

1979-64 Berry, John. "ALA Principle--Not for Sale." Library Journal 104 (March 1, 1979): 527.

Outlines ALA mail vote on the 1980 Midwinter Meeting. Background of ERA boycott is provided. Urges that librarians vote to boycott Chicago.

Letters: Comaromi, John P. "Antigone's Problem." Library Journal 104 (May 15, 1979): 1090.

Affirms Berry's high principles but argues for commitment to the Palmer House.

Evans, Charles. "Move ALA for ERA." Library Journal 104 (May 15, 1979): 1090.

Notes that ALA's boycott is meaningless unless the Association divests itself of Chicago properties and moves headquarters.

1979-65 "Politics, Politics, Politics: A Report of the Midwinter Meeting of the American Library Association, Washington, D.C., January 7-12 . . . " Library Journal 104 (March 1, 1979): 559-567.

Describes deliberation on the issue of boycotting Illinois in support of the National Organization for Women (NOW) call to boycott states which have not ratified the Equal Rights Amendment (p. 562-563). Both ALA presidential candidates Peggy Sullivan and Alice Ihrig are on record in favor of keeping ALA out of Chicago. Council discussion is also reported (p. 564).

1979-66 "ALA Antitrust Liability Fears over Boycott Believed." LJ/SLJ Hotline 8 (March 5, 1979): 1.

Reports National Organization for Women court case as decided in favor of the national boycott of states which have not ratified the ERA. The decision, still subject to appeal, is seen as possibly influencing ALA members as they vote on the Association's boycott of Illinois.

1979-67 "'Don't Waiver on ERA Boycott' Pleads Florida Librarian." LJ/SLJ Hotline 8 (March 12, 1979): 4.

Judy Mucci of Orlando, Florida urges librarians to vote for continuing boycott of states which have not ratified ERA. She points out that Florida is now close to passage of the amendment because of similar boycotts--by AFL/CIO, NAACP, and the Republican Convention.

1979-68 Bidlack, Russell E. Faculty Availability in Terms of Affirmative Action. Ann Arbor, Mich.: University of Michigan, School of Library Science, March 14, 1979. (mimeographed).

Report speculates that the composition of the student group about to receive the doctorate (which contains a larger percentage of women and minorities than in the past) may affect faculty composition in the future.

1979-69 Berry, John. "Fighting Dollar Discrimination." Library Journal 104 (March 15, 1979): 661.

Editorial notes paradox that the National Organization of Women's boycott is upheld while public library female directors still fare less well than men [1979-70]. Urges librarians to use tough tactics in the scramble for municipal funds.

  Letter: Snyder, William E. "ERA a Side Issue." Library Journal 104 (May 15, 1979): 1090.

  Argues that ALA should give moral support to social issues but not hurt its credibility by sponsoring boycotts on issues outside the main concerns of the Association.

1979-70 Heim, Kathleen M., and Kacena, Carolyn. "Sex, Salaries, and Library Support, 1979." Library Journal 104 (March 15, 1979): 675-680.

Men hold 66 percent of the directorships of large public libraries; have a 22 percent average financial advantage in per capita support; earn 23 percent more (male median salary was $28,881; female--$23,451); and pay new professionals better than women.

  Letter: Reuter, Anne. "Double Discrimination." Library Journal 104 (June 15, 1979): 1291.

Letter comments on Heim and Kacena report and observes that until women achieve true equality, efforts to improve the profession's status will not be effective.

1979-72 "Reports on the Midwinter Meeting of the American Library Association, Washington, D.C., January 7-12, 1979." Library of Congress Information Bulletin 38 (March 30, 1979): 116-124.

Report includes summaries of all three Council Meetings which debated ALA's contractual agreement with the Palmer House in Chicago, in connection with support of the National Organization of Women's boycott of states which have not ratified ERA (p. 116-118). "The Politics of Administration," a program sponsored by the LAD Women Administrators Discussion Group, is also described (p. 123-124).

1979-73 Dannreuther, Kathy. "A Selective Summary of the ASLA Executive Board Meeting, Columbus Branch Library, Tucson, January 27, 1979." ASLA Newsletter (April 1979): 4-5.

Based on a motion by Arizona State Library Association (ASLA) ALA representative, David Snider, the Board voted to conduct a referendum to determine attitudes of ASLA members toward the Equal Rights Amendment. Meanwhile, the Board voted unanimously to go on record favoring the ratification of ERA in Arizona.

1979-74 Hook, Robert D. "ALA Councilor's Report on Midwinter, 1979." Idaho Librarian 31 (April 1979): 75-76.

Much of the entire report is devoted to discussion at Council on moving ALA headquarters out of Chicago and other ERA boycott issues.

1979-75 "Letters to ALA Oppose 1980 Boycott." American Libraries 9 (April 1979): 174-175, 206.

Unsolicited letters sent to Russell Shank, American Libraries, and Robert Wedgeworth reacting to ALA Council action at the 1979 Midwinter Meeting are printed.

Letters: Alexander, Adrian W. "Heads Out of the Clouds." American Libraries 9 (April 1979): 175.

Urges librarians to face facts and recognize that stubborn allegiance to token gestures will not enhance ERA's chances.

Armstrong, Robert W. "Basic Problems Ignored." American Libraries 9 (April 1979): 206.

Author is disturbed and frustrated that ALA ignores library problems and chooses instead to support crackpot social reforms.

Cahalan, Thomas H. "No Doubt." American Libraries 9 (April 1979): 206.

"On ERA & ALA, I agree with LJ."

Crosman, Alexander C., Jr. "Illinois' ERA Vote Explained." American Libraries 9 (April 1979): 174-175.

Complains about ERA support, and accuses ALA of sexism for allowing such groups as the SRRT Task Force on Women and the LAMA Women Administrators Discussion Group to exist.

Darnall, Charles W. "Personally Accountable for Financial Loss." American Libraries 9 (April 1979): 175.

Feels that if ALA suffers a financial loss, those responsible should be held accountable.

Day, Terence L. "Inappropriate Extortion." American Libraries 9 (April 1979): 174.

Writer is outraged and revolted at ERA boycott since libraries are supposed to be neutral.

Dible, Joan B. "Credit Rating at Risk." American Libraries 9 (April 1979): 175.

Author worries that ALA's credit rating will be ruined, even though she supports the boycott in the future.

Gould, Martha. "Not ALA's Problem." American Libraries 9 (April 1979): 206.

Observes that personal, emotional support for ERA has dangerously eroded our integrity.

Hough, William E., III. "Funds for Political Action." American Libraries 9 (April 1979): 206.

Threatens to quit ALA unless cooler heads prevail.

Lynch, Laurence P. "Down Payment on Credibility." American Libraries 9 (April 1979): 174.

Supports the referendum as a down payment on credibility and notes that the price of struggle and value of dignity are costly.

Marchant, Maurice P. "ERA Boycott a Goal Displacement." American Libraries 9 (April 1979): 175.

Lengthy discussion of legal ramifications of breaking the Palmer House contract.

Marquard, Steve. "Smashed Thumbs." American Libraries 9 (April 1979): 175.

Feels that ALA's boycott will hurt ERA since political stands do more harm than good.

Severance, Rosemary. "What's One More Year?" American Libraries 9 (April 1979): 174.

Complains her blood pressure rose at hearing of Council action on behalf of ERA.

Walsh, Nina May. "Degrading Discrimination." American Libraries 9 (April 1979): 175, 206.

Author is amazed and embarrassed that her professional association would stoop to pressure tactics to make a point.

1979-76 Shepard, Mary L. "Grads Find More Work in Special Libraries--Fewer Public and Academic Posts in 1978." Feliciter 25 (April 11, 1979): 45.

Describes placement data for University of Toronto graduates. Table I, "Number of Graduates, Placements and Salaries," shows employment by sex in 1977 and 1978.

1979-77 Snider, David. "ALA Councilor Column." ASLA Newsletter (April 1979): 1-3.

Arizona State Library Association's ALA Councilor reports on ALA votes and the legal position of ALA on the issue of the ERA boycott of states which have not ratified the Equal Rights Amendment.

1979-78 Yates, Ella Gaines. "Business or Tough Tactics." Library Journal 104 (April 15, 1979): 859.

Letter describes personal voting records of the Executive Board and Council regarding ERA-related decisions. Followed by a comment from the editor that Georgia (Yates' home) has not ratified the amendment.

Letter: Eckels, Patricia W. "Cheers for Yates." Library Journal 104 (July 1979): 1394.

Protests editorial note at end of Yates' letter.

1979-79 "1980 Midwinter Returns to Chicago. Vote Reverses Council's Decision." School Library Journal 25 (May 1979): 9.

Reports on mail vote of ALA members, which was held to establish whether the membership would uphold the ALA Council's one-vote decision to boycott Chicago because Illinois had not ratified the ERA. The record vote--9,597 to return to Chicago and 5,785 against--overturned the Council's decision. Women's groups within ALA responded with a request that ALA budget money to support ERA passage.

1979-80 "ALA Membership Vote Nixes ERA Stance." Library Journal 104 (May 1, 1979): 996.

Reports that a record-breaking mail ballot of ALA membership nixed Council's tough stance on ERA by a vote of 9,597 to 5,785. History of the boycott effort is summarized. Although Midwinter 1980 will be in Chicago, states which have not ratified ERA will be boycotted for future meetings.

1979-81 Dworak, Marica. "Women in Public Library Management: How Do They Measure Up?" Public Library Quarterly 1 (Summer 1979): 147-160.

Summarizes findings of a survey of women in public library administration in Illinois. Analyzes 121 returned questionnaires sent to 177 public library administrators. Results show that as a group, the women are: somewhat older than are the men, directors of smaller libraries, have fewer responsibilities, and have less self-confidence.

1979-82 Estes, Mark E. "The Southern California Association of Law Libraries 1979 Salary Survey." Law Library Journal 72 (Summer 1979): 526-533.

Report on survey of law librarians working in the area south of Santa Barbara. Results are compared to: a Philadelphia survey of 1977 [1978-52]; the American Association of Law Libraries survey [1976-127] for salary, sex, age and experience; and to the Special Library Association Survey [1976-75] for salary.

1979-83 "Grant for Career Development Center." PNLA Quarterly 43 (Summer 1979): 20, 33.

Reports $315,316 grant from W. K. Kellogg to the University of Washington to develop a model Career Development for Women Librarians assessment center designed to help them eliminate barriers which prevent or inhibit their attaining managerial positions.

1979-84 Nystrom, Kathleen A. "Women in Librarianship." Journal of Education for Librarianship 20 (Summer 1979): 77-78.

Report of Women's Interest Group session at the Association of American Library Schools Annual Conference includes business meeting resolution to support the ALA boycott of ERA.

1979-85 Denis, Laurent G. "Full-time Faculty Survey Describes Educators." Canadian Library Journal 36 (June 1979): 107-121.

Results of a survey of seven Canadian graduate library schools in November 1978 find equal numbers of women and men in library education, but that at the highest rank, that of full professor, men outnumber women significantly.

1979-86 McGrath, Richard. "Principles or Curse?" Library Journal 104 (June 1979): 1291.

Condemns Library Journal's monthly preoccupation to further the cause of the ERA.

Letter: Paeper, Roberta. "ERA: A Matter of Survival." Library Journal 104 (November 1, 1979): 2250.

Letter responding to Richard McGrath's letter (Library Journal, June 15, 1979: 1291) which states, "Librarians must be outside of causes." Paeper notes that ERA is a matter of survival.

1979-87 Plate, Kenneth H. and Seigel, Jacob P. "Career Patterns of Ontario Librarians." Canadian Library Journal 36 (June 1979): 143-148.

Results of a questionnaire returned by Canadian library school graduates. Data show that mean salaries of men are about $1200 higher than those of women, that they supervise more people than women, and that more women graduates are unemployed. Tables, broken out by sex, (p. 145) show: "Reasons for pursuing MLS," "Factors seen as contributing to success," and "Factors perceived to hinder career success." Differences in advancement-salary patterns are not great enough to explain salary differences by sex.

1979-88 Schuman, Patricia Glass, and Weibel, Kathleen. "The Women Arisen." American Libraries 10 (June 1979): 322-326.

Traces the history of women activists in the American Library Association beginning with union leader, Maude Malone. Also mentioned are Betty Wilson, Lutie Sterns, Joan Marshall, Laura X, Ellen Gay Detlefsen, Nancy Schimmel, Pat Schuman, and Kathleen Weibel. Groups within the Association which have fought for equality are described including the Librarians for Peace Brigade, National Women's Liberation Front for Librarians, Social Responsibilities Round Table Feminist Task Force, Committee on the Status of Women in Librarianship, Reference and Adult Services Division Women's Materials and Women Library Users Discussion Group, and the Library Administration and Management Association Women Administrator's Discussion Group. Issues of concern such as the ERA, affirmative action, and comparable pay are also mentioned.

1979-89 "Women's Program Statistical Update 1978: Grade Gap Narrows Slightly, More Women in Management." Library of Congress Information Bulletin 38 (June 8, 1979): 210-212.

Study conducted in 1977 shows that in terms of the representation of women by grade level, the Library had a better record than the Federal Government as a whole, but there was still a difference of 1.8 grades between the average grades of men and women. Minority women are still concentrated in the lower grades. There is an underrepresentation of women above GS 12 at the Library of Congress (LC) and above GS 8 for the Federal Government as a whole. Blue-collar occupations are still 70 percent single sex. Of all LC jobs 48 percent were single-sex (or "men's work"). Notable progress was made in placing women in management positions. Updates "Women's Program Statistical Study" from June 1978. Contains three charts: "LC vs. Federal

Government Grade Group Data"; "Grade Gaps by LC Department"; and "Distribution of Black Women in the LC Workforce."

1979-90 "Kellogg Grant of $315,316 Has Been Awarded." LJ/SLJ Hotline 8 (June 11, 1979): 6.

The University of Washington is to receive 3-year grant to develop a "model professional assessment and in-service training program for librarians." Focuses on women. The project, which will also be of use to male librarians, has as its goal to "eliminate barriers which prevent or inhibit women from gaining administrative experiences and responsibilities." Assessment process deals with "3 areas of learning: technical, interpersonal-being competencies, and interpersonal-learning competencies."

1979-91 "Library of Congress Progress in Affirmative Action: Semi-annual Report for October 1978--March 1979." Library of Congress Information Bulletin 38 (June 15, 1979): 223-228.

Upon completion of its first definitive research project on affirmative action recruitment, the Library discovered there are "serious deficiencies in the current effort," but flaws are correctable. There were career development workshops ("Promote yourself!") and a three-day seminar ("Women on the Way Up in Government"). There has been an upgrading of part-time positions (such positions in grades GS 6 and above have increased 33 percent since November 1976). The increase "enables the library to hire minorities and women whose talents might otherwise be lost." Total employment of women among all Library employees remained constant at 52 percent. In grades GS 13 through 15, employment of women rose from 29 percent to 30 percent.

1979-92 "1978 Placement Shift." LJ/SLJ Hotline 8 (June 18, 1979): 1.

Previews placement article scheduled to appear in July, 1979 issue of Library Journal [1979-98]. Average beginning salaries: between $8,846 to $12,527 with women graduates averaging about $150 less per year than men.

1979-93 "Library Administration (and Women) Need MBAs." LJ/SLJ Hotline 8 (June 18, 1979): 6.

Refers to article [1979-53] by Joanne R. Euster, which maintains an MBA is necessary for administrative advancement, especially for women. The MBA is more profitable than the Ph.D. in Library Science. Hotline is skeptical and notes that the MBA is being devalued by the large numbers "flocking to get one." For the time being, though, it seems getting the MBA is "the only way to go."

1979-94 "Career Development and Assessment Center." Issued by Public Information Officer, Sue Fontaine. Washington State Library, June 23, 1979 (news release).

Describes model Career Development and Assessment Center for Librarians co-sponsored by the University of Washington, School of Librarianship and Washington State Library, and funded by the W. K. Kellogg Foundation for $315,316. Ruth Hamilton and Charlotte L. Wood are co-directors.

1979-95 "Xerox's Horace Becker on Special Librarians." LJ/SLJ Hotline 8 (June 25, 1979): 4-5.

Becker, Xerox engineer and executive, speaking at the SLA meeting in Hawaii, observed that special librarians are not getting paid enough and aren't being allowed to advance in management. Gives tips on how the librarian should sell him/herself and the library. Among other tips, the problem of the "aggressive" female is addressed.

1979-96 D'Elia, George P. "The Determinants of Job Satisfaction Among Beginning Librarians." Library Quarterly 49 (July 1979): 283-302.

Compares male and female job satisfaction and finds little difference.

1979-97 Hudson, Nancy. "ALA Report." High Roller 16 (July-August 1979): 14.

ALA Councilor report of the ALA Annual Conference includes reference to Council discussion on the Equal Rights Amendment. Implies that ERA is not an important issue relating to librarianship.

1979-98 Learmont, Carol L., and Troiano, Richard. "Placements & Salaries 1978: New Directions." Library Journal 106 (July 1979): 1415-1422.

Reports continued male-female differential in starting salary of new graduates of ALA-accredited library education programs.

Letter: Learmont, Carol L. "Placement Correction." Library Journal 107 (March 15, 1980): 652.

Letter corrects survey report and provides a new table for median male and female salaries.

1979-99 "The Numbers of Number 98: An Account of the 1979 Dallas Annual Conference." American Libraries 10 (July-August 1979): 406-414, 423-425, 446.

Under the heading, "Women's Activities" (p. 424), article reports that women's groups at the Annual Conference assumed a low profile.

Much activity was directed towards supporting the Equal Rights Amendment. Discusses the Bailey K. Howard-World Book Encyclopedia ALA Goal Award to the Committee on the Status of Women in Librarianship for the planned pilot study of women in the library profession. Two other programs, the SRRT Task Force on Women presentation featuring feminist author Alix Kates Shulman, and a comparable pay meeting are mentioned.

1979-100 "UW to Develop Nat'l Model to Train Women Managers." Library Journal 104 (July 1979): 1409.

Announcement of Kellogg grant funding the Career Development and Assessment Center for Librarians at the University of Washington School of Librarianship with the Washington State Library. Aim of the project is described by Washington State Librarian, Roderick Schwartz and School of Librarianship Director, Peter Hiatt as "to eliminate barriers which prevent or inhibit women from gaining administrative experience and responsibilities." The problem of getting more women to the top will be addressed.

1979-101 "Open Questions in Dallas: The 98th Annual Conference of ALA." Library Journal 104 (August 1979): 1517-1536.

Describes the conference-long debate on how the Association should show support for the Equal Rights Amendment. Includes information on ERAmerica; the ERA Task Force to be chaired by Kay Ann Cassell and Alice Ihrig; and photos of ERA supporters dressed in white: Miriam Crawford, Ellen Gay Detlefsen, Betty-Carol Sellen and Joan Marshall.

1979-102 "Career Development Assessments Offered." Noted for the Alumni No. 42 (Fall 1979): 1.

Newsletter of the University of Washington School of Librarianship describes Career Development and Assessment Center for Librarians.

1979-103 "The First Meeting of the Steering Committee for the Career Development and Assessment Center for Librarians Was Set for October 3, 1979." PNLA Quarterly 44 (Fall 1979): 21.

Advisory Council of the Career Development and Assessment Center for Librarians is noted.

1979-104 Norsworthy, James A., Jr. "Highlights of the 98th Annual ALA Conference in Dallas." KLA Bulletin 43 (Fall 1979): 52-53.

Kentucky ALA Councilor reports his surprise that social responsibilities are a top ALA priority. Norsworthy notes that he abstained on the vote to grant $10,000 for ERA work and voted "no" to give $1.00 per member for ERA action.

1979-105 Prosser, Judith. "WVLA-ALA Councilor's Report." West Virginia Libraries 32 (Fall 1979): 17-20.

Starting the report with, "Hallelujah, my last year as ALA Councilor," article launches into complaints about the issues which had concerned Council in the last five years. Most scorn is heaped on the ERA.

1979-106 Ward, James E. "ALA Councilor Report." Tennessee Librarian 31 (Fall 1979): 7-9.

Describes Council and membership debate on the Equal Rights Amendment at the ALA Annual Conference in Dallas. Author reports that he voted against the motion (which passed) to set aside $10,000 for ALA ERA support because he did not feel that the money would be helpful and that "one should recognize that . . . many ALA members . . . are not supporters of its ratification." Suggests voluntary donations instead and notes that 1980 ALA membership application forms will offer the opportunity to contribute to ERA efforts.

1979-107 "ALA Meets Peacefully in Big D." Wilson Library Bulletin 54 (September 1979): 15-26.

Reports ALA Executive Board discussion on how best to show support of the Equal Rights Amendment. Dismissing a proposal by Drexel University GSLIS, a compromise motion was made to recommend that Council set aside $10,000 to assist chapters in states which had not ratified ERA (p. 16); Council supported the motion (p. 18), and the Executive Board also approved a motion to set up a board to receive personal member donations to ERAmerica.

1979-108 Gerhardt, Lillian N., Cheatham, Bertha M., and Pollack, Pamela D. "Roundup in Dallas." School Library Journal 26 (September 1979): 35-40.

General conference coverage includes membership support of ERA described under the heading, "Issues" (p. 35), and report of an open hearing on sexism in adolescent materials (p. 40).

1979-109 Sink, Darryl L. "Employment Trends for Media Graduates: Business and Industry Emerging." Audiovisual Instruction 24 (September 1979): 36-37.

Media graduate employment report includes table displaying degree production by sex.

1979-110 Vincent, Ida. "Academic Library Administrators and Part Time Work." Australian Academic Research Libraries 10 (September 1979): 150-161.

A survey of attitudes of administrators of university and college libraries in New South Wales towards part-time work, conducted in November and December of 1978, found that academic libraries in New South Wales seemed to offer comparatively few opportunities for part-time work. Statistics from the Australian Bureau of Statistics showed that 16 percent of employees classified as "professional and technical" work part-time, compared with 6.6 percent of professional librarians in the survey. Of the women in that classification 29.8 percent worked part-time, a significant comparison for the predominantly female library profession.

1979-111 "Continuing Reports on the 98th Annual Conference of the American Library Association, Dallas, Texas, June 23-29, 1979." Library of Congress Information Bulletin 39 (September 28, 1979): 410-412.

Describes membership debate and action on the resolution that ALA contribute $1.00 per member towards ERA ratification. A detailed report by Sarah Pritchard on the activities of the SRRT Task Force on Women and the Committee on the Status of Women in Librarianship is also included.

1979-112 Wallach, John S. "ALA Councilor's Report." Ohio Library Association Bulletin 49 (October 1979): 11.

Reports ERA action at 1979 ALA Annual Conference.

1979-113 "ALA/SRRT Task Force on Women to Boycott Chicago Midwinter." LJ/SLJ Hotline 8 (October 1, 1979): 4.

Announces the SRRT Task Force on Women decision to boycott the Midwinter Meeting in Chicago, in keeping with the 1977 membership decision to hold no conferences in states which have not ratified the Equal Rights Amendment.

1979-114 "Women's Information Service Award for 1980." LJ/SLJ Hotline 8 (October 1, 1979): 4.

A $1000 award for the best plan to improve information services to women is offered by the Business and Professional Women's Association, the ALA Committee on the Status of Women, the SRRT Task Force on Women, and Women Library Workers.

1979-115 "Concluding Reports on the 98th Annual Conference of the American Library Association, Dallas, Texas, June 23-29, 1979." Library of Congress Information Bulletin 39 (October 5, 1979): 416-420.

ALA Council actions, including ERA resolutions, are reported.

1979-116 "ALA/ERA Task Force." School Library Journal 26 (November 1974): 12.

Reports appointees to the ERA Task Force and their plans. Includes comments of committee Co-chair, Kay Cassell, on those who protested meeting in Chicago because of a SRRT directive to boycott the Midwinter Meeting.

1979-117 Gerhardt, Lillian N. "Sulking to Oblivion." School Library Journal 26 (November 1979): 9.

Editorial on the SRRT Task Force on Women and their call to their 500 members to boycott the Midwinter Meeting in Chicago. Compares this "sulk" to other activities, such as the "Dramatic Departure," "Awful Silence," "Bypassed Pout," and the "Non-Join Sulk." A pragmatic commentary which observes that the boycott might be detrimental since those absent will not be working in their appointed slots to advance library service in other areas. This may affect future appointments. (An interesting editorial by a long-time supporter!)

Letters: Thibodo, Sharon. "A Yea for Boycott." School Library Journal 26 (January 1980): 4.

Believes support for the Equal Rights Amendment is not "narrow dedication to a single cause" but a much wider issue. Writes with wholehearted support for the boycott supported by the SRRT Task Force on Women.

LeBarron, Suzanne. "Awfully Cute." School Library Journal 26 (February 1980): 3.

Suggests that some statements may be misleading. Writes that "oblivion will hardly be the fate" of the Task Force on Women and individual ALA members who are participating in the boycott. Mentions the "Women in a Woman's Profession: Strategies II" pre-conference to be held at the 1980 ALA Annual Conference.

Williams, Helen E. "A 'Magnum Opus.'" School Library Journal 26 (March 1980): 71.

Believes that the editorial is well written. Hopes it encourages nonparticipants to express their concerns openly.

1979-118 "Task Force on Women Urges Midwinter Boycott." School Library Journal 26 (November 1979): 11-12.

Report of a September press release sent by Suzanne LeBarron of the SRRT Task Force on Women advising ALA committee members to notify committee chairs and ALA division heads that they will not attend the Midwinter Meeting in Chicago because of the Equal Rights Amendment boycott.

1979-119 Boucias, Karen, Moore, E. Catherine, and O'Hara, Catherine. "Been Down So Long It Looks Like Up to Me; A Course in Women Librarianship." Journal of Education for Librarianship 19 (Winter 1979): 273-278.

Discusses course offered on "Women in Librarianship" at one unnamed library school. Includes written purposes of the course, a breakdown of students who enrolled, an outline of the course (naming the required texts), and topics discussed. Maintains that library schools have the responsibility for making students aware of "women (in)-equality in librarianship." New professionals entering the field should be made aware of discrimination which exists against women.

1979-120 Hall, Hal W. "Chapter Councilor's Report: ALA Midwinter Meeting, January 1979." Texas Library Journal 55 (Winter 1979): 7.

Urges ALA members to vote in February mail ballot on moving the Midwinter Meeting of 1980 out of Chicago because of the boycott in support of ERA. Council votes on the issue from 1977 to January 1979 are listed chronologically.

1979-121 Reid, Marion T. "1976-77 Professional Salaries and Fringe Benefits in Louisiana Academic Libraries." Louisiana Library Association Bulletin 41 (Winter 1979): 50-54.

A "Questionnaire on Salary Statistics of Academic Library Staffs" sent to 32 libraries shows that men have higher mean salaries in ranked categories and fewer median years of service (p. 53; Tables IV, V).

1979-122 "ALA's For ERA." American Libraries 10 (December 1979): 663-664.

Reports ERA Task Force progress. The Task Force met in Pittsburgh August 17-18, 1979 to develop strategies with Suone Cotner of ERAmerica. Questionnaires were sent to state chapters to determine needs. Illinois, Florida, and Missouri were targeted. Brochures explaining ALA's position were developed [1980-01].

1979-123 Braunagel, Judith Schiek. "Job Mobility of Men and Women Librarians and How It Affects Career Advancement." American Libraries 10 (December 1979): 643-647.

Top prize winner in American Libraries article competition examines mobility as a contributor to women's depressed status in librarianship. Findings indicate that mobility factors do not account for status difference.

1979-124 Foster, Dona Lyn. "ALA & ERA." The Sourdough 16 (December 1979): 14.

Notes that Alaska was the second state to ratify the Equal Rights Amendment in 1972. Lists some occupational imbalances and suggests that since ALA has shown strong support of ERA that the Alaska Library Association do the same.

1979-125 "Librarians Charge Pay Discrimination." Feliciter 25 (December 1979): 1, 3.

When librarians employed at the Canadian National Library and 37 other federal departments found that they were paid 35 percent less than men employees of the Historical Research section for comparable work, they took their complaint to the Canadian Human Rights

Commission. Report gives a brief history of the sex-typed positions, the steps taken by the women librarians, and future action planned.

1979-126 "The SLA Salary Survey, 1979." Special Libraries 70 (December 1979): 559-589.

Fifth triennial SLA salary survey reports that in every percentile rank women earned less than men. Female median salary was $17,400; male, $21,000. (Note: Errors in Table 3, p. 562; and in interpretation on p. 562, column 1. These were corrected in the December 1980 issue [1980-135].)

1979-127 Wilkins, Barratt. Survey of State Library Agencies, 1977. (Occasional Paper No. 142) Urbana: University of Illinois, Graduate School of Library Science, December 1979.

"Staff" report summarizes tables 8, 9, 9a, and 10 (p. 18-23). Two-thirds of full-time professional employees were women. Administrative services were performed by 21.4 percent of men; public services were 35.2 percent men, 42.8 percent women; technical services were performed by 11.4 percent men and 19.6 percent women.

1979-128 "Taking the Library Pulse for the 1977-79 Biennium." LJ/SLJ Hotline 8 (December 10, 1979): 2-3.

Sneak preview of [1980-42a].

1979-129 Yates, Ella Gaines. "Sexism in the Library Profession." Library Journal 104 (December 15, 1979): 2615-2619.

Explores the nature of sexist attitudes in the light of the roles played by women and men library administrators. Discusses the relationships of age and color with sexism, concluding with advice to women who seek administrative roles. Suggests that grooming and appearance are important, as well as marketing and verbal skills.

Letter: Schwebke, Ruth N. "Sex and Race." Library Journal 105 (March 1, 1980): 540.

Suggests that treatment of women's movement has not dealt completely with discrimination against black women.

1980-01 "ALA's for ERA." Chicago: ALA ERA Task Force, 1980.

Brochure carries the opening text of the United States Constitution and the question, "What's missing?" Inside page describes the ALA, its record of action, and its position on social responsibilities. The text of the Equal Rights Amendment is reprinted on the back page and the purpose of the ERA Task Force is explained.

1980-02 Bevis, Dorothy L. "The Librarian-Adventurers." In What Else You Can Do With a Library Degree. Edited by Betty-Carol Sellen. Syracuse, N.Y.: Gaylord Professional Publications, in Association with Neal-Schuman Publishers, 1980: 72-76.

94   1980-03   Annotated Bibliography

Describes the Career Development and Assessment Center for Librarians (established at the University of Washington and co-sponsored by the Washington State Library) as intended for women who are already in the field and want to develop managerial skills.

1980-03   Biblo, Mary. "Social Responsibilities Round Table." In ALA Yearbook 1980. Edited by Robert Wedgeworth. Chicago: ALA, 1980: 293.

Reports activities of the SRRT Task Force on Women.

1980-04   Bidlack, Russell E. "Faculty." In Association of American Library Schools Library Education Statistical Report 1980. State College, Pa.: AALS, 1980.

Seventh in the Faculty Report series includes breakdown of data on library education faculty by sex. Notes that 58 percent of the total are male. Men hold 79.1 percent of Dean and Directorship positions, 67.4 percent are employed as professors, and 61.3 percent are associate professors. Women and men are nearly even at the assistant professor level (men 48.6 percent; women 51.4 percent). Men's salaries are generally higher at all levels.

1980-05   Bidlack, Russell E. A Statistical Survey of the Full-time Faculty in Library Education, 1979-1980. Arlington, Va.: ERIC Document Reproduction Service, 1980: ED 194 098.

Microreproduction of [1980-04].

1980-06   Cheatham, Bertha M. "SLJ News Report, 1979." In Bowker Annual, 25th ed. New York: Bowker, 1980: 26-28.

Reprint of [1980-35].

1980-07   Chisholm, Margaret E. "College Administration." In What Else You Can Do With A Library Degree. Edited by Betty-Carol Sellen. Syracuse, N.Y.: Gaylord Professional Publications in Association with Neal-Schuman Publishers, 1980: 273-281.

In an article on opportunities in higher education administration, the special concerns of women are noted. The Career Development and Assessment Center for Librarians at the University of Washington is described.

1980-08   Cuesta, Yolanda. "Personnel and Employment: Affirmative Action." In ALA Yearbook 1980. Edited by Robert Wedgeworth. Chicago: ALA, 1980: 233-234.

Report includes section on women and discussion of Washington State's Career Development and Assessment Center for Librarians.

1980-09   *Drake, Sunniva. "Kuinka Kirjastonhoitjan ammatista tuli naisvaltainen ja alipalkattu (Why Are Librarians Women and Underpaid?) Kirjastolehti 73 (7-8) 1980: 372-374. (Abstracted in LISA as 81/3360.)

"Graphs show the numbers of male and female staff in the Helsinki public libraries and in the Helenski University Library. Women earn 30 percent less on average than men because their job descriptions are different."

1980-10 Fenster, Valmai. "Women's Contributions to the Library School: 1895-1939." In University Women: A Series of Essays, Volume II-Wisconsin Women: Graduate School and the Professions. Edited by Marian J. Swoboda and Audrey J. Roberts. Madison: University of Wisconsin System. Office of Women, 1980: 21-27.

Focuses on women who founded and developed the Library School at the University of Wisconsin at Madison.

1980-11 Gasaway, Laura N. "Women in Special Libraries." In Special Librarianship: A New Reader. Edited by Eugene B. Jackson, Metuchen, N.J.: Scarecrow, 1980: 85-92.

Essay suggests that special libraries offer wide opportunities for women librarians. Management positions are more plentiful, the service element is greater, creative public service is welcomed, and subject specialties are in greater demand. Under headings such as "Getting a Job," and "What Women Need For Success in Special Libraries," librarians attracted to the field are given general hints and suggestions.

1980-12 Getz, Malcolm. Public Libraries: An Economic View. Baltimore: John Hopkins University Press, 1980: 62-63.

Discussion of sex ratio of employment and local labor market for librarians observes that some libraries may recruit women in order to pay a lower salary.

1980-13 Grant, W. Vance, and Eiden, Leo J. Digest of Education Statistics: 1980. Washington, D.C.: GPO, 1980. (NCES 80-401).

Includes data on men and women librarians in school library media centers for 1973-74 and 1978-79 (Table 191, p. 221) as well as information on library science degree recipients and enrollment for advanced degree programs by sex.

1980-14 Heim, Kathleen M. "Women in Librarianship." In ALA Yearbook 1980. Edited by Robert Wedgeworth. Chicago: ALA, 1980: 317-322.

Annual report includes: coverage of ALA/ERA actions, including the formation of an ERA Task Force; the Special Libraries Association ERA boycott; surveys of placements and salaries; degree distribution

96   1980-15   Annotated Bibliography

by sex; career development for women; comparable pay for comparable work; sexism; Women Library Workers; the Association for Women in Computing; scholarship; awards; and library science courses on women in the profession.

1980-15   Heim, Kathleen M. and Kacena, Carolyn. "Sex, Salaries and Library Support, 1979." In Bowker Annual, 25th ed. New York: Bowker, 1980: 334-344.

Reprint of [1979-70].

1980-16   Heller, Dawn. "Illinois." In ALA Yearbook 1980. Edited by Robert Wedgeworth. Chicago: ALA, 1980: 365-367.

Notes that a top legislative concern of the Illinois Library Association is ERA ratification.

1980-17   Jackson, Eugene B. Three Grandes Dames of Dayton, Ohio As a Well-Spring of Women Special Librarians. Arlington, Va.: ERIC Document Reproduction Service, 1980: ED 184 503.

Discusses the role of women librarians in special libraries in Dayton. The careers of three librarians are compared in the light of the historical background of the three institutions investigated: General Motors, the U.S. Air Force McCook Field Library, and National Cash Register Company Library.

1980-18   Josey, E. J. "Social Responsibilities." In ALA Yearbook 1980. Edited by Robert Wedgeworth. Chicago: ALA, 1980: 286-293.

Mentions that the most up-to-date information on women in librarianship is to be found in the newsletter of the American Library Association SRRT Task Force on Women, Women in Libraries.

1980-19   Kim, Ung Chon. "A Statistical Study of Factors Affecting Salaries of Academic Librarians at Medium-Sized State-Supported Universities in Five Midwestern States." Ph.D. thesis. Indiana University, 1980. DAI no. 8016431.

Variables of education, experience, supervisory level, faculty rank, publication, professional activity, mobility, age, and sex are examined. Controlling all variables reveals that sex is the variable which returns salaries consistently lower for women.

1980-20   Ladenson, Alex. "Law and Legislation." In ALA Yearbook 1980. Edited by Robert Wedgeworth. Chicago: ALA, 1980: 167-169.

Includes report of complaints filed by San Diego Public Librarians with the city's Equal Employment Investigation Officer, and by Temple University librarians with the Equal Employment Opportunities Commission. Both complaints are based on the argument that librarians earn lower salaries because they work in a women's profession.

1980-21 Learmont, Carol L. "Students." In Association of American Library Schools Library Education Statistical Report 1980. State College, Pa.: AALS, 1980: Student Report.

Provides enrollment, profile, financial and placement data broken down by sex and ethnicity.

1980-22 Learmont, Carol L. and Troiano, Richard. "Placements and Salaries, 1978: New Directions." In Bowker Annual, 25th ed. New York, Bowker, 1980: 321-344.

Reprint of [1979-98].

1980-23 Leavitt, Judith A. Network Directory 1980. Muncie, Ind., 1980.

Directory compiled for the Indiana Library Association Division on Women in Indiana Libraries. Contains approximately 30 names, addresses and interests of Indiana librarians who are interested in networking. Also contains some "do's" and "don'ts" of networking and bibliography.

1980-24 Lundy, Kathryn Renfro. Women View Librarianship: Nine Perspectives. (ACRL Publications in Librarianship no. 41) Chicago: ALA, 1980.

Interviews with Virginia Lacy Jones, Connie R. Dunlap, Annette L. Phinazee, Martha Boaz, Page Ackerman, Helen Welch Tuttle, Patricia Battin, Sarah Rebecca Reed, and Margaret Knox Goggin include subjects' remarks on the role of women in the profession.

1980-25 Melber, Barbara D. and McLaughlin, Steven D. Evaluation of the First Year of the Librarian Career Development and Assessment Center Project. Seattle, Wash.: Battelle Human Affairs Research Centers, 1980.

Issued with the Annual Report [1980-97] of the Career Development and Assessment Center, the Evaluation presents the research and evaluation instruments developed in the Center's pilot phase and discusses empirical findings.

1980-26 Pepin, Andrew J. and Wells, Agnes Q. Earned Degrees Conferred 1977-78. Washington, D.C.: GPO, 1980. (NCES 80-346).

Bachelor's, master's, and doctoral degrees are reported by sex with percentage changes.

1980-27 Savage, Noël. "LJ News Report, 1979." In Bowker Annual, 25th ed. New York: Bowker, 1980: 3-28.

Reprint of [1980-44].

1980-28 SHARE: A Directory of Feminist Library Workers, 4th ed. Berkeley, Calif.: Women Library Workers, 1980.

Fourth edition of the national SHARE directory continues [1975-18; 1976-58; 1978-28].

1980-29 Sink, Darryl L. "Employment Trends for Media Graduates 1978-1979." In Educational Media Yearbook 1980, 6th ed. Edited by James W. Brown. Littleton, Colo.: Libraries Unlimited, 1980: 68-72.

Degree production for media graduates is reported by sex.

1980-30 Slater, Margaret. Career Patterns and the Occupational Image: A Study of the Library/Information Field. (Aslib Occasional Publication No. 23) London: ASLIB, 1980.

Study of librarians' career patterns, completed in 1977, includes discussion of the image of the library and information field.

1980-31 Strong, Gary E. "Washington." In ALA Yearbook 1980. Edited by Robert Wedgeworth. Chicago: ALA, 1980: 411-412.

Includes description of the Career Development and Assessment Center for Librarians.

1980-32 U.S. Equal Employment Opportunity Commission. Hearings before the U.S. Equal Employment Opportunity Commission on Job Segregation and Wage Discrimination, April 28-30, 1980. Washington, D.C.: GPO, 1980.

Includes testimony by Margaret Myers, Director of the American Library Association Office for Library Personnel Resources, on the topic as it relates to librarians.

1980-33 Your Assessment Center in Action: Career Development and Assessment Center for Librarians. Seattle: Career Development and Assessment Center for Librarians, 1980.

Brochure describes the function of the Center, and the roles of assessees and assessors.

1980-34 "Career Development for Women Librarians." Spokeswomen 10 (January 1980): 4.

Because of the discrepancy between the ratio of women in the library profession (82 percent) and those in management (32 percent) the Career Development and Assessment Center for Librarians was launched in 1979 in the state of Washington. Includes brief description of the project.

1980-35 Cheatham, Bertha M. "Library News of the Year in Retrospect." School Library Journal 26 (January 1980): 29-33.

tary grants to be given to assist state chapters in ERA activities, and programs planned for the New York Annual Conference to teach lobbying techniques (p. 137). Activities of the Committee on the Status of Women in Librarianship are also reported (p. 142).

1980-61 "The Saga of the Lady Librarian." Circum-Spice no. 24, N.S. (Spring 1980): 1-3.

Newsletter of the City College of New York includes excerpts from Role of Women in Librarianship [1979-28] which are summarized with the question, "How does the situation at City College measure up?" A brief history of the status of women at City College Library is provided with the surprising result that women are on top!

1980-62 Gerhardt, Lillian N., Cheatham, Bertha M., and Pollack, Pamela D. "SLJ's Report on the ALA 1980 Midwinter Meeting." School Library Journal 26 (March 1980): 91-96.

The American Library Association ERA Task Force reports raising $1600 for ERA activities as a result of member checkoffs on membership forms.

1980-63 Hubbell, Sue. "Disquiet in the Stacks." Working Woman 3 (March 1980): 53-54, 58, 60, 73, 106.

Article describing women's place in the library profession, although filled with factual inaccuracies, does highlight the disparity between high job requirements and low salaries.

Letter: Barber, Peggy. "In Defense of Libraries." Working Woman 3 (July 1980): 24.

Provides some positive facts about librarians' careers.

Clarification: "ALA Staff Answers Working Woman Misstatements with Hard and Useful Facts about Librarianship." American Libraries 11 (September 1980): 496, 498.

Peggy Barber, Margaret Myers, Jeniece Guy, and Peggy O'Donnell provide a detailed response to the article on librarians in Working Woman, correcting the factual errors and providing the positive side of careers of librarians.

1980-64 McNamee, Gil. "Report of ALA Chapter Councilor." The Newsletter: California Library Association 23 (March 1980): 3.

Report includes survey of ALA's actions on behalf of ERA.

1980-65 Miller, Rae Jean. "Women Have Always Managed." Show Me Libraries 31 (March 1980): 30-32.

Description of a seminar on special concerns of women in management.

1980-66 "Reports on the Midwinter Meeting of the American Library Association Chicago, IL, January 20-25, 1980." Library of Congress Information Bulletin 39 (March 14, 1980): 85-92.

Council noted that the Executive Board "has pursued the goal of ERA ratification vigorously" (p. 86).

1980-67 "A New Ball Game on the Hill." Library Journal (March 15, 1980): 673-680.

ERA activity is commented upon in a photo caption (p. 675) of ERA Task Force Chair, Kay Cassell, and COSWL member, Elizabeth Futas.

1980-68 "Williams and Wilkins Counsel Heads Ringer Replacement Search." LJ/SLJ Hotline 9 (March 17, 1980): 1.

News note on search for new Register of Copyrights recounts the difficulty the retiring Register, Barbara Ringer, had in attaining the post. Her successful sex discrimination case against the Library of Congress is recalled.

1980-69 "ALA Supports ERA in Missouri." Missouri Library Association Newsletter 11 (April 1980): 8.

Notes that an ERA Task Force grant of $1,500 was awarded to Missouri Women in Libraries Committee for state ERA action.

1980-70 "ASIS Preliminary Report." Speakeasy 6 (April 1980): 9-13.

Tables display the results of a one-page questionnaire returned by 1,877 ASIS members. Breakdown by sex (Table VII) shows that women comprise 55.9 percent and men 43.1 percent of the membership.

1980-71 Dialogue: Newsletter of the Women's Caucus 1, n.1 (April 1980).

Newsletter of the Women's Caucus, Social Sciences Group, New York Chapter of SLA focuses on women's (sexual harassment, salaries) and professional (networking, career advancement) issues. Sent to over 400 subscribers in the United States and Canada, it includes information about national SLA meetings, the position of the Women's Caucus in SLA, topical bibliographies, and other items of interest to women in the profession.

1980-72 Hippenhammer, Craighton T. "In Praise of Nurture and Other Nasty 'Female' Qualities." School Library Journal 26 (April 1980): 43.

Calls for more balance in sex-role controversies. Criticizes Caroline Coughlin's article [1978-38] which called for school librarians to be more assertive, and comes out in favor of nurturance--a quality not totally lacking in men. Writer urges children's libraries to "crow" about their emotional strengths--not apologize for them.

1980-73 Isaacson, David. "Reference Librarian As General Fact Totem." Wilson Library Bulletin 54 (April 1980): 494-500.

Letters: Forman, Jack. "Pronoun Quirks." Wilson Library Bulletin 54 (June 1980): 64.

Objects to use of pronouns which refer to a librarian as "she" and an intellectual as "he."

Klauber, Julie. "Pronoun Quirks." Wilson Library Bulletin 54 (June 1980): 614.

Letter criticizes Isaacson's implication that patron-intellectuals are males and librarians are females, and other sexist stereotypes in article.

Note: Editor's note: Defends pronouns as a result of editing to introduce a variety which would avoid identification with either sex.

1980-74 Shaw, Louise C. "1980 Salary Survey." Datamation (April 1980): 110-118.

The first survey of data processing personnel and salaries which includes data by sex reveal women in the categories of data entry, production control and librarians. Salary tables show librarian salaries to be considerably lower than others (p.113).

1980-75 Shepard, Mary L. "Graduates Find Part-Time Positions." Feliciter 26 (April 1980): 6-7.

Describes placement information for Canadian library school graduates.

1980-76 "SLA Salary Review Finds Women Gaining." Library Journal 105 (April 15, 1980): 905.

Reports that, although women special librarians earn less than men in every category, their gains are starting to outpace men's. (Note: this report is based on incorrectly reported data. [1980-135] provides correction.)

1980-77 "Two New Members Have Been Selected to Serve on the Women's Program Advisory Committee." Library of Congress Information Bulletin 39 (April 25, 1980): follows p. 140.

Announcement names new members.

1980-78 "ALA Report." American Libraries (May 1980): 291-293.

In reference to discussion on determining a lowest-recommended salary for professional librarians, the Office for Library Personnel Resources suggests that the Association put more effort into "equal pay for jobs of equal worth." Notes that OLPR will testify before the Equal Opportunity Employment Commission and will collect and disseminate information as a result of the Council resolution on comparable wages.

1980-79 Cassell, Kay and Ihrig, Alice. "Reckoning from ERA'ers." American Libraries 11 (May 1980): 255.

Letter from the Co-Chairs of the ERA Task Force thanks members for contributions which totaled $2,931 to the Task Force and $2,045 to ERAmerica.

1980-80 Cherry, Susan Spaeth. "SLA Chapter Woman's Caucus." American Libraries 11 (May 1980): 306.

Announces the formation of the New York City Chapter of the Special Libraries Association Social Science Division Women's Caucus. At the first SLA caucus focusing on the concerns of women special librarians, the two meetings drew capacity crowds.

1980-81 Cherry, Susan Spaeth. "Women Library Workers Expands Monthly Newsletter." American Libraries 11 (May 1980): 306.

Displays the WLW logo and describes new format for WLW Journal: News/Views/Reviews for Women and Libraries.

1980-82 "Task Force on the Status of Women Establishes Network." Focus on Indiana Libraries 34 (May-June 1980): 6.

Blank form for librarians to complete for the publication of Network Directory 1980.

1980-83 Turner, Robert L. "Femininity and the Librarian--Another Test." College and Research Libraries 41 (May 1980): 235-241.

Presents a brief but to-the-point analysis of sex-role orientation tests used to determine femininity or masculinity as they have been used with librarians. Demonstrates innate bias of these tests. Uses the Bem-Sex Role Inventory (a scale corrected for misconceptions found in earlier tests) to show there are no significant differences on the masculinity, femininity and androgyny scores between male library science students and the normative male group.

1980-84 "ALA Executive Board Spring Meeting." LJ/SLJ Hotline 9 (May 19, 1980): 6.

Notes that 1984 Midwinter Meeting of ALA will be held in Washington, D.C. rather than Chicago unless Illinois ratifies the ERA.

1980-85 Bartol, Kathryn M. "An Addendum to the Sex Structuring of Organizations: The Special Case of Traditionally-Female Professions." Journal of Library Administration 2 (Summer 1980): 89-94.

Career orientation by sex is reported with some discussion of librarianship in the general context of women in organizations and their career prospects. Article is a continuation of author's "Sex Structuring of Organizations," reprinted in the Journal of Library Administration (Summer 1980): 75-88.

1980-86 Creth, Sheila. "The Impact of Changing Life Styles on Library Administration." Southeastern Librarian 30 (Summer 1980): 74-81.

Reviews impact of changing lifestyles on administration in organizations and libraries. Discusses alternative personnel arrangements such as flex-time, permanent part-time employment, and job sharing.

1980-87 Myers, Margaret. "Equal Employment Opportunity Issues and Staff Development." Journal of Library Administration 1 (Summer 1980): 39-46.

General discussion of the topic includes observations on women and equal employment opportunity.

1980-88 Rensel, Jeanne. "The Status of Women Librarians in Washington State." PNLA Quarterly 44 (Summer 1980): 18-25.

Describes results of study to determine if library women in the state of Washington were being by-passed for top jobs in favor of men. Data were gathered to support the work of the Washington State Career Development and Assessment Center for Librarians. Results showed that males (23 percent of all librarians in Washington State) hold 60 percent of the top positions.

1980-89 "State Council for Social Legislation." North Carolina Libraries 38 (Summer 1980): 105.

The North Carolina Library Association, a member of the State Council for Social Legislation, helped adopt items for consideration. The ERA is a top priority.

1980-90 "ALA Marches for ERA in Chicago Rally." American Libraries 11 (June 1980): 311.

Report of 100 librarians marching with ALA President-elect, Peggy Sullivan, at the national rally for ERA ratification May 10, 1980.

1980-91 "ALA Testifies on Sex Bias at EEOC Hearings." American Libraries 11 (June 1980): 311.

Report of testimony by Margaret Myers of the ALA Office for Library Personnel Resources before the Equal Opportunity Employment Commission. Myers described ALA's efforts to get equal pay for work of equal value, and summarized comparable worth studies in librarianship. Elaine Clever (Temple University), Sue Galloway (University of California-San Diego), Anna Martinez (San Diego Public), and Helen Josephine (Berkeley, California) also testified.

1980-92 "Something for Everyone: Program-Picking at the Big Orchard 99th Annual ALA Conference, New York City, June 28-July 4, 1980." American Libraries 11 (June 1980): 356-358.

Includes a short report on activities planned for the SRRT Task Force on Women COSWL pre-conference, "Women in a Woman's Profession--Strategies II."

1980-93 Berry, John. "The Conference Program: An Editor's Choice." Library Journal 105 (June 1, 1980): 1276.

List of important ALA Conference events includes: joint SRRT Task Force on Women and Committee on the Status of Women in Librarianship pre-conference, "Women in Librarianship--the Politics of the Profession"; "Countdown to ERA"; "Women's Library Information Services"; and "Career Stress and Career Change."

1980-94 "Affirmative Action and Women's Program Office." Library of Congress Information Bulletin 39 (June 6, 1980): 192-193.

Reports the Library's efforts to enhance the status of women and minorities through its TAP (Training Appraisal and Promotion) Program.

1980-95 "Semiannual Report on Developments at the Library of Congress, October 1, 1979, Through March 31, 1980." Library of Congress Information Bulletin 39 (June 6, 1980): 191-208.

Notes status of the Training, Appraisal and Promotion (TAP) Program under the heading, "Affirmative Action and Women's Program Office" (pp. 192-193).

1980-96 "Seventh Library Education Faculty Survey Breaks New Ground." LJ/SLJ Hotline 9 (June 23, 1980): 1.

Reports on Bidlack study [1980-04] and continuing male domination of top posts in library education.

1980-97 Your Assessment Center in Action: First Annual Report. Seattle, Wash.: Career Development and Assessment Center for Librarians, June 30, 1980.

Detailed discussion includes: report of Principal Investigator, Peter Hiatt; first year highlights; plans for the second year; fiscal reports; a research report [1980-25] and appendixes.

1980-98 Hook, Robert D. "ALA Councilor's Report. Idaho Librarian 32 (July 1980): 146-148.

Coverage of the ALA Annual Conference includes a summary of the keynote speech by James Rutherford, Assistant Secretary of Education, who listed "assisting women to move up in the library ranks more than they have" as a priority. Council action and the report of the ERA Task Force are also described.

1980-99 "Order from Chaos: Highlights of the 99th Annual Conference of the American Library Association." American Libraries 11 (July-August 1980): 420-220.

Under the heading, "Women Get Action," ALA Annual Conference report notes the speech of Sharon Percy Rockefeller, Co-Chair of ERAmerica. The jointly sponsored Committee on the Status of Women in Librarianship and SRRT Task Force on Women pre-conference, "Women in a Women's Profession--Strategies II," and the resulting seven action items for Council are described. Activities of the ERA Task Force are also reported. Estabrook and Heim's career-profile survey is described, as well as other numerous COSWL projects. Final mention is made of the name change of the SRRT Task Force on Women to the SRRT Feminist Task Force.

1980-100 "Putting Your Best Foot Forward." Focus on Indiana Libraries 34 (July-August 1980): 3.
Notes that the Task Force on the Status of Women in Indiana Libraries has been granted Division status by the Indiana Library Association.

1980-101 "Women's Program Statistical Update: 1979." Library of Congress Information Bulletin 39 (July 4, 1980): 238-240.
Statistics prepared by the Library of Congress Women's Program show little change in women's status; however, analysis of three years (chart I) shows some improvements.

1980-102 Connelly, Sherryl. "The New Librarian: How Does She Stack Up?" Daily News. New York: July 27, 1980: YOU section: 1-5.
Newspaper coverage of 1980 ALA New York Annual Conference includes discussion of pay differential for women, ERA activities, and children's librarianship.

1980-103 American Library Association. Office for Library Personnel Resources. Degrees and Certificates Awarded by U.S. Library Education Programs 1976-1979. Chicago: ALA, August 1980 (mimeographed).
Continues [1975-79, 1977-39, and 1978-02]. Reports numbers and types of degrees and certificates awarded by U.S. library education programs, broken down by sex and ethnic group.

1980-104 Davis, Lorraine. "Between Us . . . Age No Problem." Vogue 170 (August 1980): 2.
News item describes Career Development and Assessment Center for Librarians at the University of Washington.

1980-105 Gerhardt, Lillian N., Cheatham, Bertha M., and Pollack, Pamela D. "The New York Experience: ALA's 99th Conference." School Library Journal 26 (August 1980): 25-34.
ALA Annual Conference coverage includes discussion of seven resolutions prepared by the Social Responsibilities Round Table Task Force

on Women and ALA's Committee on the Status of Women in Librarianship. Of them, six were sent to Council and one was passed by membership. They include: training for two ALA members at the University of Washington's Career Development and Assessment Center; free child care service at Annual Conference; and a charge to the Committee on the Status of Women in Librarianship to develop coalitions with other women-dominated organizations and to report at the 1981 Midwinter Meeting.

1980-106 King, Donald W., Krauser, Cheri, and Sague, Virginia M. "Profile of ASIS Membership." Bulletin of the American Society for Information Science 6 (August 1980): 9-17.

Profile includes data on the relative position of responsibility of men and women. Women earn less and hold fewer positions of responsibility.

1980-107 "An Odd Euphoria." Library Journal 105 (August 1980): 1575-1598.

Coverage of 99th Annual ALA Conference held in New York includes discussion of women's issues (p. 1584); reports on the ERA (p. 1585 and pp. 1590-1591); and service to women (p. 1591).

1980-108 "Reports on the 99th Annual Conference of the American Library Association, New York City, June 28-July 4, 1980." Library of Congress Information Bulletin 39 (August 1, 1980): 268-276.

Reports ALA Council extension of the ERA Task Force through 1982.

1980-109 "Continuing Reports on the 99th Annual Conference of the American Library Association, New York City, June 28-July 4, 1980." Library of Congress Information Bulletin 39 (August 29, 1980): 325-331.

General ALA Annual Conference coverage includes detailed summary of Social Responsibilities Round Table Task Force on Women Pre-conference, "Women in a Women's Profession--Strategies II," held at Rutgers June 26-27 (by Sarah Pritchard and Linda Tepp: pp. 327-392); and a report of the LAMA Women Administrators Discussion Group program on "Career Stress and Career Change" (by Sharon S. Horowitz: p. 327).

1980-110 Cassell, Kay Ann, and Weibel, Kathleen. "Public Library Response to Women and Their Changing Roles." RQ (Fall 1980): 70-75.

The current and historical response of the public library to the information and service needs of women are discussed, including some background on clubwomen's role in establishing and supporting public libraries.

1980-111 Cowell, Penny. "Not All in the Mind: The Virile Profession." Library Review 29 (Autumn 1980): 167-175.

Discusses media treatment of librarians as "frustration personified." Notes that the profession needs to become "in all senses more virile" to revise its image and redefine its role.

1980-112 Deutrich, Mabel E. and DeWhitt, Ben. "Survey of the Archival Profession--1979." The American Archivist 43 (Fall 1980): 527-535.

Report of a survey of over 1000 members of the Society of American Archivists describes member status with personal, employment and institutional information. Women returned 467 questionnaires (45.6 percent of the respondents). Mean salary data showed that the general trend is toward lower salaries for women. Related analyses appear in the SAA Women's Caucus Newsletter 5 (February 1981). For a history of the SAA women's caucus, see the November 1980 issue of the SAA Women's Caucus Newsletter.

Letters: Lytle, Richard H. "Letter." The American Archivist 44 (Summer 1981): 195-196.

Congratulates the SAA Committee on the Status of Women on its survey of the archival profession, but suggests some different interpretations of the data. Using original data analyses, Lytle observes that there is less salary variation at the highest educational levels, and women on the whole seem to have fewer academic credentials.

DeWhitt, Ben. "Letter." The American Archivist 44 (Summer 1981): 196.

Thanks Lytle for his interest in the study.

1980-113 Yerkey, A. Neil. "Values of Library School Students, Faculty, and Librarians: Premises for Understanding." Journal of Education for Librarianship 21 (Fall 1980): 122-135.

Study of values demonstrated quite different rankings by sex among the groups studied. Females over 30 valued freedom as most important [males valued it least]; and males valued social recognition as most important [females felt it was least important].

1980-114 Hlava, Marjorie M. K. "Online Users Survey 1980." Online Review 4 (September 1980): 294-299.

Profile of online users developed from questionnaire mailed in January 1980 includes sex and salary data. Figures 6 and 7 (p. 298) show that women's salaries are consistently higher than men's in the lower ranges, but that 35 percent of the men make over $26,000 as compared to 10 percent of the women. Of the searchers studied, 76 percent were women and 24 percent were men.

1980-115 "Continuing Reports on the 99th Annual Conference of the American Library Association, New York City, June 28-July 4, 1980." Library of Congress Information Bulletin 39 (September 5, 1980): 343-348.

Describes ALA membership consideration of seven motions developed at the pre-conference on "Women in a Women's Profession."

1980-116 "News from the Women's Program Office." Library of Congress Information Bulletin 39 (September 19, 1980): follows p. 366.

Notes national coverage of efforts of the Library of Congress Women's Program to increase numbers of women and minorities in management and supervisory positions.

1980-117 Anwar, Mumtaz A. "The Profile of the Librarian; A State-of-the Art." Libri 30 (October 1980): 307-320.

A social profile of the librarian includes discussion of marital status and the librarian's image. Shows percentage of women by type of library.

1980-118 Fluellin, Gwendolyn F. "Changing the Traditional Role of the Librarian: From Matron to Manager." Georgia Librarian 17 (November 1980): 6.

Refers to the traditional stereotype of female librarians as stern, old, strict, unmarried.

1980-119 Gerhardt, Lillian N. and Cheatham, Bertha M. "AASL's First National Conference." School Library Journal 27 (November 1980): 31-37.

Editor of MS. Magazine, Gloria Steinem, speaking at an American Association of School Librarians program, "Feminism in the Future," suggests that since women are predominant in school library media centers they are in a good position to "start a revolution." She notes a "near absence" of women among library school deans, major city or academic library directors, or as editors of library periodicals.

1980-120 Plotnik, Art. "In the Limelight at Last." American Libraries 11 (November 1980): 598-597.

Summarizes speech by Gloria Steinem to school librarians on the status of women in school libraries.

1980-121 Silver, Constance. "Male Volunteers a Minority." American Libraries 11 (November 1980): 591.

Letter objects to published photo of a male volunteer (American Libraries September 1980, p. 471). Notes that the majority of volunteers are women and that 89 percent of librarians in Michigan are women.

1980-122 Caswell-Pierce, Sara L. "Sexist Writing." Library Journal 105 (November 1, 1980): 2245.

Letter protests review of Ellsworth Mason's book which uses the quote "this library has two systems of supports, like a well-braced woman--one for the central structure and one for the cantilever." Editorial note reports that the Library Journal female staff were split evenly on their reactions to the quote.

1980-123 Learmont, Carol L. "Placements and Salaries 1979: Wider Horizons." Library Journal 105 (November 1, 1980): 2271-2277.

Annual survey of placements and salaries reports that the female salary median is lower ($12,885) than the male salary median ($13,103) for new professionals.

1980-124 "Career Planning Workshop Set for December 8." Library of Congress Information Bulletin 39 (November 14, 1980): follows p. 442.

Announces Women's Advisory Committee Workshop, "It's Your Career--Take Charge!"

1980-125 "1979 Annual Business Meeting." The American Archivist 43 (Winter 1980): 134-137.

Reprints a statement read by Nancy Sahli at the fall meeting of the Society of American Archivists, which states that a number of SAA members are attending the 1979 meeting in Illinois to show commitment to the profession, but that they are showing protest against meeting in a state which has not ratified ERA by distributing buttons which read, "Archivists for ERA."

Letters: Settani, Joseph Andrew. "Letter." American Archivist 43 (Summer 1980): 281.

Author places ERA in the category of "pet peeves," considers SAA support of ERA a "highly nonprofessional and detrimental" activity, and may seriously reconsider membership in SAA.

Stroup, Timothy. "Letter." American Archivist 44 (Winter 1981): 8.

Replies that while diversity in a profession is laudable, unity over fighting sex discrimination is essential, since it affects hiring, promotion, and salaries for all.

1980-126 Bailey, Robert. "Harriet C. Long: A.L.A. Warrior." PNLA Quarterly 44 (Winter 1980): 11-15.

Biographical sketch of Long includes discussion of male dominance of posts in World War I library service. Female protests within ALA, however, and an increasing need for personnel soon gained women slots in war service.

1980-127 Shank, Beverly. "Librarians Who Change Careers." Bay State Librarian 69 (Winter 1980): 9-11.

In a discussion with Massachusetts librarians who changed careers, former librarians were asked whether the fact that 85 percent of library jobs are held by women affected their decisions. Responses ranged from those anxious to move into more male-dominated fields to those who noted that women's subservient position in libraries was endemic to the structure of the profession.

1980-128 Shediac, Margaret. "Private Law Libraries Special Interest Section 1979 Salary Survey." Law Library Journal 73 (Winter 1980): 218-226.

Table 2 cross-correlates age, sex, and salary. Women earn less in the 20-29 and 40-49 age categories.

1980-129 Cheatham, Bertha M. "'80 Library News." School Library Journal 27 (December 1980): 23-27.

Notes name change of SRRT Task Force on Women to the Feminist Task Force and its work to see that ERA is ratified. Also reports that the Task Force will reintroduce the child care services resolution at the 1981 ALA Midwinter Meeting.

1980-130 Dale, Doris C. Career Patterns of Women Librarians with Doctorates. (Occasional Papers series No. 147) Urbana: University of Illinois, Graduate School of Library Science, December 1980.

Analyzes responses of 150 women librarians with doctorates earned before 1975 to describe the population in terms of education, experience, position, salary, and professional contributions.

1980-131 DeWath, Nancy V. and Cooper, Michael D. 1981-82 Library Human Resources: Study of Supply and Demand--Conceptual Overview. Rockville, Md.: King Research, December 1980.

Prepared for the National Center for Education Statistics, this conceptual overview of study intended to update Library Manpower report [1975-13] since the end of the projection period is approaching. The final King Research report, to be issued in 1983, will include: projections of the supply and demand for librarians to 1990; discussion of skills most in demand; identification of factors affecting supply and demand; discussion of non-traditional employment trends, staffing patterns, hiring requirements, and employment and training impact of new procedures and services; a compilation of sources of data on employment in libraries; and methodology for projecting supply and demand for librarians. Of special interest to women are sensitivity of replacement demand to assumption about the future sex composition of the profession (p. 8); salary difference between women and men (p. 20); ALA COSWL study (p. 33); replacement demand (pp. 33-34); and women's issues (pp. 35-36).

1980-132 Estabrook, Leigh S. and Heim, Kathleen M. "A Profile of ALA Personal Members." American Libraries 11 (December 1980): 654-659.

Preliminary report of Committee on the Status of Women in Librarianship study shows that female ALA members earn less, have less supervisory responsibility, hold fewer state and national offices in professional associations and publish less than male members.

Letters: Rosaschi, Jim. "Sex and Salaries in Academia." American Libraries 12 (March 1981): 123.

Looks for more analysis of the Heim-Estabrook data.

Heim, Kathleen M. and Estabrook, Leigh. "Relationship Proves Complex." American Libraries 12 (March 1981): 123.

Admits a complex relationship between gender, salary, and educational attainment.

Munn, Ellie. "Success Is Genderless." American Libraries 12 (May 1981): 241.

Contrasts findings reported in Heim and Estabrook study [1980-132] with comments of women in Lundy's Women View Librarianship [1980-24].

1980-133 Fretwell, Gordon. ARL Annual Salary Survey 1979-80. Washington, D.C.: Association of Research Libraries, December, 1980.

Fourth ARL salary survey to break down data by sex highlights continued male domination of managerial positions and higher salaries.

1980-134 Reed, Kaye. "'80 and Beyond: Gloria Steinem Visits AASL." Technicalities 1 (December 1980): 2-3.

Reports Steinem's remarks on the devaluation of librarianship because of the high proportion of women in the field.

1980-135 "SLA 1980 Salary Survey Update." Special Libraries 71 (December 1980): 541.

"Update" notes incorrect table and misleading interpretation of female salary data reported in SLA's fifth triennial survey [1979-126].

1980-136 Stagg, Lynn. "Women in Library Work." Assistant Librarian 73 (December 1980): 164-165.

Describes a London conference on women in library work planned by the Feminist Library Workers Group focusing on the position of women in libraries and the feminist librarian's role in book selection.

1980-137 "UW Career Development and Assessment Center." Watermark no. 11 (December 1980): 2.

Oregon State Library newsletter includes description of the Career Development and Assessment Center for Librarians in Washington state.

1980-138 "Equal Pay Breakthrough Looms in Canada." LJ/SLJ Hotline 9 (December 7, 1980): 2.

Reports Human Rights Commission findings of salary discrimination against female-dominated library science group.

1981-01 American Library Association. Office for Library Personnel Resources. Pay Equity: Comparable Worth Action Guide, (Topics in Personnel, (TIP) No. 2) Chicago: ALA, 1981.

Packet developed by Helen Josephine on comparable worth includes general information plus action steps which may be taken to document and fight inequities. This TIP kit, developed for OLPR and the Committee on the Status of Women in Librarianship, includes case summaries of library-related actions and a comprehensive bibliography.

1981-02 American Library Association. Office for Library Personnel Resources. The Racial, Ethnic and Sexual Composition of Library Staff in Academic and Public Libraries. Chicago: ALA, 1981.

Reports national statistics on race, ethnicity, and sexual composition of the academic and public library work force gathered in April 1980. The "LIBGIS I Public Library Universe--1973" tape (updated in 1978) from the National Center for Education Statistics (NCES) was used to obtain a stratified random sample of 750 public libraries. Two NCES tapes, "Library Statistics of Colleges and Universities" and "Institutional Characteristics of College and Universities" were used to select 483 academic libraries with probabilities proportionate to the number of librarians on the staff. Statistics are provided on the total academic-public library work force (72 percent female), the academic work force (62.3 percent female), and public work force (78.6 percent female) by sex and ethnic origin. Information is also provided by library type for three positions: director, branch and department head, and beginning professional. Female academic directors earned a median salary of $24,999 while males earned $32,999. Female public directors earned a median of $18,554 to men's $28,250. The majority of directors of both types of libraries are male, with academic libraries exhibiting the most striking disparity. This study provides bench mark data for affirmative action planning.

1981-03 Baker, Curtis O. <u>Earned Degrees Conferred 1979-80</u>. Washington, D.C.: National Center for Education Statistics, 1981. (NCES 81-363).

Provides data on library science by sex for bachelor's, master's and doctoral degrees.

1981-04 Baker, Curtis O. <u>Earned Degrees Conferred: An Examination of Recent Trends</u>. Washington, D.C.: National Center for Education Statistics, 1981. (NCES 81-359).

Includes information on bachelor's degrees awarded, by discipline division and to women for the fifty states and D.C., 1971 and 1980 (Table 9, p. 29); master's degrees (Table 12, p. 32) and doctor's degrees (Table 14, p. 34).

1981-05 Biblo, Herbert. "Social Responsibilities Round Table." In <u>ALA Yearbook 1981</u>. Edited by Robert Wedgeworth. Chicago: ALA, 1981: 277-278.

Report includes coverage of Feminist Task Force and mention of the Illinois Library Association's SRRT program on the ERA.

1981-06 Bidlack, Russell E. "Faculty." In <u>Association of American Library Schools Library Education Statistical Report 1981</u>. State College, Pa.: AALS, 1981.

Eighth report in Faculty Report series includes information on library education administrators and faculty broken down by sex, and by fiscal and academic year appointments. Men dominate at full professor (70.5 percent), associate professor (54.3 percent), and assistant professor (54 percent) levels and account for 80.3 percent of the top administrative posts. Men earn more than women at all levels: dean or director (men, $43,799; women, $37,622), professor (men, $32,402; women, $30,075), associate professor (men, $24,878; women, $24,376), assistant professor (men, $20,591; women, $20,384). Data are also analyzed by ethnic background.

1981-07 Bryan, James, et al. <u>1980-81 Administrative Compensation Survey</u>. Washington, D.C.: College and University Personnel Association, 1981.

Data for 1,587 college and universities include information on library administrators. Women librarians' salaries are shown (p. 78) to lag behind men's.

1981-08 Cheatham, Bertha M. "SLJ News Report, 1980." In <u>Bowker Annual</u>, 26 ed. New York: Bowker, 1981: 33-41.

Notes "Goodbye Palmer House" action to support the ERA boycott and work of the ALA Feminist Task Force (p. 35).

1981-09 Childers, Martha. SHARE: A Directory of Feminist Librarians in Illinois. Urbana: Women Library Workers, Graduate School of Library and Information Science, 1981.

Assisted by Women Library Workers Susan Beck, Anita Bell, Irene Elrod, Judy Forsythe, Marsha Fulton, Kris Lipkowski and Katharine Phenix, Martha Childers produced the Illinois SHARE Directory with the largest number of feminist librarians entries of all SHARE directories. Annotations include library work, interests, skills and resources for those included. The directory is indexed by geographical location and subject.

1981-10 Cuesta, Yolanda J. "Personnel and Employment: Affirmative Action." In ALA Yearbook 1981. Edited by Robert Wedgeworth. Chicago: ALA, 1981: 217-219.

Includes coverage of sex discrimination, the Office for Library Personnel Resources survey of Racial/Ethnic/Sexual Composition of Library Staffs in Academic and Public Libraries, [1981-02], and other EEOC actions.

1981-11 Dale, Doris C. Career Patterns of Women Librarians With Doctorates. Arlington, Va.: ERIC Document Reproduction Center, 1981: ED 197 755.

Microreproduction of [1980-130].

1981-12 Engelbarts, Rudolf. Librarian Authors: A Bibliography. Jefferson, N. C.: McFarland, 1981.

Notes several items of interest: Dewey dumbfounded the regents of Columbia College by admitting women on an equal basis with men; schools were founded and brought to bloom by women directors (pp. 48-49); and William Frederick Poole spoke out for women in the profession (p. 125).

1981-13 Fontaine, Sue. "Washington." In ALA Yearbook 1981. Edited by Robert Wedgeworth. Chicago: ALA, 1981: 373-374.

Coverage includes short report on Career Development and Assessment Center for Librarians at the University of Washington School of Librarianship.

1981-14 Ford, Barbara J. "Illinois." In ALA Yearbook 1981. Edited by Robert Wedgeworth. Chicago: ALA, 1981: 337-338.

Includes report of Illinois Library Association ERA Task Force activities.

1981-15 Frances, Carol, and Mensel, R. Frank. Women and Minorities in Administration of Higher Education Institutions: Employment Patterns and Salary Comparisons 1978-79, An Analysis of Progress toward Affirmative Action Goals 1975-76--1978-79. Washington, D.C.: College and University Personnel Association, 1981.

Includes information on head librarians by ethnicity and sex.

1981-16 Fretwell, Gordon. ARL Annual Salary Survey, 1979-1980. Arlington, Va.: ERIC Document Reproduction Service 1981: ED 198 830.

Microreproduction of [1980-133].

1981-16a Gasaway, Laura. Equal Pay for Equal Work. New York: Special Libraries Association, 1981.

Revised edition of [1976-04].

1981-17 Grant, W. Vance, and Eiden, Leo J. Digest of Education Statistics: 1981. Washington, D.C.: GPO, 1981 (NCES 81-400).

Includes data on men and women in school library media centers for 1973-74 and 1978-79 (Table 192, p. 214), and general statistics of public libraries by populations served which break down statistics on professional librarians by sex (Table 190, p. 212). Library science degrees conferred and enrollment in advanced degree programs by sex are also provided.

1981-18 Hamlin, Arthur T. The University Library in the United States: Its Origins and Development. Philadelphia: University of Pennsylvania Press, 1981.

Passing comments on women are included (pp. 51; 55; 92; 117-119; 131-132) and the book is dedicated "to the hundreds of librarians, mostly women, who devoted their lives to the service of scholarship in secondary positions with little recognition and often at bare subsistence salaries, in the first half of the 20th century."

1981-19 Heim, Kathleen M. Women and Minorities in Academic Libraries. Arlington, Va.: ERIC Document Reproduction Service, 1982: ED 208 888.

Summarizes data on women holding directorships of academic libraries, based on the College and University Personnel Association 1977 summary [1981-44].

1981-20 Heim, Kathleen M. "Women in Librarianship." In ALA Yearbook 1981. Edited by Robert Wedgeworth. Chicago: ALA, 1981: 299-303.

Report includes coverage of the second pre-conference to examine the status of women in a women's profession, "Strategies II," sponsored by the SRRT Task Force on Women and the ALA Committee on the Status of Women in Librarianship and held at Cook College of Rutgers University June 26-27, 1980. Resolutions generated at the pre-conference are reproduced. Includes summaries of: surveys, degree distribution, career development, ALA-related activities, comparable wages, other women's organizations, awards, scholarship and the popular press.

1981-21 Heintze, Robert A. and Hodes, Lance. Statistics of Public School Libraries/Media Centers, Fall 1978. Washington, D.C.: GPO, 1981. (NCES 81-254).

Summary data include educational levels of library-media center staff by sex and employment status (p. 30).

1981-22 Hyman, Karen. "Dignity in Work?" Unabashed Librarian 39 (1981): 5.

Reflects that, while librarianship may be considered more dignified than meat packing, public ignorance of the profession leads people to call librarians 'girls.' (Reprinted from Libraries Unlimited Newsletter, Orange, N.J., November 1980.)

1981-23 Irvine, Betty Jo. "ARL Academic Library Leaders of the 1980's: Men and Women of the Executive Suite." In Options for the 80's. Edited by Michael D. Kathman and Virgil F. Massman. Ann Arbor, Mich.: University Microfilms, 1981: fiche 4 of 11.

Reports survey to determine career patterns and demographic characteristics of ARL directors. Fuller report available in author's doctoral dissertation to be released early 1982.

1981-24 Learmont, Carol L. "Placements and Salaries, 1979: Wider Horizons." In Bowker Annual, 26th ed. New York: Bowker, 1981: 231-246.

Reprint of [1980-123].

1981-25 Learmont, Carol L. "Students." In Association of American Library Schools Library Education Statistical Report 1981. State College, Pa.: Association of American Library Schools, 1981.

Second report in AALS series provides student enrollment information by program and sex. For the 1980-1981 academic year at accredited schools (67 reporting) 798 men and 2861 women were enrolled in master's programs; 83 men and 113 women in doctoral programs. Degrees and certificates are broken down by school, sex, and ethnic origin. A greater number of women received the doctoral degree.

1981-26 Lynch, Mary Jo. "Research on Libraries and Librarianship in 1980: An Overview." In Bowker Annual, 26th ed. New York: Bowker, 1981: 263-267.

Reports personnel-related studies including the ALA Office for Library Personnel Resources study, Racial, Ethnic, Sexual Composition of Library Staff in Academic and Public Libraries [1981-02] and the COSWL study to investigate careers of librarians [1980-132].

1981-27 Mann, Margaret. <u>Library Manpower Planning: A Bibliographical Review</u>. (British Library Research and Development Reports No. 5614) Boston Spa, Wetherby, West Yorkshire: Publications, British Library Lending Division, 1981.

Section 2.6 discusses women in the field and refers readers to the Weibel and Heim bibliography [1979-28] for further reference.

1981-28 <u>Meetings/1980</u>: LJ Special Report No. 20 New York: Bowker, 1981.

A collection of <u>Library Journal</u> reports of major library conferences of 1980 includes discussion of SRRT Task Force on Women meetings in New York June 28-July 4 and miscellaneous reports of such activities as the Ohio Library Association's Women on the Rise in Library Management Task Force.

1981-29 Myers, Margaret. "Recent Library Personnel Surveys." In <u>Bowker Annual</u>, 26th ed. New York: Bowker, 1981: 223-231.

Summarizes selected sources of information on library personnel statistics for specific types of libraries or positions, for particular geographical areas, and by a variety of organizations or associations. Useful for affirmative action data acquisition since those sources breaking down data with race or sex as a variable are noted.

1981-30 Samore, Theodore. "NCES Survey of College and University Libraries, 1978-1979." <u>Bowker Annual</u>, 26th ed. New York: Bowker, 1981: 287-303.

Data from National Center for Education Statistics 1979 survey of academic libraries include data on staff by sex for professionals and nonprofessionals.

1981-31 Savage, Noël. "<u>LJ News Report, 1980.</u>" In <u>Bowker Annual</u>, 26th ed. New York: Bowker, 1981: 3-32.

Notes that the economy crunch has dampened progress in improving wages and mobility of female librarians but highlights successful action at California State University (p. 24). Under "Women's Rights" (p. 29) ERA efforts in ALA are noted as well as action at the ALA New York Conference.

1981-32 Sherman, Claire Richter, and Holcomb, Adele M. <u>Women As Interpreters of the Visual Arts, 1820-1979</u>. Westport, Conn.: Greenwood Press, 1981.

Discussion of individual women who made significant contributions to the art world as historians, educators, critics and curators. Describes the careers of Myrtilla Avery, Sara Yorke Stevenson, and other women librarians (p. 47-48). Background on professional opportunities for women in librarianship is provided by references to Dee Garrison's "The Tender Technicians" [1972-73].

1981-33 Shiflett, Orvin Lee. The Origins of American Academic Librarianship. Norwood, N.J.: Ablex, 1981.

Based on dissertation [1979-25]. Expands on the role of women in libraries (see chapter 5, "Neither Power Nor Dignity").

1981-34 Sink, Darryl L. "Employment Trends for Media Graduates: 1979-1980." In Educational Media Yearbook, 1981, 7th ed. Edited by James W. Brown. Littleton, Colo.: Libraries Unlimited, 1981: 81-86.

Reports degree production by sex for media graduates.

1981-35 Treiman, Donald J., and Hartmann, Heidi I. Women, Work, and Wages: Equal Pay for Jobs of Equal Value. Washington, D.C.: National Academy Press, 1981.

Prepared by the Committee on Occupational Classification and Analysis, Assembly of Behavioral and Social Sciences, National Research Council. Report developed in response to requests from the Department of Labor and the Equal Employment Opportunity Commission for examination of the issues involved in a "comparable worth" concept of job compensation. Librarians are among the groups who have argued that their jobs are underpaid relative to jobs of comparable worth (pp. 1-2). Highlights efforts of Women Library Workers in California (pp. 2-3).

1981-36 U.S. Congress. Senate. Committee on Labor and Human Resources. Sex Discrimination in the Workplace, 1981. Washington, D.C.: GPO, 1981.

Testimony includes a table on bachelor's degrees awarded to women in 1971 and 1977 including library science (p. 434).

1981-37 Williamson, Jane. Equality in Librarianship: A Guide to Sex Discrimination Laws. Chicago: ALA, 1981.

Pamphlet written for the American Library Association Committee on the Status of Women in Librarianship intended to make women librarians aware of job rights in areas such as sex discrimination, equal pay, pregnancy and sexual harassment. Outlines procedures for filing a Title VII complaint, remedies through the workplace, state law, and professional associations. Includes addresses and phone numbers of Equal Employment Opportunity Commission Field Offices, Federal Contract Compliance Regional Offices, and State Labor Departments or Human Rights Commissions.

1981-38 "Women in Libraries: A Special Issue." <u>Librarians for Social Change</u> 9, no. 1 (1981).

In addition to the following articles, issue includes topics of general concern such as feminist books, women in management, and accounts of job sharing.

1981-38a Jespersen, Sherry. "The Problems Faced by Women in Libraries: Why We Formed a Group." <u>Librarians for Social Change</u> 9, no. 1 (1981): 3-5, 10.

Describes reasons for the formation of the group, Women in Libraries. Group objectives are to "demand equality, opportunity and even positive discrimination for all women who work in libraries" and to "demand that library stock does not include material which portrays women in a way that is sexist or derogatory."

1981-38b Little, Janet. "Censorship or Selection? Looking at the Content of Library Materials." <u>Librarians for Social Change</u> 9, no. 1 (1981): 6-8, 10.

Suggests that women in libraries are in a position to reevaluate library selection policies to create a "positive" collection, free of sexist materials.

1981-38c Allen, Jane. "Feminism in the Public Library." <u>Librarians for Social Change</u> 9, no. 1 (1981): 9-10.

Describes the feminist collection set up by staffers of a branch library. Some resistance was met from men in senior management, but the group felt that they had generated positive interest in women's issues in the community.

1981-38d Taylor, Jackie. "The Lowest of the Low: Library Assistant in Public Libraries." <u>Librarians For Social Change</u> 9, no. 1 (1981): 14-15.

Library assistants often do more work than their positions require. While unmarried workers are of both sexes, married library assistants are almost exclusively female. Low pay is justified because the income of these women is considered supplemental. Author notes that budget cutbacks have affected the library staff, and suggests that membership in a trade union can offer some job security and protection.

1981-38e Allen, Jane. "Women Workers, Union Power and Positive Action." <u>Librarians for Social Change</u> 9, no. 1 (1981): 16-19.

NALGO, fourth largest union with the second largest female membership, has little representation in its upper echelons.

1981-38f Wade, Maureen. "Job-sharing in a Public Library." <u>Libraries for Social Change</u> 9, no. 1 (1981): 27.

Describes job sharing at Camden Libraries Department.

1981-38g Newton, Mary. "Libraries, Automation and Women." Librarians for Social Change 9, no. 1 (1981): 28-29.

The tasks of librarians will change with automation. Author warns against women's loss of status by the changes and believes this time of change provides an opportunity for women to be involved in major decisions.

1981-39 Young, Arthur P. Books for Sammies: The American Library Association and World War I. Pittsburgh, Pa.: Beta Phi Mu, 1981.

Book based on dissertation [1976-98] notes the struggle of women librarians to work in camps during World War I (pp. 33-35).

1981-40 Zipcovitz, Fay, and Bergman, Sherrie S. "Never Mind Who's Watching the Store, Who's Stocking the Pool? The Status of Women in Academic Library Management." In Options for the 80's. Ann Arbor, Mich.: University Microfilms, 1981: fiche 11 of 11.

In spite of affirmative action men still dominate library administration positions. Men are groomed more consciously. Suggestions are made to encourage women to go for management positions.

1981-41 "COSWL Study of ALA Gives Membership Data." School Library Journal 27 (January 1981): 12-13.

Summary of [1980-132].

1981-42 Cummins, Julie. "Re Working Couples." School Library Journal 27 (January 1981): 3.

Responds to School Library Journal article, "Men and Women Working Together in Changing Times," (September 1980) asking for an article on married librarians. Suggests that the study of factors relating to career advancement, salaries, and personal relationships would be "interesting."

1981-43 Donovan, Ruth. "Sullivan Keynotes MPLA." Technicalities 1 (January 1981): 5.

Mountain Plains Library Association Conference report mentions shorter hair but just as many beards on men, more skirts and fewer pantsuits on women, and fewer long skirts on anyone.

1981-44 Heim, Kathleen M. "Women and Minorities in Academic Libraries." College & Research Libraries 42 (January 1981): 3.

Summary of [1981-19] which highlights data from the College and Personnel Association survey of minorities and women in higher education administration. Shows that female discrimination in library positions is compounded by the relatively low status of library administrators within their institutions.

1981-45 Carmichael, Carole A. "Librarian Jobs Scarce, Pay Low--Especially for Women." Chicago Tribune (January 4, 1981).

Reports lower salaries for women in the field.

1981-46 "Semiannual Report on Developments at the Library of Congress, April 1, 1980, Through September 30, 1980." Library of Congress Information Bulletin 40 (January 9, 1981): 9-28.

Summarizes report of the Women's Program office, which showed gains for women at the Library (p. 10).

1981-47 Savage, Noel. "News in Review, 1980." Library Journal 106 (January 15, 1981): 109-124.

Section on "Women's Rights" (p. 123) reviews the American Library Association ERA boycott, resolutions passed at the 1980 New York Conference, the name change of the Task Force on Women to Feminist Task Force, and ERA fundraising.

1981-48 Borchardt, D. H. "What of the Future?" Incite 2 (January 23, 1981): 7.

Complains about a sketch which appeared in an article in the Library Association of Australia Bulletin of November 18, 1980. The sketch [reprinted] shows a woman wearing glasses who is shelving books. Borchardt asks, how typical is the sketch, and why not show a "bright young lass showing plenty of leg," or "lad bearded and long-haired telling stories in a children's library?" Calls for a correction of librarians' public image.

Letters: Colley, H. W. "To See Ourselves . . ." Incite 2 (February 20, 1981): 9.

Contends that Borchardt's sneer at "the typical librarian, a middle-aged lady who finds you nice books to read" is not really an anachronistic rarity but doesn't constitute a threat to "real" librarians. Asks, why fret about the public image?

Lodewycks, K. A. "Destruct the Image." Incite 2 (February 20, 1981): 9.

Agrees with Borchardt that the traditional image of librarians undercuts the status of the profession as it attempts to upgrade itself.

Meredith, P. J. "Death to the Spectre." Incite 2 (February 20, 1981): 9.

Urges all librarians to see that the spectre in black is laid to rest.

Stall, Ray. "Flesh Out!" Incite 2 (February 20, 1981): 9.

Agrees with Borchardt but suggests he avoid sexist and patronizing remarks concerning women.

1981-49 Ball, Joyce. "The New Director . . . Is a Woman." Technicalities 1 (February 1981): 10+.

Brief profile of Ball, director of Sacramento State University Library, includes her observations on women in management.

1981-50 White, Paul. "ALA Councilor's Report: Midwinter 1981." Missouri Library Association Newsletter 12 (February-March 1981): 9.

Includes notice of ERA Task Force activities and notice that Missouri has been allocated $1,500 for ERA work in the state.

1981-51 "Women Name 41 Nestle Products." American Libraries 12 (February 1981): 98.

Reprints list of Nestle products published in Women in Libraries which membership voted to boycott in June 1980.

1981-52 "Sarah Weddington." Library of Congress Information Bulletin 40 (February 12, 1981): follows p. 56.

Notes letter written to Librarian of Congress by Sarah Weddington, former Assistant to President Carter, commending the program, "Bringing Dead Ends Back to Life."

1981-53 "Women, Co-op, Technology Are Focus at OLA." Library Journal 106 (February 15, 1981): 414-415.

Report of Ohio Library Association Conference notes activities of the Women on the Rise in Library Management Task Force, including its networking activities.

1981-54 "ALA Report: Divided We Stand: ALA Weathers a 'Me-Too' Midwinter in Washington, D.C." American Libraries 12 (March 1981): 124-34.

Midwinter Meeting coverage of women's issues includes ERA Task Force activities (p. 126); presidential candidates' remarks at a SRRT Feminist Task Force forum (p. 128); photo of Elizabeth Futas, quotes as stating (on salary differentials), "Women just don't stand a chance" (p. 128); and report on a panel discussion on mentoring sponsored by the LAMA Women Administrator's Discussion Group (p. 131).

1981-55 "Career Development and Assessment Center for Librarians Established." The Newspoke (March-April 1981).

Newsletter of the Alaska Library Association includes description of the Career Development and Assessment Center for Librarians.

1981-56 Deutrich, Mabel. "Ms. vs. Mr. Archivist: An Update." SAA Women's Caucus Newsletter 5 (February 1981): [3-6].

Provides tabular data to support assertions made in [1980-112] which discussed women's depressed status in the archival profession.

1981-57 Dougherty, Richard M. "Affirmative Action: Will the Commitment Hold Firm?" Journal of Academic Librarianship 1 (March 1981): 3.

Uses Bendix Corporation's William Agee-Mary Cunningham liaison to illustrate "how close to the surface sexual discrimination still lurks." Noting the small gains women have made in ARL member libraries in the past decade, this editorial urges "the profession to strive for fairness in appointments, promotions, and salaries."

1981-58 Englebert, Alan. "Women in Corrections." Show-Me Libraries 32 (March 1981): 21-24.

Individual case of a woman librarian working at a correctional facility leads to a discussion of discrimination in general against women working in such institutions.

1981-59 Gerhardt, Lillian N., Cheatham, Bertha M., and Pollack, Pamela D. "SLJ Reports ALA Midwinter 1981." School Library Journal 27 (March 1981): 97-104.

Kay Cassell of the Equal Rights Amendment Task Force reports cash grants to four state library associations. ALA Executive Board gives permission to join a National Organization for Women signature campaign, and new ERA buttons are announced.

1981-60 Leavitt, Judy. "Network Directory." Focus on Indiana Libraries 35 (March 1981): 5.

Requests entries for the 2nd ed. of the NETWORK Directory to be published by the Indiana Library Association Division on Women in Indiana Libraries. Announces a program on mentors and networking held at the ILA/ILTA (Indiana Library Trustee Association Conference) 1981.

1981-61 "Midwinter in Reagan's Washington: An ALA Conference Report." Wilson Library Bulletin 55 (March 1981): 497-502, 557.

General coverage of 1981 ALA Midwinter Meeting in Washington, D.C. includes Kay Cassell's report to Council II on ERA Task Force Activities (p. 499), appearance of 1982 ALA presidential candidates at SRRT-Feminist Task Force meetings (pp. 501-502), and a side trip to the Capital for "Women's Rights Day" in Congress (p. 502).

1981-62 "Status of Women in Librarianship." Tar Heel Libraries 4 (March-April 1981): 2.

Describes the first organizational meeting of the North Carolina Library Association's Round Table on the Status of Women in Librarianship. Program included a keynote address by ERA Task Force Co-Chair, Alice Ihrig, and a reactor panel. A brief business meeting followed during which a formal steering Committee was established. Originators' names and affiliations are listed.

128   1981-63 Annotated Bibliography

1981-63   "For Men Only." Incite 2 (March 6, 1981): 4.

Reprints a letter by W. H. Ifould from the Library Record of Australasia 2 (1902) for readers of Incite. Ifould referred readers to Chennell's attack on women in public libraries [1902-03] and pointed out that Australia would soon have the same problems.

Letters: "For Gentlewomen." Incite 2 (April 3, 1981): 2.

Prompted by the reprint of the 1902 Ifould letter another librarian submits a quote from an 1880 publication, Occupations Accessible to Women, in which it is suggested that a single woman might enjoy the work of a librarian since she would be capable of living on a pittance while a married man with a family would not.

Whyte, J. P. "Cheap Labour." Incite 2 (April 17, 1981).

Notes that Ifould did employ women when he became a librarian since they worked more cheaply than men.

Gawler, Kathleen. "Women Librarians." Incite 2 (May 1981): 5.

States that 1880 and 1902 acts and deeds of discrimination against women have nothing on 1947. On writing to the public library at Perth in that year the author was told categorically, "we do not employ women librarians in our library."

Arnot, Jean. "Women in Librarianship." Incite 2 (June 1981): 9.

Writer, who worked under Ifould, relates early history of women librarians in New South Wales, including the fact that N. B. Kibble was the first woman employed at the Public Library of New South Wales in 1899.

Lukis, Mollie. "Unsafe for Women." Incite 2 (July 17, 1981): 8.

Responds to Gawler's letter. Notes that the principal Librarian at that time, Dr. J. S. Battye, believed it unsafe for women to leave the library at night due to the dangerous neighborhood. Author relates lower salaries paid to women at that time.

1981-64   "SRRT Feminist Task Force Picks Horrocks for President." LJ/SLJ Hotline 10 (March 9, 1981): 5.

Notes Feminist Task Force endorsement of Norman Horrocks for president of ALA.

1981-65   "Canadian Federal Librarians Win Bias Back Pay." Library Journal 106 (March 15, 1981): 601.

Reports Canadian Human Rights Commission award of $2.3 million to Canadian librarians.

1981-66   "ALA Chapter Councilor Report." The Newsletter California Library Association 23 (April 1981): 1-2.

Report by Gil McNamee notes that the ERA Task Force of ALA is working with ERAmerica members on a national petition campaign.

1981-67 "Assessment Center Extends Service." Password 4 (April 1981): 2.

Describes training of assessors at the Career Development and Assessment Center for Librarians. Notes that the Center was one of the sponsors of a conference, "Achieving Pay Equity; Strategies for Change," held at the University of Washington on April 4, 1981.

1981-68 Black, Sandra M. "Personality--Librarians as Communicators." Canadian Library Journal 38 (April 1981): 65-71.

Cites Presthus' [1970-06] conclusion that "the vast majority of librarians, i.e. women, have a tenuous commitment to change and innovation" and offers alternative viewpoints.

1981-69 "Canadians Win Equal Pay for Work of Equal Value." American Libraries 12 (April 1981): 175-176.

The librarians in the National Library of Canada and women in the Public Archives complaint filed in 1979 wins a settlement which provides back pay to March 1, 1978. ALA Office for Library Personnel Resources assistance, available to librarians in the United States, is described.

1981-70 "Feminist Task Force Endorses Horrocks." Library Journal 106 (April 1981): 701.

Horrock's responses to questions posed by Feminist Task Force members and his voting record secures their support.

1981-71 Shepard, Mary L. "Full-time Jobs Are Scarce for Grads." Feliciter 27 (April 1981): 8-9.

Continues reports on graduates of Canadian library schools.

1981-72 "Solidarity, Sisters." Assistant Librarian 74 (April 1981): 45.

Editor's column welcomes the formation of "Women in Libraries" as a nationwide pressure group to improve the position of women within the profession.

Letters: Pateman, John. "You Can Prove Anything." Assistant Librarian 74 (July-August 1981): 112.

In response to "Solidarity Sisters" (Assistant Librarian April 1981), author notes that since 11 out of 13 national officers of Association of Assistant Librarians are men, perhaps the Association ought to "put its own house in order."

Walsh, P. "With Figures." Assistant Librarian 74 (July-August): 112.

Notes that the proportion of women among the national officers has increased from 8 percent in 1980 to 15 percent in 1981.

130   1981-73 Annotated Bibliography

1981-73   "Women's Program Statistical Update: 1980." <u>Library of Congress Information Bulletin</u> 40 (April 3, 1981): 109-112.

Reports status of women at Library of Congress. A grade difference is still evident.

1981-74   "Reports on the Midwinter Meeting of the American Library Association, Washington, D.C., January 31-February 5, 1981." <u>Library of Congress Information Bulletin</u> 40 (April 10, 1981): 117-120.

Report of the lengthy agenda of the Feminist Task Force by Sarah Pritchard (p. 119).

1981-75   "Another Equal Pay Complaint Launched in Canada." <u>LJ/SLJ Hotline</u> 10 (April 13, 1981): 4.

Reports 52 National Research Council Librarians in Ottawa, mostly women, are earning an average of $4,000 less than other public service librarians who recently won a case for parity with male researchers.

1981-76   "The Career Development and Assessment Center for Librarians (CDACL)." <u>The Tuesday News</u> (April 21, 1981).

Washington State Library Staff newsletter includes status of assessor training at the Career Development and Assessment Center for Librarians.

1981-77   "Downs, Kaser, Metcalf and Shera at Eastern Illinois." <u>LJ/SLJ Hotline</u> 10 (April 27, 1981): 3.

Notes Metcalf's comments on women in library work. He noted that the predominance of women devalued librarianship and kept salaries down.

1981-78   Adamson, Martha C., and Zamora, Gloria J. "Publishing in Library Science Journals: A Test of the Olsgaard Profile." <u>College and Research Libraries</u> 42 (May 1981): 235-241.

Reports authorship of special library articles is most often male. Tables and figures display data.

1981-79   Carmack, Bob and Olsgaard, John N. "Population Characteristics of Academic Librarians." <u>College and Research Libraries</u> 42 (May 1981): 141-142.

Sample survey of academic librarians shows variation in the concentration of women academic librarians by geographic region. Women are also found to supervise fewer professionals than men.

1981-80   "Illinois Library Association Legislative Platform for 1981." <u>Illinois Libraries</u> 63 (May 1981): 388.

Support of efforts to ratify the Equal Rights Amendment in Illinois is listed as the first issue in "Special Concerns."

1981-81 "Salaries Up, But Variance Still High." College and Research Libraries 42 (May 1981): 142.

Notes data compiled annually by the College and University Personnel Association which include information on library directors by sex and race.

1981-82 "Status of Women in Librarianship." Tar Heel Libraries 4 (May-June 1981): 3.

Announces names of leaders elected to the Steering Committee of the North Carolina Library Association Round Table on the Status of Women in Librarianship and upcoming workshop activities.

1981-83 "ALA's Feminist Task Force Rallies Support for Council Favorites." LJ/SLJ Hotline 10 (May 11, 1981): 4.

Notes Feminist Task Force endorsements for 1981 ALA elections.

1981-84 Adamson, Martha C. and Zamora, Gloria J. "Authorship Characteristics in Law Library Journal." Law Library Journal 74 (Summer 1981): 527-533.

Bibliometric analysis of authorship in five special library publications reports that women publish least in the Journal of the American Society for Information Science (23.5 percent) and most in Online (59.3 percent). A "gender ratio" is used to compare association membership with authorship.

1981-85 "Association Activities." Journal of Education for Librarianship 22 (Summer-Fall 1981): 104.

Report of Association of American Library Schools 1981 conference session on "Trends and Issues in Field Experience." Includes update on the Career Development and Assessment Center for Librarians.

1981-86 Heim, Kathleen M. and Estabrook, Leigh S. "Career Patterns of Librarians." Drexel Library Quarterly 17 (Summer 1981): 35-51.

Based on survey done by authors for the ALA Committee on the Status of Women in Librarianship, the report shows that men predominate in administrative positions, are more mobile, more likely to be married, and exhibit somewhat different career patterns than women. Professional achievement, as measured by association involvement and publishing, also varies for men and women.

1981-87 Heim, Kathleen M. "Toward a Work-Force Analysis of the School Library Media Professional." School Media Quarterly 9 (Summer 1981): 235-249.

Summarizes general demographic and economic data about school media professionals. Sections highlight entry-level personnel, the universe of school librarians, and salaries. Men earn more than women in most cases.

1981-88 Holman, Norman D. "Comparable Worth and Library Employment." Drexel Library Quarterly 17 (Summer 1981): 27-34.

Summarizes major legislation and court cases on comparable worth. Discusses problems in reducing wage discrimination throughout the personnel hierarchy.

1981-89 Monroe, Margaret E. "Issues in Field Experience as an Element in the Library School Curriculum." Journal of Education for Librarianship 22 (Summer-Fall 1981): 57-72.

Describes the Career Development and Assessment Center for Librarians in Washington state as a major model of analysis for the design of competency-based education.

1981-90 "NCLA Receives $7,500 for ERA Efforts." North Carolina Libraries 39 (Summer 1981): 48.

Reports grant from ALA to the North Carolina Library Association for ERA ratification activities.

1981-91 Collins, Margaret. "Social Responsibilities Round Table." Illinois Libraries 63 (June 1981): 454.

Annual report describes ERA as a top priority issue for the Illinois Library Association SRRT. Presents favorable report on the program, "ERA: What's the Big Deal," at the ILA Annual meeting, where the impact of the passage of ERA on libraries was discussed.

1981-92 Grefrath, Richard W. "Will the Real Librarian Please Stand Up?" Technicalities 1 (June 1981): 17-19.

Informal look at the portrayal of librarians in the Occupational Outlook Handbook includes observations on photographs and appearance of men in them.

Letter: Galloway, R. Dean. "Letter to the Editor." Technicalities 1 (August 1981): 2.

Offers insight into some pictures in the Occupational Outlook Handbook and suggests authors' assumptions are unwittingly sexist.

1981-93 Heim, Kathleen M. "ILA-ERA Task Force." Illinois Libraries 63 (June 1981): 435.

Summary of the Illinois Library Association ERA Task Force efforts to support passage of the ERA.

1981-94 Mallory, Mary, and Heim, Kathleen M. Directory of Library and Information Profession Women's Groups. Chicago: ALA, June, 1981.

As part of its coalition-building responsibilities, the ALA Committee on the Status of Women in Librarianship (COSWL) sponsored publication of this Directory to provide a central source for addresses, contact persons, meeting dates, and purposes of library and information profession women's groups. National groups include: ALA and its various sub-sections on women's issues (COSWL, ERA Task Force, LAMA Women Administrator's Discussion Group, RASD Women's Materials and Women Library Users Discussion Group, and the SRRT Feminist Task Force); Association for Women in Computing; Society of American Archivists; Women Library Workers; and the Women's History Research Center. State groups from Illinois, Indiana, Louisiana, Missouri, New York, North Carolina, Ohio and Wisconsin are listed. One British organization, Feminist Library Workers Group, is included. Forms for updating are provided, and it is noted that future editions are planned.

1981-95 "Racial, Ethnic and Sexual Composition of Library Staff in Academic and Public Libraries, (Findings)." American Libraries 12 (June 1981): 363, 366.

Summarizes major affirmative action study [1981-02] conducted by the ALA Office for Library Personnel Resources.

1981-96 Wasylycia-Coe, Mary Ann. "Profile: Canadian Chief Librarians by Sex." Canadian Library Journal 38 (June 1981): 159-163.

Reports data on chief librarians from the 1975-76 national study [1977-35]. In relative terms 11 percent of women and 21 percent of men hold top posts. Men earned a median of $20,896 compared to women's $16,444. Other variables examined include starting point and length of career, career pattern, hours worked, job evaluation, social background, age, and education.

1981-97 West, Celeste. "The Library as Motherlode." Small Press Review 13 (June 1981).

Describes libraries as "repositories of patriarchy." Suggests that women claim the territory: invite representatives of women's groups to speak in libraries, join Women Library Workers and the SRRT Feminist Task Force, use alternative reviewing sources to select feminist titles, revise sexist subject headings and classification schemes, and create a community.

1981-98 "Semiannual Report on Developments at the Library of Congress, October 1, 1980, through March 31, 1981." Library of Congress Information Bulletin 40 (June 5, 1981): 184-204.

General overview mentions the Women's Program Office of the Library. The Office collected materials on sexual harassment, conducted a work force analysis, co-sponsored career development workshops, and was praised by the Federal Women's Program for its presentation, "Bringing Dead Ends Back to Life." Other activities of the Office are also reported.

1981-99 "ALA Awash the Third Wave: Illumination or Wetness?" American Libraries 12 (July-August 1981): 403-413, 426-430.

Reports Executive Board vote of seven to three to appropriate $5000 to the ERA Task Force. Includes Wedgeworth quote, "It's a point of pride for ALA to stand up and be counted as supporters who held up until the end" (p. 407). Under the heading "Women's Groups Keep Busy," activities of the Feminist Task Force and the Committee on the Status of Women are reported. Special attention is given to the Feminist Task Force's successful campaign to remove exhibitor Showcard Machine Co.'s "offensive . . . tasteless" sign. The Women Administrators Discussion Group panel presentation on mentoring is also reported.

1981-100 "Another Equal Pay Complaint Filed by Librarians." Library Journal 106 (July 1981): 1372.

National Research Council librarians lodge a complaint with the Canadian Human Rights Commission asking for equal pay.

1981-101 "Contributed Papers." College & Research Libraries News 42 (July-August 1981): 230.

Description of papers presented at the 1981 ACRL National Conference in Minneapolis includes an abstract of Fay Zipkovitz's and Sherrie S. Bergman's "Never Mind Who's Watching the Store Who's Stocking the Pool? The Status of Women in Academic Library Management" [1981-40]. States that the men predominate in management positions because they are groomed and prepared for them. Suggests encouraging women to assume management roles.

1981-102 "Library Workers Lead Strikers in Comparable Pay Fight." American Libraries 12 (July-August 1981): 397.

Reports on the Concerned Library Activist Workers organization involvement in the comparable worth struggle in San Jose.

1981-103 Ward, Patricia Layzell. "Do Not Make the Coffee." Library Association Record 83 (July 1981): 349.

Reviews of Dale's paper, Career Patterns of Women Librarians with Doctorates [1981-11] and Lundy's Women View Librarianship [1980-24].

1981-104 Yerkey, A. Neil. "The Psychological Climate of Librarianship: Values of Special Librarians." Special Libraries 72 (July 1981): 195-200.

Compares value survey of special librarians with results from public librarians, library school faculty, and library students [1980-113]. Author notes that "not surprisingly, faculty were predominately male, while students were predominately female."

1981-105 "Beyond 'Librarian' to 'Information Executive.'" Library Journal 106 (August 1981): 1499-1502.

Reports on SLA Women's Caucus program, "Comparable Pay for Comparable Worth," at SLA Conference.

1981-106 "The Operating Agreement." Library Journal 106 (August 1981): 1479-1498.

ERA Task Force donations are enumerated in Annual Conference coverage. Mentions RTSD Board vote to ask ALA to look into restoring Chicago as a conference site if the ERA boycott is ended.

1981-107 Weigand, Wayne A. "American Library Association Executive Board Members, 1876-1917: A Collective Profile." Libri 31 (August 1981): 153-166.

Analysis of socioeconomic and professional characteristics of early ALA Executive Board Members includes a focus on gender differences and tabular information on sex of members.

1981-108 "Continuing Reports on the Annual Conference of the American Library Association, San Francisco, California, June 26-July 2, 1981." Library of Congress Information Bulletin (August 21, 1981): 280-288.

General conference coverage includes: (1) summary of ALA-SRRT Feminist Task Force programs, (by Sarah Pritchard, pp. 280-281); (2) a detailed report on the joint SRRT-Feminist Task Force, RASD Women's Materials and Women Library Users Discussion Group (WMWLU), and Committee on the Status on Women in Librarianship (COSWL) program, "With Reference to Women: Indexing and Computerizing Information on Women," (by Irene Schubert, pp. 281-282); (3) description of slide show, "Barriers to Service"; discussion of NEH "Women in the Community Project"; and need for information on women's health care issues--all part of a joint RASD-WMWLU and COSWL program (by Janet Hays, pp. 282-283).

1981-109 Hamilton, Ruth. "Career Development and Assessment Center for Librarians." Noted for the Alumni 46 (Fall 1981).

University of Washington School of Librarianship newsletter includes description of the Career Development and Assessment Center for Librarians.

1981-110 Cargill, Jennifer, and Alley, Brian. "Rating the Library Director's Job Performance." Technicalities 1 (September 1981): 1, 3-5, 15.

Report of a questionnaire sent to library staffs and anonymously returned to determine 'good' and 'bad' characteristics of library directors. Relatively few women were identified in any of the categories. The good director group was 82 percent male. No percentage of males is reported for the 'bad' director group.

1981-111 "Carolina Libraries Interface '81." Tar Heel Libraries 5 (September-October 1981): 1.

Highlights of the Joint Conference of NCLA-SCLA include program by Round Table on the Status of Women in Librarianship featuring Working Woman editor, Kate Rand Lloyd.

1981-112 Maag, Albert F. "So You Want to Be a Director." Journal of Academic Librarianship 7 (September 1981): 213-217.

Research on 122 librarians who had new appointments that were announced in three library journals are studied for career path data. Hiring patterns reveal "women are still disadvantaged in the library director sweepstakes."

1981-113 "Minnesota Library Workers Seek Pay Parity in 13-Week Strike." American Libraries 12 (September 1981): 454.

Second longest library strike in history results in a slight narrowing of the wage gap for librarians in Dakota County.

1981-114 "Pursuing Happiness in the Golden State: ALA Conference Report." Wilson Library Bulletin 56 (September 1981): 17-26.

Notes ERA Task Force report and Board vote to provide another $5000 to, as Wedgeworth states, "go out in style" (p. 18). Reviews RASD Women's Materials and Women Library Users Discussion Group program, "With Reference to Women."

1981-115 Heim, Kathleen M., and Kacena, Carolyn. "Sex, Salaries and Library Support . . . 1981." Library Journal 106 (September 15, 1981): 1692-1699.

Provides sex and salary information for directors of major public libraries. Demonstrates continuing advantage of men in per capita support and new professionals' salaries.

1981-116 "Continuing Reports on the Annual Conference of the American Library Association, San Francisco, Calif. June 26-July 2, 1981." Library Congress Information Bulletin 40 (September 25, 1981): 333-340.

Records Council Meeting during which Kay Cassell, co-chair of the ERA Task Force, reported ERA activities and stated that ALA's participation in and support of the ERA ratification effort was an important part of the nationwide movement. Cassell expressed appreciation for the continued support of the Association (p. 334).

1981-117 Cargill, Jennifer, and Alley, Brian. "Rating the Library Director's Job Performance Part II." Technicalities 1 (October 1981): 4-6.

Of the public library directors analyzed in the survey, 62 percent were male. Continues [1981-110].

1981-118 Sherman, Claire Richter. "Women Librarians As Interpreters of the Visual Arts." ARLIS/NA 9 (October 1981): 185-189.

Offers two complementary approaches to examining the professional development of women librarians who promoted public and scholarly understanding of the visual arts. Relates underlying connections between public libraries and art museums and briefly analyzes conditions favoring women's involvement with the visual arts. Individual biographical examples of women whose careers demonstrate achievement as librarians and interpreters of the visual arts are included. Based on research for [1981-32].

1981-119 Tolliver, Barbara. "Career Development and Assessment Center for Librarians." The Sourdough 18 (October-November-December 1981): 1-3.

History and description of the Career Development and Assessment Center for Librarians in Washington state.

1981-120 Learmont, Carol L., and Van Houton, Stephen. "Placements and Salaries 1980: Holding the Line." Library Journal 106 (October 1, 1981): 1881-1887.

Annual placement and salary survey of new graduates finds female median salary is $13,500 and male median is $14,112.

1981-121 "The Conference Papers--Personnel." LJ/SLJ Hotline 10 (October 12, 1981): 7.

Coverage of ACRL Conference includes summary of paper by Betty Jo Irvine, "ARL Academic Library Leaders of the 1980s: Men and Women of the Executive Suite." [1981-23].

1981-122 "California Librarians Eye Equal Pay Bill." LJ/SLJ Hotline 10 (October 26, 1981): 5.

A California bill to establish equal pay for female-dominated professions is reported as a topic at the CLA meeting.

1981-123 Methven, Liz, and Long, Jan. "Women in Libraries: A Student View." Assistant Librarian 74 (November 1981): 144-145.

Reflections by students after attending Feminist Librarians' Group Conference, Women in Libraries--Their Position and Role. Low chances for female success are compounded by male domination of the Library Council of the Library Association (L.A.) and even by such minor affronts as the L.A. tie (eventually followed up after protest by the L.A. scarf for the female majority). Proposes a Library Association Women's Group.

Letters: Henney, Janice. "Jobs for the Mums?" Assistant Librarian 75 (March 1982): 42.

Describes her experience with career and children conflicts. Requests responses from other women librarians with children.

Goddard, Ann. "Dad Blocks Mums." Assistant Librarian 75 (May 1982): 74.

Agrees with Henney and suggests list of 3 questions--How many married women are in this position; What genuine difficulties exist; What solutions are available. Believes the work could be done by "enthusiastic but unemployed mum with professional ambitions."

Saunders, Ann. "Proving the Rule." Assistant Librarian 75 (May 1982): 75.

Describes hiring practices in her district. One-third of the senior staff are married women, four out of five deputy chief librarians have been women. Believes that married women are given equal consideration.

1981-124 Fischer, Russell G. "Pay Equity and the San Jose Strike." Library Journal 106 (November 1, 1981): 2079-2085.

Interview with Patt Curia, San Jose Public Library senior librarian and member of the union negotiating team of the Municipal Employees Federation of San Jose. Summarizes July 5-14, 1981 strike against the city of San Jose, California, believed to be the first public employees strike in which the main issue was equal pay for jobs of comparable worth. Curia notes that "Pay parity for librarians can mean as much as a 30 percent salary increase," and observes, "Why should librarians and women in general, subsidize good service by accepting low salaries?" Article also outlines the Hay associates job evaluation study which provided data for the strike and found a strong relationship between pay and the predominant sex of members of a job class.

1981-125 Campbell, Ann Morgan. "Council Programs Committee." The American Archivist 44 (Winter 1981): 79.

Report of the Society of American Archivists Council includes the proposal by the Status of Women Committee that a questionnaire be distributed to employers advertising in the Employment Bulletin or the SAA Newsletter to determine whether employers comply with Equal Opportunity-Affirmative Action regulations. Council voted to request details of the project from the Status of Women Committee.

1981-126 Lloyd, Kate Rand. "The Working Woman: Leadership for the '80's." North Carolina Libraries 39 (Winter 1981): 31-37.

In a general discussion on working women, librarianship is mentioned as a female-intensive occupation.

1981-127 Wiegand, Wayne A., and Greenway, Geri. "A Comparative Analysis of the Socioeconomic and Professional Characteristics of American Library Association Executive Board and Council Members, 1876-1917." Library Research 4 (Winter 1981): 309-325.

Discusses socioeconomic characteristics of early ALA leaders. Finds that male dominance of the Executive Board continued throughout the period studied. Although female representation on Council increased during this period, most power remained vested with the Board (p. 321).

1981-128 "ALA Survey Reports on Library Work Force." School Library Journal 28 (December 1981): 8.

Summary of [1981-02].

1981-129 Pankhurst, Rita. "Women and Libraries: Part 1--Women in Polytechnic Libraries: a Preliminary Report on Their Representation at Various Salary Levels." Information and Library Manager 1 (December 1981): 88-90.

Reports under-representation of women in top professional posts in polytechnic libraries. Although six out of ten professional staff members are women they hold only 10 percent of posts with annual salaries over £11,000. Women held 85 percent of the posts at the lowest salary ranges and 90 percent of nonprofessional positions.

1981-130 "Quotable Quotes." Technicalities 1 (December 1981): 1.

"The applicant pool (for deanship and directorships) is stocked primarily with men who have been preselected for that pool since it is stocked by those already in power." From [1981-40].

1981-131 Ritchie, Sheila. "Women and Libraries: Part 2--The Position of Women in Public Libraries." Information and Library Manager 1 (December 1981): 89-90.

Reports 1977-78 survey of public library positions. Top posts were held by 106 men; 2 women; Deputy (second-level posts) by 98 men; 16 women. Third level posts by 112 women compared to 487 men. Ritchie also discusses two "myths" about women employed in libraries: less career commitment, and less ambition. She calculates that men have odds of 25 to 1 in gaining top posts; women 2,000 to 1.

1981-132 Wolf, Milton T. "A Conversation with Pat Schuman." Technicalities 1 (December 1981): 6-7, 13-15.

Pat Schuman answers questions about the status of women in librarianship, the existence of sexism in the profession, and success orientation vs. service orientation. Refutes the perception that there is an emerging "old girl" network.

1981-133 "Photo." Library of Congress Information Bulletin 40 (December 25, 1981): follows p. 458.

Formal photograph of the members of the Women's Program Advisory Committee with caption.

Author Index

Adamson, Martha C., 1981-78, 1981-84
Alexander, Adrian W., 1979-75 (letter)
Allen, Jane, 1981-38C, 1981-38E
Alley, Brian, 1981-110, 1981-117
Almquist, Elizabeth M., 1978-01
Ambrose, Karen S., 1977-63 (letter), 1978-35
Anwar, Mumtaz A., 1980-117
Archuleta, Alyce, 1978-80
Armstrong, Robert W., 1979-75 (letter)
Arnot, Jean, 1981-63 (letter)
Ayers, Jill, 1979-63 (letter)

Baer, Mark, 1977-01
Bailey, Nancy P., 1978-75
Bailey, Robert, 1980-126
Baker, Curtis O., 1976-78, 1976-79, 1977-02, 1981-03, 1981-04
Baker, Gladys L., 1976-99
Ball, Joyce, 1981-49
Ballard, Bob, 1975-99
Barber, Peggy, 1980-63 (letter)
Bartol, Kathryn M., 1980-85
Bauer, Caroline Feller, 1979-40
Beardwood, Louise B., 1980-59
Beasley, Clarence, Jr. 1978-49

Beazley, Richard M., 1979-01
Beede, Benjamin R., 1977-04
Behn, Jan, 1979-02
Berger, Patricia W., 1978-76
Bergman, Sherrie S., 1981-40
Bergmann, Martha, 1974-70
Berry, John, 1977-65, 1978-53, 1978-71, 1978-98, 1978-99, 1979-64, 1979-69, 1980-93
Bevis, Dorothy L., 1980-02
Biblo, Herbert, 1981-05
Biblo, Mary, 1979-03, 1980-03
Bidlack, Russell E., 1977-36, 1978-57, 1979-50, 1979-68, 1980-04, 1980-05, 1981-06
Biggs, Mary, 1979-28 (review)
Black, Sandra M., 1981-68
Blackburn, Mary, 1978-125
Blades, William, 1957-07, 1966-11
Blankenship, W. C., 1971-42
Blau, Francine D., 1978-03
Bobinski, George S., 1979-11 (review)
Boisse, Josette Anne, 1977-03
Bolino, August C., 1968-18, 1969-24
Borchardt, D. H., 1981-48
Boucias, Karen, 1979-119

Boyd, Barbara Gray, 1978-41 (letter)
Braunagel, Judith Schiek, 1979-123
Broadley, Pamela R., 1979-14
Brown, George H., 1978-04, 1978-05, 1979-04, 1979-05
Brown, Gretchen Davidson, 1977-56
Brugh, Anne E., 1977-04
Bryan, James, 1981-07
Buck, Vernon E., 1979-06
Bushbin, O. Mell, 1978-70
Byam, M. S., 1979-11 (review)

Cahalan, Thomas H., 1979-75 (letter)
Cambre, Marjorie, 1977-42, 1977-49
Campbell, Ann Morgan, 1981-125
Campbell, Jean W., 1973-72
Cargill, Jennifer, 1981-110, 1981-117
Carmack, Bob, 1981-79
Carmichael, Carole A., 1981-45
Carpenter, Ray L., 1977-27
Carter, Jane Robbins, 1978-58
Casey, Marion, 1979-11 (review)
Casey, Philip, 1977-48 (letter)
Cassell, Kay, 1980-79, 1980-110
Caswell-Pierce, Sara L., 1980-122
Chapman, Liz, 1978-77
Chase, Julie Ann, 1978-124
Cheatham, Bertha M., 1976-80, 1977-41, 1977-75, 1977-91, 1978-06, 1978-62, 1978-107, 1978-138, 1979-07, 1979-60, 1979-108, 1980-06, 1980-35, 1980-62, 1980-105, 1980-119, 1980-129, 1981-08, 1981-59
Cheda, Sherrill, 1977-05, 1978-37
Cherry, Susan Spaeth, 1979-28 (review), 1980-47, 1980-80, 1980-81
Childers, Martha, 1981-09
Chisholm, Margaret E., 1980-07
Christofferson, Rea, 1977-45

Clubb, Barbara, 1978-100
Coble, Gerald M., 1978-78 (letter)
Cohen, Sylvia, 1979-63 (letter)
Colley, H. W., 1981-48 (letter)
Collins, Carol, 1977-74
Collins, Judith, 1975-100
Collins, Margaret, 1981-91
Collins, Rosann Webb, 1980-36
Comaromi, John P., 1979-64 (letter)
Connelly, Sheryl, 1980-102
Cooney, Jane, 1978-30 (letter)
Cooper, Michael D., 1978-07, 1980-131
Corkill, Cynthia M., 1976-93
Corth, Annette, 1978-76
Corts, Ans, 1978-130J
Coughlin, Caroline M., 1978-38
Courain, Margaret E., 1979-51
Cowell, Penny, 1980-111
Creth, Sheila, 1980-86
Crosman, Alexander C., Jr., 1979-75 (letter)
Cuesta, Yolanda, 1980-08, 1981-10
Cummins, Julie, 1981-42

Dale, Doris C., 1980-130, 1981-11
Dannreuther, Kathy, 1979-73
Darling, Richard L., 1977-14, 1977-59, 1978-19, 1978-92
Darnall, Charles W., 1979-75 (letter)
Davis, A. F., 1979-11 (review)
Davis, Eileen, 1979-63 (letter)
Davis, Lorraine, 1980-104
Day, Terence, 1979-75 (letter)
Day, Virginia, 1979-63 (letter)
D'Elia, George P., 1979-96
Dempsey, Frank L., 1979-08
Denis, Laurent G., 1979-85
Detlefsen, Ellen Gay, 1978-16b (commentary)
Deutrich, Mabel E., 1980-112, 1981-56

Deveny, Mary Alice, 1979-11 (review)
DeWath, Nancy V., 1980-131
DeWhitt, Ben, 1980-112
Dible, Joan B., 1979-75 (letter)
Dickinson, Elizabeth, 1976-81, 1977-06, 1977-32E, 1978-08, 1979-41
DiMattia, Ernest A., 1979-11 (review)
Donovan, Ruth, 1981-43
Dougherty, Richard M., 1979-57, 1981-57
Drabble-Versteeg, Atie, 1978-130C
Drake, Miriam A., 1979-52
Drake, Sunniva, 1980-09
Dworak, Marcia, 1979-81

Echelman, Shirley, 1978-78
Eckard, Helen M., 1978-09
Eckels, Patricia W., 1979-78 (letter)
Eggleton, Richard, 1980-36
Eldridge, Marie D., 1976-82
Eiden, Leo J., 1980-13, 1981-17
Elkins, Deborah, 1978-79
Ellenberger, Jack S., 1976-127
Ellsworth, Diane J., 1979-28
Engelbarts, Rudolf, 1981-12
Engelberg, Laurie, 1978-24
Englebert, Alan, 1981-58
Estabrook, Leigh S., 1980-132, 1980-132 (letter), 1981-86
Estes, Mark E., 1979-82
Euster, Joanne R., 1979-09, 1979-53
Evans, Charles, 1979-64 (letter)

Fennell, Janice Clinedinst, 1978-10
Fenster, Valmai, 1980-10
Ferber, Marianne A., 1973-76
Field, Carolyn W., 1977-48 (letter)
Filter, Nancy H., 1969-22, 1970-34

Fischer, Linda, 1977-35
Fischer, Russell G., 1981-124
Fletcher, Janet, 1978-99
Fluellin, Gwendolyn F., 1980-118
Fontaine, Sue, 1981-13
Ford, Barbara J., 1981-14
Forman, Jack, 1980-73 (letter)
Foster, Dona Lyn, 1979-124
Frances, Carol, 1981-15
Frankie, Suzanne, 1977-07, 1978-11, 1978-12, 1978-133, 1979-10
Frarey, Carlyle J., 1970-35
Freedwomen, Janet, 1977-62
French, Mary Blake, 1979-11 (review)
Fretwell, Gordon, 1980-48, 1980-133, 1981-16
Frye, Larry, 1977-72

Galloway, R. Dean, 1981-92 (letter)
Galloway, Sue, 1978-80, 1978-125
Garland, Henry Walter, III, 1975-98
Garrison, Dee, 1979-11
Gasaway, Laura N., 1980-11, 1981-16a
Gaver, Mary, 1979-11 (review), 1979-28 (review)
Gawler, Kathleen, 1981-63 (letter)
Geidel, Patti, 1979-02
Gelshenen, Linda, 1979-59 (letter)
Genaway, David C., 1978-54
Genova, B. K. L., 1977-08
Gerhardt, Lillian N., 1977-32A, 1977-41, 1977-75, 1978-41, 1978-62, 1978-107, 1979-59, 1979-60, 1979-108, 1979-117, 1980-49, 1980-62, 1980-105, 1980-119, 1981-59
Getz, Malcolm, 1980-12
Ginzberg, Eli, 1966-12
Glasser, L., 1976-121
Goddard, Ann, 1981-123 (letter)

Goldstein, Harold, 1978-16a, 1978-16b
Goldstein, Rachael, 1977-63, 1978-13, 1980-37
Gottleib, Ann K., 1978-76
Gould, Lewis L., 1979-11 (review)
Gould, Martha, 1979-75 (letter)
Graham, Patricia Albjerg, 1973-74
Grant, LaRue Tucker, 1978-104
Grant, W. Vance, 1976-84, 1977-09, 1978-14, 1979-12, 1980-13, 1981-17
Gray, Robert, 1976-120
Greenway, Geri, 1981-127
Grefath, Richard W., 1981-92
Griffen, Agnes M., 1978-15, 1979-13
Grimm, James W., 1978-16
Grotzinger, Laurel A., 1978-16a, 1978-81, 1979-11 (review)

Hall, Hal W., 1978-105, 1979-120
Hamilton, Beth A., 1979-13a, 1979-15a
Hamilton, Ruth, 1981-109
Hamlin, Arthur T., 1981-18
Harkess, Shirley, 1978-33
Harris, Patricia R., 1976-85, 1977-10
Hartmann, Heidi I., 1981-35
Havens, Shirley, 1978-99
Haycock, Ken, 1977-54 (letter)
Heim, Kathleen M., 1979-13a, 1979-14, 1979-28, 1979-70, 1980-14, 1980-15, 1980-42a, 1980-50, 1980-132, 1980-132 (letter), 1981-19, 1981-20, 1981-44, 1981-86, 1981-87, 1981-93, 1981-94, 1981-115
Heintze, Robert A., 1981-21
Heller, Dawn, 1980-16
Henney, Janice, 1981-123 (letter)
Herbert, Clara W., 1939-06
Herman, Mary Lou, 1979-02
Hill, Dorothy R., 1980-37

Hills, Kate, 1979-28 (review)
Hinding, Andrea, 1979-15
Hippenhammer, Craighton T., 1980-72
Hlava, Marjorie M. K., 1980-114
Hodes, Lance, 1981-21
Hoke, William Neff, 1977-53, 1978-32
Holbourn, Cheryl, 1979-63 (letter)
Holcomb, Adele M., 1981-32
Holcomb, Morrigene, 1977-61
Holley, Edward G., 1976-87, 1978-16c, 1979-15a
Holman, Norman D., 1981-88
Hook, Robert D., 1978-91, 1979-74, 1980-39, 1980-98
Horrocks, Norman, 1977-46
Hough, William E., III, 1979-75 (letter)
Hubbell, Sue, 1980-63
Hudson, Nancy, 1979-97
Hunt, Sally, 1979-32
Hurst, Lannie, 1977-55
Hyman, Karen, 1981-22

Ihrig, Alice B., 1979-61, 1980-51, 1980-79
Irvine, Betty Jo., 1981-23
Isaacson, David, 1980-73

Jackson, Eugene B., 1980-11, 1980-17
James, Minnie Stewart Rhodes, 1957-08, 1966-13
Jensen, J. Eide, 1978-130I
Jespersen, Sherry, 1981-38A
Johnson, Richard D., 1977-11, 1978-17
Josephine, Helen B., 1977-32B, 1977-32C, 1979-11 (review), 1979-28 (review)
Josey, E. J., 1975-95, 1976-88, 1977-12, 1980-18

Kacena, Carolyn, 1979-70, 1980-15, 1980-42a, 1981-115

Kadanoff, Diane Gordon, 1977-32D
Kahl, Anne, 1974-72
Kato, Komei, 1978-18
Kellum-Rose, Nancy, 1976-89, 1977-48
Kelley, Gloria A., 1977-48 (letter)
Kenney, Brigitte L., 1977-37
Kickbusch, Ilona, 1976-122, 1978-130F
Kim, Ung Chon, 1980-19
King, Donald W., 1980-106
Klauber, Julie, 1980-73 (letter)
Klotzburger, Kay, 1973-75
Kraus, Joe W., 1950-05

Ladd, Jay L., 1979-11 (review)
Ladenson, Alex, 1979-16, 1980-20
Land, Brian, 1976-90, 1979-17
Lansman, Jeanne, 1977-45 (letter)
Lawson, Venable A., 1977-13
Learmont, Carol L., 1977-14, 1977-59, 1978-19, 1978-92, 1979-18, 1979-98, 1979-98 (letter), 1980-21, 1980-22, 1980-123, 1981-24, 1981-25, 1981-120
Leavitt, Judith A., 1980-23, 1981-60
Lebare, Lynn, 1979-33
LeBarron, Suzanne, 1979-117 (letter)
Lee, Joel M., 1979-13a, 1979-15a
Leinbach, Anne E., 1980-59
Leita, Carole, 1977-32C, 1978-28
Lemons, J. S., 1979-11 (review)
Lester, Daniel W., 1978-76
Levitt, Eleanor Sosnow, 1970-33
Lillard, R. S., 1969-25
Lind, C. George, 1976-84, 1977-09, 1978-14, 1979-12
Lipow, Ann, 1971-44
Little, Janet, 1981-38B
Little, Robert David, 1978-20, 1978-21
Lloyd, Kate Rand, 1981-126

Lockhart, Helen, 1976-105
Lodewycks, K. A., 1981-48 (letter)
Loeb, Jane W., 1973-76
Long, Jan, 1981-123
Lowenthal, Helen, 1978-106
Luethe, Marie, 1977-15
Lukis, Mollie, 1981-63 (letter)
Lundy, Kathryn Renfro, 1980-24
Lynch, Beverly P., 1977-16, 1977-17
Lynch, Laurence P., 1979-75 (letter)
Lynch, Mary Jo., 1981-26
Lytle, Richard H., 1980-112 (letter)

Maag, Albert F., 1981-112
Mallory, Mary, 1981-94
Mann, Margaret, 1981-27
Marchant, Maurice P., 1977-18, 1979-33, 1979-75 (letter)
Marquard, Steve, 1979-75 (letter)
Martin, Jean Krieg, 1978-22, 1979-54
Martinez, Anna, 1979-19
Martinez, Julio, 1979-19
Maxwell, Margaret F., 1978-84
McAnally, Arthur M., 1958-04, 1971-45
McFarland, C. K., 1979-11 (review)
McGrath, Richard, 1979-86
McKay, J. R., 1976-93
McLaughlin, Steven D., 1980-25
McNamee, Gil, 1980-64
Melber, Barbara D., 1980-25
Mensel, R. Frank, 1981-15
Meredith, P. J., 1981-48 (letter)
Methven, Liz, 1981-123
Metz, Paul, 1978-109
Miele, Tony, 1978-110
Milden, James W., 1977-38
Miller, Deborah, 1980-52
Miller, Rae Jean, 1980-65
Minudri, R., 1979-28 (review)

Author Index

Molenda, Michael, 1977-19, 1977-42, 1977-49
Monroe, Hamilton, 1978-137
Monroe, Margaret E., 1981-89
Moon, Brenda E., 1979-28 (review)
Moore, E. Catherine, 1979-119
Morlock, Laura, 1973-77
Mullins, Stephanie, 1976-91, 1979-20
Munn, Ellie, 1980-132 (letter)
Muriuki, M. N., 1978-23
Myers, Margaret, 1977-48 (letter), 1978-08, 1980-87, 1981-29

Newton, Mary, 1981-38G
Norsworthy, James A., Jr., 1979-55, 1979-104
Nyren, Karl E., 1976-113, 1977-20, 1978-99
Nystrom, Kathleen A., 1979-84

O'Hara, Catherine, 1979-119
Olsgaard, Jane Kinch, 1980-40
Olsgaard, John N., 1980-40, 1981-79
Orr, Nancy A., 1978-41 (letter)
Osborne, Jeanne, 1979-28 (review)
Osso, Nicholas, 1977-21
Ott, Mary Diederich, 1977-22

Paeper, Roberta, 1979-86 (letter)
Pankhurst, Rita, 1981-129
Parsons, Jerry L., 1976-109, 1977-87 (letter)
Partington, Dorothy, 1976-91, 1979-20
Pateman, John, 1981-72 (letter)
Patterson, Michelle, 1978-24
Pearson, Lois R., 1980-53
Pepin, Andrew J., 1980-26
Perkins, Stephanie, 1977-56
Peterson, Gary T., 1974-71, 1976-110, 1977-23, 1977-50, 1978-25

Pierce, Sydney, 1977-24, 1977-48 (letter)
Plate, Kenneth H., 1979-87
Platt, Judith, 1973-80
Plotnik, Art, 1980-120
Pollack, Pamela D., 1977-41, 1977-75, 1978-62, 1978-107, 1979-60, 1979-108, 1980-62, 1980-105, 1981-59
Prosser, Judith, 1979-105

Ratner, Jane, 1979-28 (review)
Ray, Jean M., 1979-21
Reagan, Agnes Lytton, 1957-09, 1958-05
Reed, Kaye, 1980-134
Reed, Sarah R., 1975-101
Ried, Marion T., 1979-121
Reinshagen, Bill, 1979-22
Rensel, Jeanne, 1980-88
Reuter, Anne, 1979-70 (letter)
Ricker, Ann, 1980-50
Ritchie, Shelia, 1978-26, 1979-63, 1981-131
Ritzer, George, 1977-25
Roberts, Audrey J., 1980-10
Robertson, S. E., 1975-97
Rosaschi, Jim, 1980-132 (letter)
Rosenfeld, Harriet E., 1978-114, 1979-43
Rossi, Alice S., 1973-78
Rudy, Michele, 1977-73
Rufe, Charles P., 1977-87 (letter)

Sague, Virginia M., 1980-106
Salazar, Marilyn, 1977-48 (letter)
Samore, Theodore, 1981-30
Sandler, Rhoda, 1973-80
Saunders, Ann, 1981-123 (letter)
Savage, Noel, 1976-92, 1977-20, 1978-27, 1978-46, 1979-23, 1979-36, 1980-27, 1980-44, 1981-31, 1981-47
Schick, Frank L., 1950-06
Schuman, Patricia Glass, 1979-88
Schwebke, Ruth N., 1977-87 (letter), 1979-129 (letter)

Seigel, Jacob P., 1979-87
Sellen, Betty-Carol, 1977-87 (letter)
Sergean, R., 1976-93, 1977-26
Settani, Joseph, 1980-125 (letter)
Severance, Rosemary, 1979-75 (letter)
Shank, Beverly, 1980-127
Shank, Russell, 1979-24
Shapiro, Lillian L., 1977-48 (letter)
Shaw, Louise C., 1980-74
Shearer, Kenneth D., 1977-27
Shediac, Margaret, 1978-52, 1980-128
Shepard, Mary L., 1976-111, 1977-43, 1979-76, 1980-75, 1981-71
Sherman, Claire Richter, 1981-32, 1981-118
Shiflett, Orvin Lee, 1979-25, 1981-33
Shubert, Joseph F., 1979-26
Silver, Constance, 1980-121
Simon, Barry, 1976-94
Singh, Jennifer, 1976-123
Sink, Darryl L., 1978-116, 1979-109, 1980-29, 1981-34
Slanker, Barbara O., 1976-95, 1978-02, 1978-29
Slater, Margaret, 1978-128, 1980-30
Smith, Karen F., 1978-63
Smith, Nathan M., 1977-18
Smith, Ralph E., 1978-30
Smith, Stanley V., 1977-28, 1978-31
Snider, David, 1979-45, 1979-77
Snyder, William E., 1979-69 (letter)
Stagg, Lynn, 1980-136
Stall, Ray, 1981-48 (letter)
Stangl, Peter, 1977-53, 1978-32
Stineman, Esther R., 1979-28 (review)
Stirling, Keith H., 1977-18
Strable, Edward G., 1976-96
Stromberg, Ann H., 1978-33

Strong, Gary E., 1980-31
Stroup, Timothy, 1980-125 (letter)
Swoboda, Marian J., 1980-10

Taylor, Jackie, 1981-38D
Tedder, Henry Richard, 1957-10, 1966-14
Tees, Miriam, 1977-29
Teich, Steve, 1977-63 (letter)
Thibodo, Sharon, 1979-117 (letter)
Thorne, Barbara, 1978-59
Thornton, John L., 1957-07, 1957-11, 1966-13, 1966-15
Tolliver, Barbara, 1981-119
Toth, George, 1976-119
Treiman, Donald J., 1981-35
Troiano, Richard, 1979-98, 1980-22
Turner, Robert L., 1980-83

Van Alystyne, Carol, 1977-57
Van Houton, Stephen, 1981-120
Vazhko, O., 1976-124
Vincent, Ida, 1978-139, 1979-110

Wade, Maureen, 1981-38F
Walker, Susan, 1977-54
Wallach, John S., 1979-112
Walsh, Nina May, 1979-75 (letter)
Walsh, P., 1981-72 (letter)
Ward, James E., 1979-106
Ward, Patricia Layzell, 1978-130G, 1981-103
Wasylycia-Coe, Mary Ann, 1977-35, 1981-96
Watson, Elbert L., 1979-27
Wehrl-Einhorn, Juanita L., 1978-01
Weibel, Kathleen, 1977-30, 1978-34, 1979-28, 1979-88, 1980-110
Wells, Agnes Q., 1976-78, 1976-79, 1977-02, 1978-31, 1980-26
Wert, Lucille M., 1977-90
West, Celeste, 1981-97

Westenberger, Jane W., 1979-56
White, Paul, 1981-50
Whyte, J. P., 1981-63 (letter)
Wiegand, Wayne, 1979-11 (review), 1979-29, 1981-107, 1981-127
Wilkins, Barratt, 1979-127
Williams, Helen E., 1979-117 (letter)
Williams, Janet, 1978-117
Williamson, Jane, 1978-43, 1981-37
Williamson, William Landram, 1963-09
Wolf, Milton T., 1981-132
Wolfskill, Mary, 1977-69
Wood, Frances E., 1975-96
Wrose, I., 1976-122 (letter)

Yaffe, Phyllis, 1977-35
Yates, Ella Gaines, 1979-78, 1979-129
Yerkey, A. Neil, 1980-113, 1981-104
Yohalem, Alice M., 1979-30
Young, Arthur Price, 1976-98, 1981-39

Zamora, Gloria J., 1981-78, 1981-84
Zimmerman, Lee Frank, 1932-03
Zipcovitz, Fay, 1981-40

Title Index

'80 and beyond: Gloria Steinem visits AASL, 1980-134
'80 library news, 1980-129
The 1976 AECT member opinion survey: income comparisons, 1977-42
The 1976 member opinion survey, 1977-49
1976-77 professional salaries and fringe benefits in Louisiana academic libraries, 1979-121
1977 conference-editorial viewpoint, 1977-90
1977 news roundup in children's and young adult services, 1978-06
1978 placement shift, 1979-92
1978 update on women in libraries, 1978-106
1979 annual business meeting, 1980-125
1980 Midwinter returns to Chicago; vote reverses Council's decision, 1979-79
1980 salary survey, 1980-74
1980-81 Administrative Compensation Survey, 1981-07
1981-82 Library Human Resources: Study of Supply and Demand--Conceptual Overview, 1980-131
2000 to 1: a sex oddity, 1979-63

AALS conference summary, 1977-37
AASL's first national conference, 1980-119
Abschied von der Eule der Minerva; Frauen--offentlicher Dienst Bibliothek, 1976-122
The Academic and Professional Education of College and University Librarians, 1932-03
Academic libraries, 1977-11, 1978-17
Academic Library Administrators and Part Time Work, 1979-110
Academic library management: a comparison of females and males, 1979-54
Academic Women on the Move, 1973-72, 1973-74, 1973-75, 1973-77, 1973-78

150   Title Index

Academics shave own pay to aid library colleagues, 1980-53
An addendum to the sex structuring of organizations: the special case of traditionally-female professions, 1980-85
Administrative detail program begun, 1978-121
Administrative succession in the academic library, 1978-109
<u>Advances in Librarianship</u>, 1978-08
AECT member opinion survey: 1975-1976, 1977-19
Affirmative action, 1978-69
Affirmative action and American librarianship, 1978-08
Affirmative action and charges of reverse bias, 1976-113
Affirmative action and Women's Program Office, 1980-94
Affirmative action in libraries, 1977-48
Affirmative action in Md.: Fairfax update AA plan, 1976-126
Affirmative action in Tucson: library develops written plan, 1978-135
Affirmative action plans in review: a report from Equal Employment Opportunity Subcommittee, 1979-41
Affirmative action/reverse bias, 1976-102
Affirmative action: will the commitment hold firm?, 1981-57
ALA & ERA, 1979-124
ALA antitrust liability fears over boycott relieved, 1979-66
ALA at 100, 1976-87
ALA awash the third wave: illumination or wetness?, 1981-99
ALA Chapter Councilor, 1979-61, 1980-51
ALA Chapter Councilor report, 1981-66

ALA Chicago decision faces mail vote, 1979-37
ALA Councilor column, 1979-77
ALA Councilor report, 1979-106
ALA Councilor's report, 1979-112, 1980-39, 1980-98
ALA Councilor's report: Midwinter 1981, 1981-50
ALA Councilor's report on Midwinter, 1979, 1979-74
ALA Equal Employment Subcommittee guidelines for library affirmative action plans, 1976-114
ALA equal rights stand draws Louisiana protest, 1977-93
ALA/ERA Task Force, 1979-116
ALA/ERA--where do you stand?, 1977-71, 1978-136
ALA Executive Board Spring meeting, 1980-84
ALA marches for ERA in Chicago rally, 1980-90
ALA meets peacefully in big D, 1979-107
ALA membership vote nixes ERA stance, 1979-80
ALA Midwinter--a happening in Washington D.C., 1979-55
ALA Midwinter Meeting '77, 1977-41
ALA Midwinter Meeting change torpedoes Alabama governor, 1978-118
ALA Midwinter this week, 1980-45
ALA offers checklist and advisory service for affirmative action plans, 1976-115
ALA-Palmer House flap over ERA boycott unlikely to ever see court, 1979-46
ALA principle--not for sale, 1979-64
ALA report, 1979-97, 1980-78
ALA report: divided we stand: ALA weathers a 'me-too' Mid-

Title Index   151

winter, in Washington, D.C., 1981-54
ALA, SLA & ERA, 1978-98
ALA/SRRT Task Force on Women to boycott Chicago Midwinter, 1979-113
ALA steps lively through Detroit, 1977-64
ALA supports ERA in Missouri, 1980-69
ALA survey reports on library work force, 1980-128
ALA testifies on sex bias at EEOC hearings, 1980-91
ALA women's rights stand: Alabama warns of impact, 1977-87
Alabama first non-ERA state to squawk at ALA boycott plans, 1977-80
ALA's Committee on Women in Librarianship, 1977-32E
ALA's Feminist Task Force rallies support for Council favorites, 1981-83
ALA's for ERA, 1979-122, 1979-124, 1980-01
Amend equal opportunity--or abolish it, 1976-119
American librarianship, 1977-04
American Library Association, 1979-24
The American Library Association and World War I, 1976-98
American Library Association Executive Board members, 1876-1917: a collective profile, 1981-107
Analysis of Doctor's Degrees Awarded to Men and to Women, 1970-1971 through 1974-75, 1977-22
Another equal pay complaint filed by librarians, 1981-100
Another equal pay complaint launched in Canada, 1981-75

Apostles of Culture: The Public Librarian and American Society, 1987-1920, 1979-11
ARL academic library leaders of the 1980's: men and women of the executive suite, 1981-23
ARL Annual Salary Survey 1976-77, 1977-07, 1978-11
ARL Annual Salary Survey, 1977-78, 1978-133, 1979-10
ARL Annual Salary Survey 1978-1979, 1980-48
ARL Annual Salary Survey, 1979-80, 1980-133, 1981-16
ARL salaries not rising fast enough says study, 1978-65
ARL statistics and salary survey, 1976-1977, 1978-74
As Much to Learn As to Teach, 1979-13a, 1979-15a
ASIS preliminary report, 1980-70
Assessment center extends service, 1981-67
Association activities, 1981-85
Association of American Library Schools Library Education Statistical Report 1981, 1981-06, 1981-25
Association of College and Research Libraries, 1977-16
Association of Research Libraries, 1978-12
At a Midwinter career workshop, 1978-60
Attacking the 'woman's profession' barrier, 1977-60
Attorney's union calls librarians nonprofessional, 1978-123
Authorship characteristics in Law Library Journal, 1981-84
Authorship in five library periodicals, 1980-40

Bar coding and the librarian supermarket: an analysis of advertised library vacancies, 1978-54

Been down so long it looks like up to me; a course in women librarianship, 1979-119
Before--and since--Angie, 1977-32A
Beginning the second five years, 1978-116
Besoldungs--and Vergutungsgruppen von Depl.--Bibliothekaren mach der Schnellstatistik 1976/77, 1977-52
Best of both worlds: librarian/working mother, 1978-117
Between us . . . age no problem, 1980-104
Beyond awareness: women in libraries organize for change, 1977-32, 1977-32B
Beyond 'librarian' to 'information executive,' 1981-105
Bibliotekaryrket--et feministyrke ("library profession--a feminist profession?"), 1976-121
Blades on Enemies of Books, 1957-07, 1966-11
Board approves task force on women, 1978-36
Books for Sammies, 1981-39
Boycott boomerang, 1978-49
Business or tough tactics, 1979-78

California, 1976-86
California librarians eye equal pay bill, 1981-122
California librarians tell employers: equal pay for equal work!, 1977-33
California's Demand for Librarians: Projecting Future Requirements, 1978-07
Can library affirmative action succeed? the Black Caucus of ALA surveys minority librarians in 22 leading libraries, 1975-95

Canadian correspondent's report, 1976-90, 1979-17
Canadian federal librarians win bias back pay, 1981-65
Canadians win equal pay for work of equal value, 1981-69
Career Aspirations of Female Librarians in English Public Libraries, 1978-26
Career assessments underway, 1980-57
Career Development and Assessment Center, 1979-94
Career Development and Assessment Center for Librarians, 1980-46, 1981-76, 1981-109, 1981-119
Career Development and Assessment Center for Librarians established, 1981-55
Career development assessments offered, 1979-102
Career development for women librarians, 1977-89, 1980-34
The Career Paths of Male and Female Librarians in Canada: Report to the Canada Council, 1977-35
Career patterns and mobility in the library/information field, 1978-128
Career Patterns and the Occupational Image: A Study of the Library/Information Field, 1980-30
Career patterns of librarians, 1981-86
Career patterns of Ontario librarians, 1979-87
Career Patterns of Women Librarians With Doctorates, 1980-130, 1981-11
Career planning workshop set for December 8, 1980-124
A Career Profile of Women Directors of the Largest

Academic Libraries in the United States: An Analysis and Description of Determinants, 1978-10

The Careers of Professional Women: Commitment and Conflict, 1979-30

Carefully prepared campaign, 1977-74

Carolina libraries interface '81, 1981-111

Censorship or selection? looking at the content of library materials, 1981-38B

Changing the traditional role of the librarian: from matron to manager, 1980-118

Changing Times: Changing Libraries, 1978-30

Chapter Councilor's Report: ALA Midwinter Meeting, January 1979, 1979-120

Characteristics of research library directors, 1958 and 1973, how have they changed?, 1976-109

Children's librarians: managing in the midst of myths, 1978-38

Classics of Librarianship, 1957-07, 1957-08, 1957-10, 1957-11

Coalition of library groups mount major effort to keep ALA behind ERA, 1979-47

College administration, 1980-07

The coming male majority, 1979-22

Comparable worth and library employment, 1981-88

The comparable worth study, 1979-19

A comparative analysis of the socioeconomic and professional characteristics of American Library Association Executive Board and Council members, 1876-1917, 1981-127

Concluding reports on the 98th Annual Conference of the American Library Association, Dallas, Texas, June 23-29, 1979, 1979-115

Concluding reports on the Midwinter Meeting of the American Library Association, Chicago, IL, January 22-28, 1978, 1978-67

The condition of the law librarian in 1976, 1976-127

The conference papers--personnel, 1981-121

The conference program: an editor's choice, 1980-93

Continuing reports on the 98th Annual Conference of the American Library Association, Dallas, Texas, June 23-29, 1979, 1979-111

Continuing reports on the 99th Annual Conference of the American Library Association, New York City, 1980-109, 1980-115

Continuing reports on the Annual Conference of the American Library Association, Chicago, IL 1978-101, 1978-102

Continuing reports on the Annual Conference of the American Library Association, Detroit, Michigan, June 17-23, 1977, 1977-68

Continuing reports on the Annual Conference of the American Library Association, San Francisco, California, 1981-108, 1981-116

Continuing reports on the Midwinter Meeting of the American Library Association, Washington D.C., January 30-February 5, 1977, 1977-44

Contributed papers, 1981-101

154   Title Index

A conversation with Pat Schuman, 1981-132
COSWL study of ALA gives membership data, 1981-41
Council, ALA, 1976-85, 1977-10, 1981-114
Council Programs Committee, 1981-125
CPEC report: the last word on librarians' salaries?, 1978-125
Current activities . . . ERA, 1979-31

The data on women workers, past, present, and future, 1978-03
Degree Awards to Women: An Update, 1979-04
Degrees and Certificates Awarded by U.S. Library Education Programs 1973-1976, 1978-02
Degrees and Certificates Awarded by U.S. Library Education Programs 1974-1975, 1977-39
Degrees and Certificates Awarded by U.S. Library Education Programs 1976-1979, 1980-103
The determinants of job satisfaction among beginning librarians, 1979-96
Dewey's "splendid women" and their impact on library education, 1978-16a
Dialogue: Newsletter of the Women's Caucus, 1980-71
Digest of Education Statistics: 1975 Edition, 1976-84
Digest of Education Statistics: 1976 Edition, 1977-09
Digest of Education Statistics: 1977-78, 1978-14
Digest of Education Statistics: 1979, 1979-12
Digest of Education Statistics: 1980, 1980-13
Digest of Education Statistics: 1981, 1981-17
Dignity in work?, 1981-22

Directory of Library and Information Profession Women's Groups, 1981-94
Discipline variation in the status of academic women, 1973-77
Discrimination charged in Oakland recruitment, 1976-106
Disquiet in the stacks, 1980-63
Do not make the coffee, 1981-103
Doctoral Degree Awards to Women, 1978-04
The dominant issue was race, 1978-71
Don't waiver on ERA boycott pleads Florida librarian, 1979-67
The doubly disadvantaged: minority women in the labor force, 1978-01
Downs, Kaser, Metcalf and Shera at Eastern Illinois, 1981-77
The dynamics of securing academic status, 1958-04

Earned Degrees Conferred 1972-73 and 1973-74: Summary Data, 1976-78
Earned Degrees Conferred 1973-74: Institutional Data, 1976-79
Earned Degrees Conferred 1974-75: Summary Data, 1977-02
Earned Degrees Conferred 1975-76, 1978-31
Earned Degrees Conferred 1977-78, 1980-26
Earned Degrees Conferred 1979-80, 1981-03
Earned Degrees Conferred: An Examination of Recent Trends, 1981-04
Editors' Midwinter notebook, 1977-40
Education, library, 1977-13
The Education Professions 1971-72, Part IV: A Manpower

Title Index   155

<u>Survey of the School Library Media Field</u>, 1973-79
<u>Educational Media Yearbook</u>, 1978-25, 1980-29
Employment trends for media graduates 1978-1979, 1980-29
Employment trends for media graduates: 1979-1980, 1981-34
Employment trends for media graduates: business and industry emerging, 1979-109
<u>Enemies of Books</u>, 1957-07, 1966-11
Equal employment opportunity a statement of policy of the American Library Association, 1976-116
Equal employment opportunity issues and staff development, 1980-87
Equal pay breakthrough looms in Canada, 1980-138
<u>Equal Pay for Equal Work</u>, 1981-16a
Equal rights & libraries, 1979-32
<u>Equality in Librarianship: A Guide to Sex Discrimination Laws</u>, 1981-37
Equity and patterns of library governance, 1977-73
ERA endorsement passes, 1980-58
An era ends, a decade begins, 1980-60
ERA vs. Chicago in '80--ALA members to decide in mail ballot, 1979-43
<u>The Evaluation of Continuing Education for Professionals: A Systems View</u>, 1979-06
<u>Evaluation of the First Year of the Librarian Career Development and Assessment Center Project</u>, 1980-25
Expressing disapproval of the film, "The Speaker," 1978-40

Factors related to the representation of women in library management, 1978-22
Faculty, 1980-04, 1981-06
Faculty availability in terms of affirmative action, 1979-68
Faculty salaries of 62 library schools, 1976-77, 1977-36
Faculty salaries of 62 library schools, 1977-78, 1978-57
Fear of success theory and librarians, 1980-36
Federal libraries, 1976-83
Feminism in the public library, 1981-38C
Feminist Task Force endorses Horrocks, 1981-70
Femininity and the librarian--another test, 1980-83
A few new projects . . . the Annual Meeting of the Association of American Library Schools January 28-30, 1977, 1977-46
Fighting dollar discrimination, 1979-69
The first meeting of the Steering Committees for the Career Development and Assessment Center for Librarians was set for October 3, 1979, 1979-103
The flight from Chicago: ALA Midwinter 1979, 1979-58
For men only, 1981-63
Four new takes on 1978 activity from ALA Midwinter Meeting, 1978-61
Fourth annual placement and salary survey, 1976-111
From the desk of Tony Miele, 1978-110
Full-time faculty survey describes educators, 1979-85
Full-time jobs are scarce for grads, 1981-71
Fun place at any cost, 1979-40

The future role of the academic librarian as viewed through a perspective of forty years, 1979-21

General sessions, Women Library Workers, ILL draw conference audiences, 1978-134
Grads find more work in special libraries, fewer public and academic posts in 1978, 1979-76
Graduates find part-time positions, 1980-75
Graduates of media programs in 1972-73, 1974-71
Graduates of media programs 1975-76: an optimistic study, 1977-50
Grant for career development center, 1979-83
Greater Philadelphia Law Library Association 1977 survey, 1978-52
Greater Philadelphia Law Library Association 1979 survey, 1980-59

Handbook on Women Workers, 1969-23, 1975-94
Harriet C. Long: A.L.A. warrier, 1980-126
Head librarians: how many men? how many women?, 1971-42
Head-on collision: ALA in motor city, 1977-92
Hearings Before the U.S. Equal Employment Opportunity Commission on Job Segregation and Wage Discrimination, April 28-30, 1980, 1980-32
Heim and Estabrook to head profile, 1980-38
Helen Wheeler discrimination suit dismissed, 1978-140
Hell no, they won't go, 1978-89
The high cost of hiring, 1977-45

Highlights of the 98th Annual ALA Conference in Dallas, 1979-104
Highlights of the Annual Conference Meetings of the ACRL Board of Directors, 1978-108
The History of a Hoax: Edmund Lester Pearson, John Cotton Dana, and THE OLD LIBRARIAN'S ALMANACK, 1979-29
Honorable terms, 1978-75
How to show the queen, 1979-59

ILA-ERA Task Force, 1981-93
Illinois, 1979-08, 1980-16, 1981-14
Illinois Library Association Legislative Platform for 1981, 1981-80
The impact of changing life styles on library administration, 1980-86
In praise of nurture and other nasty 'female' qualities, 1980-72
In the limelight at last, 1980-120
Ina Coolbrith: forgotten as poet ... remembered as librarian, 1977-55
Index of Opportunity in the Library and Information Sciences, 1971; A Directory of Career Opportunities for Qualified Librarians and Information Science Specialists with Public, Private, University and Special Libraries and Information Centers, 1971-43
Indiana, 1979-27
Indiana forms task force, 1978-82
Information Management in the 1980's, 1977-81
The institute's remuneration survey, 1975-97
Interviews met bibliotheekvrouwen, 1978-130H

Is CLA in danger of being taken over by its members?, 1978-100
Issues, arguments, actions: ALA in Detroit, 1977-75
Issues in field experience as an element in the library school curriculum, 1981-89
It all boiled down to, 1977-47
It's not all fun, 1978-126

Job mobility of men and women librarians and how it affects career advancement, 1979-123
Job picture brighter for graduates of media programs in 1974-75, 1976-110
Job sharing, 1974-70
Job sharing and the woman librarian with family responsibilities, 1977-56
Job sharing at Montgomery County, 1973-80
Job-sharing in a public library, 1981-38F
Job sharing in Canadian libraries, 1978-131
Juffrouw Bits: Vrouwenwerk in de bibliotheek van vroeger, 1978-130C

Kellogg grant of $315,316 has been awarded, 1979-90
The key word was access, 1977-65
De Kommissie Vrouwenwerk in openbare bibliotheken, 1978-130D
Kuinka kirjastonhoitjan ammatista tuli naisvaltainen ja alipalkattu (why are librarians women and underpaid?), 1980-09

Law and legislation, 1979-16, 1980-20
Law library salaries, 1970-35

LC minority employment, May 1977, 1977-66
LC minority employment, May 1978, 1978-97
LC minority employment, November 1976, 1976-129
LC minority employment, November 1977, 1978-44
LC minority employment, November 1979, 1980-55
Legislative--Library Development Committee, 1979-62, 1980-52
Letters to ALA oppose 1980 boycott, 1979-75
The librarian-adventurers, 1980-02
<u>Librarian Authors: A Bibliography</u>, 1981-12
Librarian jobs scarce, pay low--especially for women, 1981-45
Librarians, 1975-92
Librarians among women on the move in Houston, 1978-42
Librarians charge pay discrimination, 1979-125
Librarians who change careers, 1980-127
<u>Librarianship and Information Work: Job Characteristics and Staffing Needs</u>, 1977-26
Librarianship as a profession, 1957-10, 1966-14
<u>Libraries and Information Services As Instruments of Transition to the 21st Century in Africa</u>, 1978-23
Libraries, automation, and women, 1981-38G
Library administration (and women) need MBAs, 1979-93
The library as motherlode, 1981-97
Library clerks seek parity with liquor clerks, 1976-104

Library issues in the seventies, 1979-15a
Library Lit 7--The Best of 1976, 1977-04
Library Manpower Planning: A Bibliographical Review, 1981-27
Library manpower planning in the USA, 1975-101
Library news of 1978, 1978-138
Library news of the year in retrospect, 1980-35
The Library of Congress equal employment opportunity plan of affirmative action for fiscal year 1977, 1976-128
Library of Congress equal employment opportunity plan of affirmative action for fiscal year 1978, 1977-82
Library of Congress leads government agencies in advancement of women, 1978-66
Library of Congress progress in affirmative action: semiannual report for October 1978-March 1979, 1979-91
Library school instruction in discrimination awareness, 1979-33
Library schools present statistical reports for 1975-76, 1977-83
Library service to Illinois women, 1980-50
Library Statistics of Colleges and Universities, 1976 Institutional Data, 1979-01
Library Statistics of Colleges and Universities Fall 1975 Institutional Data, 1977-28
Library technicians/mysteries, 1976-123
Library union organized in Boston, 1918-08
Library wage parity suit overcomes latest obstacle, 1978-50

Library workers lead strikers in comparable pay fight, 1981-102
Library workers to meet, 1978-83
Life Styles of Educated Women, 1966-12
The lion and the lady: the firing of Miss Mary Jones, 1978-84
Literature review: women in management, 1979-56
Literatuurlijst vrouwenwerk in openbare bibliotheken, 1978-130J
Liudi odnoi professii, 1976-124
LJ news report 1975, 1976-92
LJ news report, 1978, 1979-23
LJ news report, 1979, 1980-27
LJ news report, 1980, 1981-31
London correspondent's report, 1979-20
London report, 1976-91
The lowest of the low: library assistant in public libraries, 1981-38D

Making more money as a librarian, 1977-88
Male volunteers a minority, 1980-121
Marking time in Chicago: ALA's 97th Annual Conference, 1978-107
Maryland library clerks seek parity with liquor clerks, 1976-107
Master's Degree Awards to Women, 1978-05, 1979-05
The MBA in library land, 1979-53
Media manpower and the future: survey results, 1977-23
Media manpower: trusting the trends or making them, 1978-25
Medical librarians & ERA: Dade & Atlanta boycott, 1978-66a
Medical librarians vote to boycott Dade and Atlanta, 1978-48

Meet the college librarian, 1950-06
Meetings/1980, 1981-28
Midwinter in Reagan's Washington: an ALA conference report, 1981-61
Midwinter Meeting moves to Washington, D.C., January 5-12, 1978-93
Midwinter notebook, 1979-42
Milestones to the Present, 1978-16a, 1978-16b (commentary), 1978-16c
Minnesota library workers seek pay parity in 13-week strike, 1981-113
Minnie Stewart Rhodes James, 1957-11, 1966-15
MLA: a membership profile, 1970-34
The M.L.S., Affirmative Action, Equal Employment Opportunity and Equivalency: a report to the Board of Directors of the California Society of Librarians, 1975-98
Mobility and flexibility key factor for U of T grads, 1977-43
The month in review, 1977-76
More on ALA's Equal Rights Amendment stand, 1977-86
Ms. vs. Mr. archivist: an update, 1981-56
Multi-cultural graduate library education, 1978-58

National Librarians Association backs ERA boycott, 1980-43
NCES 1974 survey of school library/media centers, 1976-82
NCES survey of college and university libraries, 1978-1979, 1981-30
NCLA receives $7,500 for ERA efforts, 1981-90
Network directory, 1981-60
Network Directory 1980, 1980-23

Never mind who's watching the store, who's stocking the pool? The status of women in academic library management, 1981-40
A new ball game on the hill, 1980-67
The new director . . . is a woman, 1981-49
New Horizons for Academic Libraries, 1979-09, 1979-21
The new librarian: how does she stack up?, 1980-102
New members named to Women's Program Advisory Committee, 1978-132
New members sought for the Women's Program Advisory Committee, 1977-70, 1978-103
New statistics, 1978-47
New Women's Survival Sourcebook, 1975-92
New York, 1979-26
The New York experience: ALA's 99th conference, 1980-105
News from the Women's Program Office, 1980-116
News in review, 1980, 1981-47
News report 1976, 1977-20
News report 1977, 1978-27, 1978-46
News report 1978, 1979-36
News report 1979, 1980-44
Not all in the mind: the virile profession, 1980-111
Notes from a cold, cold capitol, 1979-45
The numbers of number 98: an account of the 1979 Dallas Annual Conference, 1979-99

Oakland job goes to a woman, 1976-108
An odd euphoria, 1980-107
Of bottom lines and top jobs, 1978-41

160   Title Index

Off the air videotaping, intellectual freedom, and ERA, 1978-94
On principal university librarians, 1969-25
Online users survey 1980, 1980-114
Open questions in Dallas: the 98th Annual Conference of ALA, 1979-101
The operating agreement, 1981-106
De opkomst van de man in een vrowenberoep, 1978-130E
Options for the 80s, 1981-23, 1981-40
Order from chaos: highlights of the 99th Annual Conference of the American Library Association, 1980-99
The Origins of American Academic Librarianship, 1979-25, 1981-33

Palmer House threat of $ $ lawsuit faces ALA, 1979-35
Pay equal but not opportunities, 1978-77
Pay equity and the San Jose strike, 1981-124
Pay Equity: Comparable Worth Action Guide, 1981-01
Personality--librarians as communications, 1981-68
Personnel Administration in Public Libraries, 1939-06
Personnel and employment: affirmative action, 1976-81, 1977-06, 1978-15, 1979-13, 1980-08, 1981-10
Personnel and employment: salaries, 1976-94
Personnel in Libraries, 1979-19
Photo, 1981-133
Pilot profile of ALA women, 1980-41
Placements and salaries 1975: a difficult year, 1977-14

Placements and salaries 1976: a year of adjustment, 1977-59, 1978-19
Placements and salaries 1977: the picture brightens, 1978-92, 1979-18
Placements and salaries, 1978: new directions, 1979-98, 1980-22
Placements and salaries 1979: wider horizons, 1980-123, 1981-24
Placements and salaries 1980: holding the line, 1981-120
Plowing through Chicago: SLJ's report on ALA's Midwinter Meeting '78, 1978-62
Plus ca change, 1978-79
Political action by academic women, 1973-75
Politics, politics, politics: a report of the Midwinter Meeting of the American Library Association, Washington, D.C., January 7-12 . . . 1979-65
Population characteristics of academic librarians, 1981-79
Power, women and MLA, 1978-35
Preconference on women and library politics, 1980-47
Preliminary report on salary survey, 1977-51
Principles or curse?, 1979-86
Private law libraries special interest section 1979 salary survey, 1980-128
The pro/con ERA mail vote, 1979-38
Pro ERA supporters asked for $5 donations, 1979-48
The problems faced by women in libraries: why we formed a group, 1981-38A
Professional education: some comparisons, 1979-13a
Professional librarians of Temple University have filed a class

action sex discrimination complaint with the Equal Employment Opportunity Commission against the university administration on the basis of the low salaries paid to those who work in a women's occupation, 1977-77
The Professional Women, 1971-42
Profile: Canadian chief librarians by sex, 1981-96
A profile of ALA personal members, 1980-132
Profile of ALA women for June Conference, 1980-42
Profile of ASIS membership, 1980-106
The profile of the librarians; a state-of-the-art, 1980-117
Prospects for women in the paid labor market, 1978-30
The psychological climate of librarianship values of special librarians, 1981-104
Public Libraries: An Economic View, 1980-12
Public Libraries and Affirmative Action; Exploiting the Resources of ALA, 1977-24
Public Library response to women and their changing roles, 1980-110
Public library statistics: analysis of NCES survey, 1978-20
Public library support and salaries in the seventies, 1977-27
Public school library media center statistics: analysis of NCES survey, 1978-21
Publishing in library science journals: a test of the Olsgaard profile, 1981-78
Pursuing happiness in the golden state: ALA conference report, 1981-114
Putting your best foot forward, 1980-100

The qualifications of university librarians 1948 and 1953, 1950-05
The qualm before the storm, 1978-111
Quotable quotes, 1981-130

The Racial, Ethnic and Sexual Composition of Library Staff in Academic and Public Libraries, 1981-02, 1981-95
Racism/sexism training contract going begging, 1978-119
Rating the library director's job performance, 1981-110
Rating the library director's job performance part II, 1981-117
Re working couples, 1981-42
Recent ALA action and policy on the employment of library workers, 1976-117
Recent library personnel surveys, 1981-29
Recent study surveys employment of women at the library, 1978-55
Reckoning from ERA'ers, 1980-79
Reference librarian as general fact totem, 1980-73
Report from the ALA Councilor, 1978-91
Report of ALA Chapter Councilor, 1980-64
Report of the ALA Councilor, 1976-105
Report of the Commission on the Supply of and Demand for Qualified Librarians, 1977-31
Report on pilot study of woman graduates in the library service field, 1974-69
Report on the ALA Annual Conference Chicago, June 1978, 1978-105
A Report on the Status of Women Employed in the Library of the University of California,

Berkeley, with Recommendations for Affirmative Action, 1971-44
A Report on the Supply and Training of Librarians, 1968-17
Report recommends center, 1978-112
Reports on the 66th Annual Conference of the Special Library Association, 1977-79
Reports on the 99th Annual Conference of the American Library Association, New York City, June 28-July 4, 1980, 1980-108
Reports on the Midwinter Meeting of the American Library Association Chicago, Il., January 20-25, 1980, 1980-66
Reports on the Midwinter Meeting of the American Library Association, Washington, D.C., January 7-12, 1979, 1979-72
Reports of the Midwinter Meeting of the American Library Association, Washington, D.C., January 31-February 5, 1981, 1981-74
Representation, performance and status of women on the faculty at the Urbana-Champaign campus of the University of Illinois, 1973-76
Research, 1976-95, 1978-29
Research Librarianship: Essays in Honor of Robert B. Downs, 1971-45
Research on libraries and librarianship in 1980: an overview, 1981-26
Resolution to hold Midwinter 1979 in Washington, D.C., 1978-127
The role of women in African librarianship--the next 25 years, 1978-23

The Role of Women in Librarianship 1876-1976: The Entry, Advancement and Struggle for Equalization in One Profession, 1979-28
Roll call on E.R.A. Council vote, 1978-113
Roundup in Dallas, 1979-108
Running to--and from Illinois-- Annual Conference report, 1978-95

SAA Women's Caucus Newsletter, 1975-102
The saga of the lady librarian, 1980-61
Salaries to buy less for academic librarians, 1978-51
Salaries up, but variance still high, 1981-81
Salaries: up in library school faculties, 1976-125
Salary differentials of female and male librarians in Canada, 1978-37
Salary discrimination program packet available, 1975-99
Salary study, 1978-96
San Diego librarians charge sex bias in wages, 1977-34
Sarah Rebecca Reed: 1914-1978-- an interview on June 8, 1978-115
Sarah Weddington, 1981-52
Scientists in librarianship and information work: a survey of former information studies students of the Postgraduate School of Librarianship and Information Science, University of Sheffield, 1964-1973, 1975-96
Scholars, gentle ladies, and entrepreneurs: American library leaders, 1876-1976, 1978-16c
Selected characteristics of members of the Music Library Association, 1969-22

Title Index   163

Selected Readings in the History of Librarianship, 1966-11, 1966-13, 1966-14, 1966-15
A selective summary of the ASLA Executive Board Meeting, Columbus Branch Library, Tucson, January 27, 1979, 1979-73
Semiannual report on developments at the Library of Congress, April 1, 1980, through September 30, 1980, 1981-46
Semiannual report on developments at the Library of Congress January 1978, 1978-45
Semiannual report on developments at the Library of Congress June 1977, 1977-58
Semiannual report on developments at the Library of Congress, October 1, 1979, through March 31, 1980, 1980-95
Semiannual report on developments at the Library of Congress, October 1, 1980, through March 31, 1981, 1981-98
Seventh library education faculty survey breaks new ground, 1980-96
Sex and salary: equal pay for comparable work, 1978-80
Sex bias at Temple U.: EEOC okays court fight, 1978-86
Sex bias charged in Milwaukee firing, 1977-85
Sex discrimination complaint: professional librarians at Temple University have filed a class action complaint, 1977-84
Sex Discrimination in the Workplace, 1981, 1981-36
Sex, salaries and library support, 1979, 1979-70, 1980-15, 1980-42a
Sex, salaries and library support ... 1981, 1981-115
Sexism & inflation: new setbacks for large public libraries, 1979-49
Sexism in the library profession, 1979-129
Sexism is the root, 1978-43
Sexist writing, 1980-122
SHARE: A Directory of Feminist Librarians in Illinois, 1981-09
SHARE: A Directory of Feminist Library Workers, 1978-28, 1980-28
SHARE: Sisters Have Resources Everywhere: A Directory of Wisconsin Women Library Workers, 1979-02
Sheehy's passages and ours, 1977-62
The Sheffield Manpower Project: A Survey of Staffing Requirements for Librarianship and Information Work, 1976-93
SLA 1980 salary survey update, 1980-135
SLA Chapter Woman's Caucus, 1980-80
SLA faces the Equal Rights Amendment, 1978-76
SLA in Kansas City: ERA/copyright/continuing education and etc., 1978-90
SLA joins boycott, 1979-44
SLA salary review finds women gaining, 1980-76
SLA salary survey 1976, 1976-118
The SLA salary survey, 1979, 1979-126
SLA's 69th Annual Conference: out of date in Kansas City, 1978-114
SLJ news report, 1978, 1979-07
SLJ news report, 1979, 1980-06
SLJ news report, 1980, 1981-08
SLJ news roundup 1975, 1976-80
SLJ reports ALA Midwinter 1981, 1981-59
SLJ's 1977 news roundup, 1977-91
SLJ's report on the ALA 1980 Midwinter Meeting, 1980-62
Snow job: ALA Midwinter Meeting 1978, 1978-64

164 Title Index

So you want to be a director, 1981-112
Social responsibilities, 1976-88, 1977-12, 1980-18
Social Responsibilities Round Table, 1976-89, 1979-03, 1980-03, 1981-05, 1981-91
Solidarity, sisters, 1981-72
Some issues relating to SLA and ERA, 1978-78
Something for everyone: program-picking at the big orchard 99th Annual ALA Conference, New York City, June 28-July 4, 1980, 1980-92
The Southern California Association of Law Libraries 1979 salary survey, 1979-82
Special issue on women in public libraries, 1978-130
Special librarians report salary gains, 1980-56
Special librarians vote ERA boycott action, 1979-34
Special Librarianship: A New Reader, 1980-11
Special libraries, 1976-96, 1977-29
Special Libraries Association, 1977-01
Special report: WLW meets in Kenosha, 1978-124
SPSS as a Library Research Tool, 1977-18
SRRT backs Eric Moon for ALA president, 1976-112
SRRT Feminist Task Force picks Horrocks for president, 1981-64
SRRT Task Force on Women, 1977-32D
St. Paul library jobs upgraded, 1978-56
St. Paul library jobs upgraded by civil service, 1978-72
State council for social legislation, 1980-89

A statistical study of factors affecting salaries of academic librarians, 1980-19
A statistical survey of 67 library schools, 1978-79, 1979-50
A Statistical Survey of the Full-time Faculty in Library Education, 1979-1980, 1980-05
Statistics of Public Libraries, 1974, 1978-09
Statistics of Public School Library Media Centers, 1974, 1977-21
Statistics of Public School Libraries/Media Centers, Fall 1978, 1981-21
The Status of American College and University Librarians, 1958-04
Status of the university librarian in the academic community, 1971-45
The Status of Women and Ethnic Minorities Employed in the Libraries of the California State University and College System, 1977-15
Status of Women Committee C.L.A., 1977-54
Status of women in librarianship, 1981-62, 1981-82
The status of women in the administration of health sciences libraries: a five-year follow-up study, 1972-1977, 1980-37
The status of women librarians in Washington State, 1980-88
Status transitions of women students, faculty and administrators, 1973-74
Students, 1980-21, 1981-25
A Study of Certain Factors ... Which Influence Students to Become Librarians, 1957-09
A Study of Factors Influencing College Students to Become Librarians, 1958-08

A study of four career patterns and associated life history characteristics among female professional librarians, 1970-33
A Study of Salary Determinants within the SUNY Librarians Association Between 1973 and 1974, 1977-08
Sulking to oblivion, 1979-117
Sullivan keynotes MPLA, 1981-43
Summary and prospects, 1973-78
SUNYLA Salary Survey 1977-- First Report SUNYLA Personnel Policies Committee, 1978-63
Supply and Demand Analysis of Manpower Trends in the Library and Information Field, 1969-24
Survey of Federal Libraries 1972, 1975-93
Survey of librarians' salaries, 1976-120
Survey of salaries in West Virginia academic libraries, 1977-72
A Survey of Salaries of Medical School Librarians in the United States and Canada 1976-77, 1977-53, 1978-32
Survey of State Library Agencies, 1977, 1979-127
Survey of the archival profession--1979, 1980-112
A survey of the perceptions of librarians, attending the TLA/NMLA Convention, concerning the status and need of human resources as media in field of career awareness, 1978-104
A Survey of the Writings of the First Fifteen Women Presidents of the American Library Association, 1978-70

Take her up tenderly, 1980-49
Taking the library pulse for the 1977-79 biennium, 1979-128
Task Force on the Status of Women establishes network, 1980-82
Task Force on Women urges Midwinter boycott, 1979-118
Task force seeks name change, 1978-85
Tax revolt--the library defense, 1978-99
Temple librarians file sex bias complaint, 1977-78
The Texas librarian as a censor: two configural psychological profiles, 1978-137
Three Grandes Dames of Dayton, Ohio As a Well-Spring of Women Special Librarians, 1980-17
Tied up in Washington: SLJ's report on ALA's Midwinter Meeting '79, 1979-60
Top level women's professional group includes library/information science women, 1976-100
Toward a work-force analysis of the school library media professional, 1981-87
Toward professionals managing professionals: a case study of career development for women librarians, 1979-06
Trends in library manpower, 1968-18
Two new members have been selected to serve on the Women's Program Advisory Committee, 1980-77

The University Library in the United States: Its Origins and Development, 1981-18
University Women: A Series of Essays, Volume II, 1980-10
U.S. Congress, Senate, Committee on Labor and Human Resources, 1981-36

166   Title Index

UW Career Development and Assessment Center, 1980-137
UW to develop nat'l model to train women managers, 1979-100

Values of library school students, faculty, and librarians: premises for understanding, 1980-113
Vermont, 1977-03
The vote in Chicago, 1979-39
De vrouw in de britse openbare bibliotheek, 1978-130G
De vrouw in de duitse openbare bibliotheek, 1978-130F
De vrouw in de Zweedse openbare bibliotheek, 1978-130I
Vrouwenemancipatie in Nederland: een historisch overzicht, 1978-130B

Washington, 1980-31, 1981-13
What Else You Can Do With A Library Career, 1980-02, 1980-07
What of the future?, 1981-48
What's happening to jobs in the library field?, 1974-72
Who will speak for the library profession?, 1979-57
Will the real librarian please stand up?, 1981-92
William Frederick Poole and the Modern Library Movement, 1963-09
Williams and Wilkins Counsel heads Ringer replacement search, 1960-68
WLW/Journal: News/Views/Reviews for Women and Libraries, 1980-54
Woman librarianship: cases of private college and university libraries in Japan 1977, 1978-18
Womanpower! Part-time work and job sharing in libraries, 1978-139

A woman's profession in academia: problem and proposal, 1979-09
Women and Biomedical Library Administration, 1978-13
Women and employment in academic librarianship, 1977-17
Women and health sciences librarianship: an overview, 1977-63
Women and libraries: part 1-- women in polytechnic libraries: a preliminary report on their representation at various salary levels, 1981-129
Women and libraries: part 2-- the position of women in public libraries, 1981-131
Women and minorities in academic libraries, 1981-19, 1981-44
Women and Minorities in Administration of Higher Education Institutions: Employment Patterns and Salary Comparisons, 1977-57
Women and Minorities in Administration of Higher Education Institutions: Employment Patterns and Salary Comparisons 1978-79, an Analysis of Progress Toward Affirmative Action Goals 1975-76--1978-79, 1981-15
The women arisen, 1979-88
Women As Interpreters of the Visual Arts, 1820-1979, 1981-32
Women, co-op technology are focus at OLA, 1981-53
Women drop back in: educational innovation in the sixties, 1973-72
Women earn 45 percent of doctoral library degrees, 1978-129
Women gaining in French libraries, 1976-103

Women have always managed, 1980-65
Women in Canadian librarianship, 1977-05
Women in corrections, 1981-58
Women in female-dominated professions, 1978-16
Women in librarianship, 1978-59, 1979-84, 1980-14, 1981-20
<u>Women in Librarianship, 1892-1976</u>, 1976-97
Women in librarianship: jobs and careers, 1979-52
Women in librarianship, status of, 1977-30, 1978-34, 1979-14
Women in libraries: a special issue, 1981-38
Women in libraries: a student view, 1981-123
Women in library management: stop, look & listen, 1979-51
Women in library work, 1980-136
Women in male-dominated professions, 1978-24
Women in public library management: how do they measure up?, 1979-81
Women in special libraries, 1980-11
Women in the U.S. Department of Agriculture, 1976-99
Women librarians, 1957-08, 1966-13
Women librarians as interpreters of the visual arts, 1981-118
Women Library Workers, 1977-32C
Women Library Workers announce strategy to take power from men, 1976-101
Women Library Workers expands monthly newsletter, 1980-80
Women managers to speak, 1978-68
Women name 41 Nestle products, 1981-51

Women, public libraries, and library unions, 1977-38
<u>Women View Librarianship: Nine Perspectives</u>, 1980-24
Women who spoke for themselves, 1978-81
<u>Women, Work, and Wages: Equal Pay for Jobs of Equal Value</u>, 1981-35
Women workers, union power and positive action, 1981-38E
<u>Women Working: Theories and Facts in Perspective</u>, 1978-01, 1978-03, 1978-16, 1978-24
Womenpower and librarianship: the changing career pattern of female qualified librarians since 1945, 1977-31
Women's advancement at LC has come to a standstill, 1978-73
Women's contributions to the library school: 1895-1939, 1980-10
Women's equality day observed, 1977-69
<u>Women's History Sources: A Guide to Archives and Manuscript Collections in the United States</u>, 1979-15
Women's information service award for 1980, 1979-114
Women's Program panel features top managers, 1978-88
Women's Program reported, 1978-120
Women's Program statistical update 1978: grade gap narrows slightly, more women in management, 1979-89
Women's Program statistical update: 1979, 1980-101
Women's Program statistical update: 1980, 1981-73
Women's Program survey of the special recruit/intern program, 1977-61

Women's Program to offer career development workshops, 1978-122

Women's work, 1978-87

<u>Working: Conflict and Change,</u> 1977-25

The working woman: leadership for the '80's, 1981-126

WVLA-ALA Councilor's report, 1979-105

Xerox's Horace Becker on special librarians, 1979-95

You can't eat prestige, 1978-53

<u>Your Assessment Center in Action: Career Development and Assessment Center for Librarians,</u> 1980-33

<u>Your Assessment Center in Action: First Annual Report,</u> 1980-97

Subject Index

Ackerman, Page, 1980-24
academic librarians, 1950-06,
    1958-04, 1971-45, 1973-77,
    1976-109, 1977-07, 1977-08,
    1977-11, 1977-17, 1977-28,
    1977-57, 1977-72, 1978-11,
    1978-12, 1978-17, 1978-22,
    1978-47, 1978-51, 1978-53,
    1978-63, 1978-65, 1978-74,
    1978-79, 1978-109, 1978-133,
    1979-09, 1979-21, 1979-110,
    1979-121, 1980-40, 1980-48,
    1980-133, 1981-02, 1981-07,
    1981-15, 1981-19, 1981-23,
    1981-40, 1981-44, 1981-57,
    1981-79, 1981-81, 1981-121,
    1981-130
academic libraries, 1977-28,
    1977-72, 1977-79, 1978-79,
    1979-01, 1979-121, 1980-19,
  history, 1979-25, 1981-18,
    1981-33
Administrative Detail Program,
    1978-121
administrators, 1979-27, 1979-51,
    1979-129, 1981-101, 1981-103,
    1981-106
  academic libraries, 1932-03,
    1950-05, 1969-25, 1971-42,
    1973-77, 1976-109, 1978-10,
    1978-109, 1979-54, 1981-02,
    1981-07, 1981-19, 1981-23,
    1981-44, 1981-81, 1981-101,
    1981-121, 1981-130
  library schools, 1973-77, 1979-
    50
  public libraries, 1979-49, 1979-
    69, 1979-70, 1979-81, 1981-02,
    1981-115
affirmative action, 1971-44,
    1975-95, 1975-98, 1976-81,
    1976-86, 1976-102, 1976-113,
    1976-114, 1976-115, 1976-116,
    1976-117, 1976-119, 1976-126,
    1976-128, 1976-129, 1977-06,
    1977-24, 1977-35, 1977-48,
    1977-65, 1977-82, 1978-08,
    1978-15, 1978-54, 1978-69,
    1978-135, 1979-13, 1979-15a,
    1979-41, 1979-68, 1979-88,
    1979-91, 1980-08, 1980-94,
    1980-95, 1981-02, 1981-10,
    1981-29, 1981-57, 1981-95,
    1981-125
Africa, 1978-23
Alabama, 1977-80, 1977-86,
    1977-87, 1977-93, 1978-
    118
Alaska Library Association,
    1979-124, 1981-55

170 Subject Index

American Association of Law
  Libraries, 1970-35
American Association of
  School Librarians, see
  American Library Association, American Association
  of School Librarians
American Association of University Professors, 1977-78,
  1978-86
American Library Association,
  1978-98, 1979-15
  1918 Conference, 1918-09
  1919 Conference, 1977-38,
    1979-88
  1977 Annual Conference,
    1977-62, 1977-64, 1977-65,
    1977-68, 1977-75, 1977-76
  1977 Midwinter Meeting, 1977-
    40, 1977-41, 1977-45, 1977-47
  1978 Annual Conference,
    1978-95, 1978-99, 1978-101,
    1978-102, 1978-107
  1978 Midwinter Meeting,
    1978-60, 1978-61, 1978-62,
    1978-64, 1978-67
  1979 Annual Conference,
    1979-99, 1979-101, 1979-
    107, 1979-108, 1979-111,
    1979-115
  1979 Midwinter Meeting,
    1979-42, 1979-58, 1979-60,
    1979-65, 1979-72
  1980 Annual Conference,
    1980-92, 1980-93, 1980-98,
    1980-99, 1980-102, 1980-
    105, 1980-107, 1980-108,
    1980-109, 1980-115, 1981-
    28, 1981-31, 1981-47
  1980 Midwinter Meeting,
    1980-60, 1980-62, 1980-66
  1981 Annual Conference,
    1981-99, 1981-106, 1981-
    108, 1981-114, 1981-116
  1981 Midwinter Meeting,
    1981-54, 1981-59, 1981-61,
    1981-74

American Association of School
  Librarians, 1978-107, 1980-119,
  1980-120, 1980-134
Association of College and Research Libraries, 1977-11,
  1977-16, 1978-108, 1981-101,
  1981-121
Black Caucus, 1975-95
centennial, 1976-87
Committee on Committees,
  1977-41
Committee on the Status of
  Women in Librarianship, 1976-
  85, 1976-105, 1977-10, 1977-
  12, 1977-30, 1977-32, 1977-
  32E, 1977-48, 1977-62, 1977-
  86, 1977-91, 1977-92, 1978-64,
  1978-67, 1978-91, 1978-99,
  1978-107, 1979-42, 1979-88,
  1979-99, 1979-111, 1979-114,
  1980-38, 1980-47, 1980-60,
  1980-105, 1980-115, 1981-01,
  1981-31, 1981-37, 1981-47,
  1981-86, 1981-94, 1981-99,
  1981-108
  Profile of ALA members,
    1979-99, 1980-38, 1980-41,
    1980-42, 1980-99, 1980-131,
    1980-132, 1981-26, 1981-41,
    1981-86
  resolutions, 1978-91, 1978-
    102, 1978-107, 1978-108,
    1978-111, 1978-127, 1979-
    88, 1980-99, 1980-105,
    1981-31, 1981-47
Council, 1976-85, 1977-10,
  1978-91, 1978-107, 1978-
  108, 1978-111, 1978-113,
  1979-37
councilor reports, 1976-105.
  See also Equal Rights Amendment, American Library Association Councilor reports
ERA Task Force. see Equal
  Rights Amendment, American Library Association, ERA
  Task Force

Executive Board, 1977-41, 1978-62, 1979-58, 1981-99, 1981-107, 1981-114, 1981-127
goal awards, 1979-99
history, 1976-87, 1979-88, 1980-127, 1981-107, 1981-127
Intellectual Freedom Committee, 1977-40, 1977-41, 1977-47
Library Administration Division, Women Administrators Discussion Group. see Library Administration and Management Association, Women Administrators Discussion Group
Library Administration and Management Association
  Personnel Administration Section, 1977-65
  Women Administrators Discussion Group, 1977-40, 1977-47, 1977-62, 1977-64, 1977-92, 1978-64, 1978-71, 1978-99, 1979-72, 1979-75 (letters), 1979-88, 1980-109, 1981-54, 1981-99
Office for Library Personnel Resources, 1977-24, 1977-39, 1978-02, 1980-78, 1980-103, 1981-01, 1981-02, 1981-10, 1981-26, 1981-69, 1981-95, 1981-128
  Equal Employment Opportunity Subcommittee, 1976-114, 1976-115, 1977-48 (letters), 1979-41
presidents, 1978-70
Reference and Adult Services Division
  Women's Materials and Women Library Users Discussion Group, 1977-64, 1977-92, 1979-88, 1981-108, 1981-114
Resolution on Prejudice, Stereotyping and Discrimination, 1979-33
Social Responsibilities Round Table, 1976-87, 1976-89, 1976-112, 1979-03, 1979-47, 1980-03
  Feminist Task Force, 1973-75, 1976-89, 1976-97, 1977-32, 1977-32D, 1977-45, 1977-48, 1977-62, 1977-64, 1978-60, 1978-61, 1978-64, 1978-67, 1978-85, 1978-95, 1978-99, 1978-101, 1979-03, 1979-42, 1979-75 (letters), 1979-88, 1979-99, 1979-111, 1979-113, 1979-114, 1979-117, 1979-118, 1980-03, 1980-18, 1980-47, 1980-99, 1980-105, 1980-129, 1981-05, 1981-08, 1981-28, 1981-51, 1981-54, 1981-61, 1981-64, 1981-70, 1981-74, 1981-83, 1981-97, 1981-99, 1981-108
Task Force on Women see Feminist Task Force
American Society for Information Science, 1977-81, 1980-70, 1980-106
Anthony, Susan B., 1978-84
Apostles of Culture: The Public Librarian and American Society, 1876-1920, 1979-11, 1979-11 (reviews)
archivists, 1980-112, 1981-56. see also Society of American Archivists
Arizona State Library Association, 1979-73
Aslib, 1978-128
assertiveness training, 1977-54, 1978-60, 1978-71, 1979-95
Association for Educational Communications and Technology, 1977-19, 1977-42, 1977-49, 1978-75, 1978-94
Association of American Library Schools
  Women's Interest Group, 1977-37, 1977-46, 1977-90, 1978-59, 1979-84

Subject Index

Association of Assistant Librarians, 1981-72 (letter)
Association of College and Research Libraries see American Library Association, Association of College and of Research Libraries
Association of Research Libraries, 1977-07, 1978-11, 1978-22, 1978-51, 1978-53, 1978-65, 1978-74, 1978-133, 1980-48, 1981-23, 1981-57
Australia, 1979-110, 1981-48, 1981-63
Avery, Myrtilla, 1981-32

Ball, Joyce, 1981-49
Barber, Peggy, 1980-63 (letter)
Battin, Patricia, 1980-24
Beck, Susan, 1981-09
Becker, Horace, 1979-95
Bell, Anita, 1981-09
Bem-Sex Role Inventory, 1980-83
Boaz, Martha, 1980-24
Bogle, Sarah C. N., 1976-87
Boisard, Genevieve, 1976-103
Bolton, Charles K., 1918-08
Boone, Nancy W., 1977-85
Boston Area Women in Libraries, 1978-87
Boston Athenaeum, 1918-08, 1963-09, 1977-32A
Boston Public Library, 1918-08
Brown, Bonita, 1977-71
Brown, Rita Mae, 1978-99, 1978-101
Business and Professional Women's Association, 1979-114

California, 1977-55, 1978-07
California Commission on the Status of Women, 1978-125
California Library Association, 1975-98, 1976-86, 1977-60, 1978-40, 1979-36, 1981-122
California Library Employee's Association, 1978-69, 1978-80
California Postsecondary Education Committee, 1978-125
California Society of Librarians, 1975-98
California State Bar Journal, 1978-123
California State University and Colleges System, 1977-15, 1981-31
Canada, 1976-90, 1976-111, 1976-123, 1977-05, 1977-35, 1977-54, 1977-83, 1978-37, 1978-39, 1978-96, 1978-131, 1979-76, 1979-85, 1979-87, 1979-125, 1980-75, 1980-138, 1981-65, 1981-67, 1981-69, 1981-75, 1981-96, 1981-100
Canadian Human Rights Commission, 1979-125, 1980-138, 1981-65, 1981-100
Canadian Library Association, 1978-100
  Status of Women Committee, 1976-90, 1977-05, 1977-54
Carbine, Pat, 1977-79
career development, 1977-89, 1978-13, 1978-41, 1978-68, 1978-69, 1978-121, 1978-122, 1979-53, 1979-91, 1979-95, 1981-40, 1981-98
career development see also Career Development and Assessment Center for Librarians
Career Development and Assessment Center for Librarians, 1978-112, 1979-06, 1979-83, 1979-90, 1979-94, 1979-100, 1979-102, 1979-103, 1980-02, 1980-07, 1980-08, 1980-25, 1980-31, 1980-33, 1980-34, 1980-44, 1980-46, 1980-57, 1980-88, 1980-97, 1980-104, 1980-105, 1980-137, 1981-13, 1981-55, 1981-67, 1981-76,

Subject Index 173

1981-85, 1981-89, 1981-109, 1981-119

Career Paths of Male and Female Librarians in Canada: Report to Canada Council, 1977-05, 1977-54, 1978-37, 1978-39, 1978-96, 1979-17, 1981-96

career patterns, 1970-33, 1975-96, 1977-05, 1977-35, 1977-61, 1978-10, 1978-26, 1978-37, 1978-81, 1978-88, 1978-109, 1978-128, 1979-63, 1979-87, 1979-123, 1980-30, 1980-127, 1980-130, 1981-23, 1981-86, 1981-96, 1981-112

Case Western Reserve University Libraries, 1978-126

Cassell, Kay Ann, 1979-101, 1979-116, 1981-59, 1981-61, 1981-116

censorship, 1978-137, 1981-38, 1981-38B

children's librarians, 1978-38, 1980-102

City College of New York, 1980-61

Clever, Elaine, 1980-91

College and University Personnel Association, 1977-57, 1981-07, 1981-15, 1981-19, 1981-44, 1981-81

Columbia University, School of Library Service, 1974-69

Commission on the Supply of and Demand for Qualified Librarians, 1977-31

comparable worth, 1971-44, 1976-104, 1976-107, 1977-31, 1977-34, 1977-77, 1977-78, 1978-40, 1978-50, 1978-56, 1978-72, 1978-80, 1978-91, 1978-102, 1978-106, 1978-107, 1979-16, 1979-19, 1979-88, 1979-99, 1979-125, 1980-20, 1980-32, 1980-53, 1980-78, 1980-91, 1980-138, 1981-01, 1981-16a, 1981-35, 1981-65,

1981-69, 1981-75, 1981-88, 1981-100, 1981-102, 1981-105, 1981-113, 1981-122, 1981-124

competency-based education, 1981-89

Coolbrith, Ina, 1977-55

Cotner, Suone, 1979-122

Coughlin, Caroline, 1980-72

Crawford, Miriam, 1979-101

Curia, Patt, 1981-124

data processing personnel, 1980-74

Dayton, Ohio, 1980-17

Detlefsen, Ellen Gay, 1977-46, 1977-86, 1978-107, 1979-88, 1979-101

Detroit Feminist Women's City Club, 1977-62

Deutsch, Nancy, 1978-60

Dewey, Melvil, 1978-16a, 1978-16b (commentary), 1978-84, 1979-25, 1981-12, 1981-33

discrimination see salary differentials, employment discrimination

Doctoral Degree Awards to Women, 1978-129

Drexel University, Graduate School of Library and Information Science, 1979-107

Dunlap, Connie, 1978-62, 1980-24

Elizabeth II, Queen of England, 1979-59

Elmendorf, Theresa West, 1976-87

Elrod, Irene, 1981-09

employment discrimination, 1977-17, 1977-26, 1977-32, 1977-35, 1977-60, 1978-77, 1978-84, 1978-86, 1978-115, 1978-140, 1979-15A, 1979-119, 1980-68, 1980-88, 1980-127, 1981-10, 1981-37, 1981-38A, 1981-58, 1981-63

174 Subject Index

equal employment opportunity, 1975-98, 1976-114, 1976-115, 1976-116, 1976-117, 1976-119, 1976-128, 1976-129, 1978-126, 1980-87, 1981-37, 1981-125

Equal Pay for Equal Work: Women in Special Libraries, 1977-01

equal pay for work of equal value see comparable worth

Equal Rights Amendment
  Alaska, 1979-124
  American Library Association, 1978-95, 1978-98, 1978-106, 1978-138, 1979-24, 1979-32, 1979-36, 1979-57, 1979-66, 1979-88, 1979-99, 1979-108, 1980-44, 1980-66, 1980-102, 1980-107, 1980-129, 1981-08, 1981-31, 1981-47
    Association of College and Research Libraries, 1978-108
    brochure, 1980-01
    Chicago meetings, 1978-89, 1979-113, 1979-117, 1979-118, 1980-35, 1980-60
    COALITION, 1979-47, 1979-48, 1979-60
    conference relocation, 1978-93, 1979-39, 1979-40, 1979-65, 1979-78, 1980-84
    Council action, 1976-85, 1977-62, 1977-64, 1977-68, 1977-71, 1977-75, 1977-91, 1977-92, 1978-102, 1978-107, 1978-108, 1978-127, 1979-58, 1979-115
    Councilor reports, 1978-91, 1978-105, 1979-45, 1979-55, 1979-61, 1979-74, 1979-77, 1979-97, 1979-104, 1979-105, 1979-106, 1979-112, 1979-120, 1980-39, 1980-51, 1980-64, 1980-98, 1981-50, 1981-66
    dues checkoff, 1979-107, 1980-62, 1980-79
    ERA Task Force, 1979-101, 1979-116, 1980-58, 1980-60, 1980-62, 1980-67, 1980-69, 1980-79, 1980-99, 1980-108, 1981-54, 1981-59, 1981-61, 1981-62, 1981-99, 1981-106, 1981-114, 1981-116
    Executive Director, 1977-76, 1977-91, 1981-99, 1981-114
    grants awarded, 1980-69, 1981-59, 1981-90
    Headquarters relocation, 1978-107, 1978-113, 1979-42, 1980-35
    mail vote, 1979-37, 1979-38, 1979-43, 1979-59, 1979-64, 1979-79, 1979-80
    Palmer House, 1979-35, 1979-46, 1979-58
  Arizona, 1979-73
  Association for Educational Communications and Technology, 1978-94
  Association of American Library Schools, 1979-84
  Drexel University, Graduate School of Library and Information Science, 1979-107, 1979-111
  Florida, 1979-67
  Illinois Library Association, 1979-08, 1979-62, 1980-16, 1980-52, 1981-14, 1981-80, 1981-91, 1981-93
  Indiana Library Association, 1979-31
  Letters, 1977-87, 1978-49, 1978-78, 1979-59, 1979-64, 1979-69, 1979-75, 1979-78, 1979-86, 1979-117, 1980-125
  Louisiana, 1977-71, 1977-86, 1977-93, 1978-136
  Medical Library Association, 1978-48, 1978-66a
  Miele, Tony, 1977-80, 1977-86, 1977-87, 1977-91, 1978-110, 1978-118

Subject Index 175

Missouri Women in Libraries, 1980-69
Mother's Day march, 1980-90
National Librarians Association, 1980-43
National Organization for Women signature campaign, 1981-59
North Carolina Library Association, 1980-58, 1980-89, 1981-90
Society of American Archivists, 1980-125
Special Libraries Association, 1978-76, 1978-78, 1978-90, 1978-98, 1978-114, 1979-44, 1980-35
states, not ratifying, 1977-91, 1978-48
ERAmerica, 1979-101, 1979-107, 1979-122, 1980-79, 1980-99
Estabrook, Leigh, 1980-38, 1980-41

faculty status, 1958-04
Fairchild, Mary Salome Cutler, 1976-87
Fairfax County Public Library, 1976-126
fear of success theory, 1980-36
Federal libraries, 1975-93, 1976-83
Feinberg, Renee, 1979-46
Feminist Library Workers Group, 1980-136, 1981-112 (letter)
Finland, 1980-09
Florida, 1978-48
"Focus on Change: Sexism Awareness," 1978-107
Folsom, C., 1977-32A
France, 1976-103
Fulton, Marsha K., 1981-09
Futas, Elizabeth, 1980-67, 1981-54

Galloway, Sue, 1980-91
Garrison, Dee, 1978-16b, 1981-32

Gasaway, Laura, 1975-99
George Amos Memorial Library, 1977-74
Gerhardt, Lillian, 1978-75
Gilbert, Luan, 1978-60
Giraud, Lisa, 1977-33
Goggin, Margaret Knox, 1980-24
Great Britain, 1968-17, 1975-96, 1975-97, 1975-100, 1976-91, 1976-93, 1977-26, 1977-31, 1978-26, 1978-77, 1978-128, 1978-130G, 1979-20, 1979-63, 1980-136, 1981-27, 1981-38A-F, 1981-72, 1981-123 (letter), 1981-129, 1981-131
Greater Philadelphia Law Library Association, 1978-52, 1980-59
Guy, Jeniece, 1980-63 (letter)

Hamilton, Ruth, 1979-06, 1979-94
Harnden, A. B., 1963-09, 1977-32A
Hasse, Adelaide, 1978-81
Higher Education General Information Survey (HEGIS) see also Library General Information Survey, 1977-28, 1978-09, 1978-20, 1978-47, 1979-01, 1981-02
Heim, Kathleen M., 1980-38, 1980-41
Henning, Margaret M., 1978-38
Hewins, Caroline M., 1976-87
HEGIS see Higher Education General Information Survey
Hiatt, Peter, 1979-100, 1980-97
higher education administration, 1980-07
Hines, Patricia, 1978-88
Hodgins, Ellis, 1978-43
Horowitz, Sharon S., 1980-109
Horrocks, Norman, 1981-64, 1981-70
Hoy, Chris, 1977-76

Ifould, W. H., 1981-63
Ihrig, Alice, 1979-65, 1979-101

Illinois Library Association,
   1979-08, 1979-62, 1980-16,
   1980-51, 1980-52, 1981-05,
   1981-80, 1981-91, 1981-93
Illinois Women Library Workers,
   1980-50, 1981-09, 1981-14
Indiana, 1978-79
Indiana Library Association,
   1979-27, 1979-36, 1981-60
  Division on Women in Indiana
   Libraries, 1978-36, 1978-79,
   1978-82, 1979-27, 1979-31,
   1980-23, 1980-82, 1980-100,
   1981-60
  Task Force on the Status of
   Women, see Division on
   Women in Indiana Libraries
Institute of Information Scientists, 1975-97, 1975-100
International Federation of
   Library Associations, 1975-101

James, Minnie Stewart Rhodes,
   1957-11, 1966-15
Japan, 1978-18
Jardim, Anne, 1978-38
job sharing, 1973-80, 1974-70,
   1977-56, 1978-131, 1980-86,
   1981-38, 1981-38F
Jones, Clara Stanton, 1976-87
Jones, Mary, 1978-84
Jones, Virginia Lacy, 1980-24
Josephine, Helen, 1980-91,
   1981-01

Kellogg Foundation see W. L.
   Kellogg Foundation
Kenosha, Wisconsin, 1978-71
Kibble, N. B., 1981-63

Laura X, 1979-88
law librarians, 1970-35, 1976-127, 1978-52, 1979-82,
   1980-59, 1980-128, 1981-84
LeBarron, Suzanne, 1979-118
Leita, Carole, 1976-106, 1977-32C

LIBGIS see Library General Information Survey
librarians see also media professionals, music librarians,
   academic librarians, etc.
 archival sources, 1979-15
 attitudes toward, 1971-45
 characteristics, 1969-22, 1970-34, 1970-35, 1976-109, 1976-127, 1978-22, 1978-26, 1978-137, 1979-29, 1980-19, 1980-72, 1980-83, 1980-117, 1981-68, 1981-104, 1981-127
 directories, 1978-28, 1978-64, 1978-67, 1979-02, 1980-23, 1980-28, 1981-09, 1981-94
 earned degrees, 1969-24, 1973-77, 1974-71, 1976-78, 1976-79, 1976-95, 1976-111, 1977-02, 1977-09, 1977-22, 1977-39, 1978-02, 1978-04, 1978-05, 1978-14, 1978-31, 1978-116, 1978-129, 1979-04, 1979-05, 1979-12, 1979-109, 1980-13, 1980-26, 1980-29, 1980-103, 1981-03, 1981-04, 1981-17, 1981-36
 history, 1978-16a, 1978-16b, 1979-11, 1979-25, 1979-28, 1981-33
 image, 1978-56, 1978-58, 1978-123, 1980-30, 1980-49, 1980-73, 1980-111, 1980-117, 1980-118, 1981-22, 1981-48, 1981-92
 job satisfaction, 1979-96
 minorities, 1975-95, 1976-128, 1976-129, 1977-15, 1977-39, 1977-57, 1977-66, 1978-02, 1978-44, 1978-58, 1978-97, 1978-121, 1978-135, 1979-135, 1979-68, 1979-89, 1979-129, 1980-55, 1980-94, 1981-02, 1981-19, 1981-44
 placement, 1977-14, 1977-43, 1977-59, 1977-83, 1978-19, 1978-92, 1978-116, 1979-76,

Subject Index   177

1979-92, 1979-98, 1979-109,
  1980-21, 1980-75, 1980-123,
  1981-25, 1981-71, 1981-120
political action, 1973-75,
  1977-32A-E, 1977-61, 1981-93
publication activity, 1978-70,
  1980-40, 1980-132, 1981-78,
  1981-84, 1981-86
qualifications, 1969-25, 1979-
  22, 1979-53, 1979-93, 1980-
  63, 1980-130
salaries, 1918-08, 1958-04,
  1968-18, 1969-22, 1969-23,
  1970-34, 1970-35, 1971-44,
  1974-71, 1975-97, 1975-99,
  1975-100, 1976-93, 1976-94,
  1976-118, 1976-127, 1977-01,
  1977-06, 1977-07, 1977-08,
  1977-11, 1977-14, 1977-16,
  1977-17, 1977-27, 1977-29,
  1977-34, 1977-36, 1977-49,
  1977-51, 1977-52, 1977-53,
  1977-57, 1977-59, 1977-72,
  1977-83, 1978-11, 1978-12,
  1978-17, 1978-19, 1978-22,
  1978-57, 1978-63, 1978-65,
  1978-66, 1978-74, 1978-79,
  1978-92, 1978-125, 1978-133,
  1979-01, 1979-50, 1979-70,
  1979-82, 1979-87, 1979-92,
  1979-98, 1979-121, 1979-126,
  1980-04, 1980-19, 1980-42a,
  1980-48, 1980-56, 1980-59,
  1980-76, 1980-101, 1980-102,
  1980-114, 1980-123, 1980-128,
  1980-133, 1980-135, 1980-138,
  1981-02, 1981-07, 1981-45,
  1981-73, 1981-75, 1981-77,
  1981-81, 1981-87, 1981-96,
  1981-115, 1981-120, 1981-122,
  1981-124, 1981-128, 1981-129
supply and demand, 1968-17,
  1968-18, 1969-24, 1974-72,
  1975-101, 1976-93, 1977-31,
  1978-07, 1980-131, 1981-27
Librarians for Peace Brigade,
  1979-88

librarianship
  appeal to women, 1957-09, 1958-
    05, 1973-72, 1973-79, 1980-85
  late entrance, 1974-69
  re-entry, 1977-31
librarianship as a profession,
  1957-10, 1958-05, 1966-14
library administration, 1979-51,
  1979-53, 1979-56, 1979-72,
  1980-86
Library Association, 1975-100,
  1981-123
Library Bill of Rights, 1977-68
library employee unions, 1918-08,
  1977-38, 1978-106, 1981-38E,
  1981-113
Library General Information
  Survey (LIBGIS) see also
  Higher Education General
  Information Survey, 1977-28,
  1978-09, 1978-20, 1978-47,
  1979-01, 1981-02
Library Manpower--A Study of
  Demand and Supply, 1974-72,
  1976-94, 1978-30 (letter)
Library of Congress, 1976-128,
  1976-129, 1977-58, 1977-61,
  1977-66, 1977-67, 1977-68,
  1977-69, 1977-70, 1977-82,
  1978-44, 1978-45, 1978-46,
  1978-55, 1978-66, 1978-68,
  1978-73, 1978-88, 1978-97,
  1978-103, 1978-120, 1978-121,
  1978-122, 1978-132, 1979-89,
  1979-91, 1980-55, 1980-68,
  1980-77, 1980-94, 1980-95,
  1980-101, 1980-116, 1980-124,
  1981-46, 1981-52, 1981-73,
  1981-98, 1981-133
Women's Program Advisory
  Committee, 1977-58, 1977-61,
  1977-67, 1977-68, 1977-69,
  1977-70, 1978-45, 1978-73,
  1978-88, 1978-103, 1978-120,
  1978-122, 1978-132, 1979-89,
  1980-77, 1980-94, 1980-95,
  1980-101, 1980-116, 1980-124,

Library of Congress (cont.)
Women's Program Advisory Committee (cont.), 1981-46, 1981-51, 1981-73, 1981-98, 1981-133
Women's Program Office see Women's Program Advisory Committee
library schools
 curriculum, 1979-119
 faculty, 1975-125, 1977-13, 1977-36, 1978-57, 1979-50, 1979-68, 1979-85, 1980-04, 1980-40, 1980-96, 1981-06, 1981-104
 students, 1979-68, 1979-119, 1980-21, 1980-36, 1980-113, 1981-25, 1981-104, 1981-123 (letter)
Lipkowski, Kris, 1981-09
Lloyd, Kate Rand, 1981-111
Loch-Wouters, Marge, 1979-02
Long, Harriet C., 1980-126
Los Angeles Public Library, 1978-84
Louisiana, 1977-71, 1977-86, 1977-93, 1979-121
Louisiana Library Association, 1977-71, 1978-136
Louisiana State University, 1978-140
Ludington, Flora Belle, 1978-81

Malone, Maud, 1977-38, 1979-88
Mann, Margaret, 1978-81
The Managerial Woman, 1978-38
marginal professions see occupational segregation
married women, 1939-06, 1977-31, 1978-77, 1981-42, 1981-123 (letter)
Marshall, Joan, 1979-88, 1979-101
Martin, Allie Beth, 1976-87
Martinez, Anna, 1980-91
Mason, Ellsworth, 1980-122
Massachusetts Library Association, 1978-106

media professionals, 1974-71, 1976-82, 1976-110, 1977-23, 1977-42, 1977-49, 1977-50, 1978-21, 1978-25, 1978-75, 1978-116, 1979-109, 1980-13, 1980-29, 1981-17, 1981-21, 1981-34, 1981-87
 earned degrees, 1974-71, 1976-110, 1977-23, 1977-50, 1978-25, 1978-116, 1979-109, 1980-29, 1981-34
medical librarians, 1977-51, 1977-53, 1977-63, 1978-13, 1978-32, 1978-48, 1978-66a, 1980-37
Medical Library Association, 1977-63 (letter), 1978-35, 1978-48, 1978-66a, 1979-36
 Survey and Statistics Committee, 1977-53
mentors, 1981-53, 1981-60, 1981-99
Metcalf, Keyes, 1981-77
Midwest Federation of Library Associations, 1980-50
Miele, Tony, 1977-80, 1977-86, 1977-87, 1977-91, 1978-110, 1978-118
Milwaukee Public Library, 1977-85
Minnesota, 1981-113
Minnesota Multiphasic Personality Inventory, 1978-137
Missouri Library Association, 1981-50
Missouri Women in Libraries, 1980-69
mobility, 1950-05, 1969-24, 1977-15, 1978-128, 1979-123, 1981-86
modesty, 1977-32A
Moon, Eric, 1976-112
mothers, 1939-06, 1970-33, 1978-117, 1979-63 (letters), 1981-123 (letters)
Ms., 1977-79
Mucci, Judy, 1979-67
Mudge, Isadore Gilbert, 1978-81

Subject Index 179

music librarians, 1969-22, 1970-34
Music Library Association, 1969-22, 1970-34
Myers, Margaret, 1976-97, 1980-32, 1980-63 (letter), 1980-91

National Center for Education Statistics, 1975-93, 1976-78, 1976-79, 1976-82, 1976-84, 1977-02, 1977-09, 1977-21, 1977-22, 1977-28, 1978-04, 1978-05, 1978-09, 1978-14, 1978-20, 1978-21, 1978-31, 1978-129, 1979-01, 1979-04, 1979-05, 1979-12, 1980-13, 1980-26, 1980-131, 1981-02, 1981-03, 1981-04, 1981-17, 1981-21, 1981-30, 1981-116
National Libraries Association, 1980-43
National Library of Canada, 1979-125, 1981-69
National Organization for Women, 1979-65, 1979-66, 1979-69, 1979-72, 1981-59
National Plan of Action, 1978-91, 1979-88
National Research Council (Canada), 1981-100
National Women's Conference, 1978-42, 1978-64, 1979-88
National Women's Liberation Front for Librarians, 1979-88
Nemeyer, Carol A., 1978-88
Nestle boycott, 1981-51
Netherlands, 1978-130, 1978-130A, 1978-130B, 1978-130C
New South Wales, 1979-110, 1981-62 (letter)
New York Library Association Round Table on Concerns of Women, 1979-26, 1979-46
New York Public Library Employees Union, 1977-38
New Zealand Library Association, 1976-120

North Carolina Library Association, 1980-58, 1980-89, 1981-90
Round Table on the Status of Women in Librarianship, 1981-62, 1981-82, 1981-111
Norton, Meb, 1977-71
Norway, 1976-121

Oakland Public Library, 1976-106, 1976-108, 1977-12
Occupational Outlook Handbook, 1981-92
occupational segregation, 1973-74, 1977-25, 1978-02, 1978-04, 1978-16, 1978-24, 1978-30, 1978-33, 1978-130E, 1979-13a, 1979-22, 1979-110, 1980-09, 1980-20, 1980-85, 1980-127, 1980-134, 1981-122, 1981-124, 1981-126
Occupations Accessible to Women, 1981-63
O'Donnell, Peggy, 1980-63
Ohio Library Association, Women on the Rise in Library Management Task Force, 1981-28, 1981-53
old girls' network, 1977-40, 1977-47, 1981-132
"Orphans Without a Home," 1978-43

part-time work, 1978-139, 1979-110, 1980-86
Passages, 1977-62
pay equity see comparable worth
Phenix, Katharine, 1981-09
Phinazee, Annette L., 1980-24
Pierce, Sydney, 1977-46
Plummer, Mary Wright, 1976-87, 1979-25, 1981-33
Poole, William Frederick, 1963-09, 1977-32A, 1981-12
Princeton-Trenton Special Libraries Association, 1978-117
prison librarians, 1981-58

180   Subject Index

Pritchard, Sarah, 1979-111, 1980-109, 1981-74, 1981-108
professionalism, 1977-25, 1978-43
Public Archives (Canada), 1981-69
public librarians, 1978-79, 1978-130A-J, 1979-49, 1979-81, 1980-42a, 1981-02, 1981-63, 1981-115, 1981-131
public libraries, 1977-24, 1977-27, 1978-09, 1978-20, 1978-79, 1978-130A-J, 1979-49, 1979-63, 1979-70, 1979-81, 1980-12, 1980-42a, 1981-02, 1981-63, 1981-115, 1981-118, 1981-131
  history, 1979-11, 1980-110

Racial/Ethnic/Sexual Composition of Library Staffs in Academic and Public Libraries, 1980, 1981-10, 1981-26, 1981-95, 1981-128
racism, 1977-10, 1977-40, 1977-41, 1977-47, 1977-65, 1978-67, 1978-119, 1979-121
Reed, Sarah Rebecca, 1978-115, 1980-24
REFORMA, 1979-47
Reynolds, Judy, 1980-53
Ringer, Barbara, 1978-88, 1980-68
Rockefeller, Sharon Percy, 1980-99
The Role of Women in Librarianship 1876-1976: The Entry, Advancement and Struggle for Equalization in One Profession, 1979-28 (reviews), 1980-61
Royal, Norma, 1980-58
Rutherford, James, 1980-98

Sacramento State University Library, 1981-49
Sahli, Nancy, 1980-125

salary differentials, 1958-04, 1968-18, 1975-97, 1975-99, 1975-100, 1975-101, 1976-127, 1977-11, 1977-16, 1977-26, 1977-27, 1977-29, 1977-49, 1977-51, 1977-53, 1977-57, 1977-59, 1977-72, 1977-74, 1978-11, 1978-19, 1978-22, 1978-32, 1978-37, 1978-47, 1978-52, 1978-57, 1978-66, 1978-79, 1978-92, 1978-96, 1978-100, 1978-133, 1979-01, 1979-27, 1979-49, 1979-50, 1979-52, 1979-54, 1979-70, 1979-87, 1979-88, 1979-89, 1979-92, 1979-98, 1979-121, 1979-126, 1980-04, 1980-12, 1980-19, 1980-42a, 1980-48, 1980-56, 1980-59, 1980-74, 1980-76, 1980-101, 1980-102, 1980-106, 1980-112, 1980-114, 1980-123, 1980-128, 1980-131, 1980-133, 1980-135, 1981-02, 1981-07, 1981-15, 1981-45, 1981-54, 1981-63, 1981-73, 1981-75, 1981-87, 1981-96, 1981-120, 1981-124, 1981-129
San Diego, 1977-33, 1978-40, 1978-46, 1978-50, 1978-72, 1979-36, 1980-20
San Francisco Public Library, 1974-70, 1977-12, 1978-46
San Jose, 1980-53, 1981-102, 1981-124
Schimmel, Nancy, 1979-88
school librarians (includes school library media librarians), 1973-79, 1977-21, 1978-75, 1980-72, 1981-87
school library-media centers, 1976-82, 1977-21
school library media librarians see school librarians
Schubert, Irene, 1981-108
Schuman, Pat, 1979-88, 1981-132
Schwartz, Roderick, 1979-100
Seattle, Washington, 1979-36

Sellen, Betty-Carol, 1979-101
service to women, 1979-114, 1980-50, 1980-107, 1980-110, 1981-38C, 1981-108
"Sex and Salary: Achieving Parity among Professions," 1978-80
sexism, 1977-10, 1977-40, 1977-41, 1977-47, 1977-65, 1977-68, 1978-67, 1978-95, 1978-119, 1979-88, 1979-108, 1979-121, 1980-122, 1981-99, 1981-132
sexual harassment, 1981-37, 1981-98
Shank, Russell, 1979-75
SHARE Directory, 1978-28, 1978-64, 1978-67, 1979-02, 1980-28, 1981-09
Sharp, Katharine Lucinda, 1978-81, 1979-25, 1981-33
Sheehy, Gail, 1977-62
Sheffield Manpower Project, 1977-26
Shera, Jesse, 1977-56
Shulman, Alix Kates, 1979-99
Simmons College, 1979-21
Slocum, Grace, 1978-62
Society of American Archivists, 1980-112, 1980-125, 1981-125
 Status of Women Committee, 1975-101, 1980-112 (letter), 1981-125
 Women's Caucus, 1975-102, 1981-125
South Carolina Library Association, 1981-111
Southern California Association of Law Librarians, 1979-82
Soviet Union, 1976-124
The Speaker, 1978-40
special librarians, 1975-99, 1976-118, 1977-29, 1978-79, 1978-117, 1979-126, 1980-11, 1980-17, 1980-56, 1980-76, 1980-135, 1981-16a, 1981-78, 1981-104
special libraries, 1978-79, 1980-11, 1981-16a
Special Libraries Association, 1976-118, 1977-01, 1977-29, 1977-79, 1978-76, 1978-78, 1978-90, 1978-98, 1978-114, 1979-34, 1979-36, 1979-44, 1979-82, 1979-126, 1980-16a, 1980-56, 1980-76, 1980-135
 New York Chapter, Women's Caucus, 1980-71, 1980-80, 1981-105
 Special Committee on the Pilot Education Project (Salary Discrimination), 1975-99, 1976-96
SPSS, 1977-18
St. Paul, Minn., 1978-56, 1978-72, 1979-16, 1979-36
Stanford University, 1977-33
state library agencies, 1979-127
Steinem, Gloria, 1980-119, 1980-120, 1980-134
Sterns, Lutie, 1979-88
Stevens, Ernestine, 1976-99
Stevenson, Grace, 1976-87
Stevenson, Sara Yorke, 1981-32
Stroup, Elizabeth, 1978-88
Sullivan, Peggy, 1979-65, 1980-90
SUNY Librarians Association, 1977-08, 1978-63
support staff, 1976-123, 1977-05, 1978-69, 1978-72, 1981-38D
surveys
 academic libraries, 1932-03, 1950-06, 1971-42, 1977-07, 1977-08, 1977-28, 1977-57, 1977-72, 1978-11, 1978-22, 1978-23, 1978-47, 1978-79, 1978-109, 1978-133, 1979-01, 1979-110, 1979-121, 1980-19, 1980-48, 1980-133, 1981-15, 1981-79

surveys (cont.)
  academic libraries (cont.)
    American Association of Law Libraries, 1970-35, 1979-82
    American Society for Information Science, 1980-106
    Association for Educational Communications and Technology, 1977-19
    Association of Research Libraries, 1977-07, 1978-11, 1978-22, 1978-133, 1979-10, 1980-48, 1980-133
    Canada, 1976-111, 1977-35, 1977-83, 1978-37, 1979-76, 1979-85, 1979-87, 1980-75, 1981-71, 1981-96
    career patterns, 1975-96, 1977-05, 1977-35, 1977-61, 1980-30, 1981-112
    data processing personnel, 1980-74
    earned degrees, 1974-71, 1976-78, 1976-79, 1976-95, 1976-110, 1976-111, 1977-02, 1977-09, 1977-22, 1977-23, 1977-39, 1977-50, 1978-02, 1978-04, 1978-05, 1978-14, 1978-25, 1978-31, 1978-116, 1979-04, 1979-05, 1979-112, 1979-109, 1980-13, 1980-26, 1980-29, 1980-103, 1981-03, 1981-04, 1981-17, 1981-34
    Federal libraries, 1975-93, 1976-83
    Great Britain, 1968-17, 1975-96, 1975-97, 1976-93, 1977-26, 1977-31, 1978-26, 1979-63, 1981-131
    Illinois, 1979-81
    Indiana, 1978-79
    Institute of Information Scientists, 1975-97
    law librarians, 1970-35, 1976-127, 1978-52, 1979-82, 1980-128
    Library of Congress, 1977-61, 1977-66, 1978-44, 1978-55, 1978-66, 1978-73, 1978-97, 1979-89, 1979-91, 1980-55, 1980-101
    library school faculty, 1977-36, 1978-57, 1979-50, 1980-04, 1981-06
    media professionals, 1974-71, 1976-82, 1976-110, 1977-23, 1977-42, 1977-49, 1977-50, 1978-21, 1978-25, 1978-116, 1979-109, 1980-13, 1980-29, 1981-17, 1981-21, 1981-34
    medical librarians, 1977-51, 1977-53, 1978-13, 1978-32, 1980-37
    minority librarians, 1975-95, 1977-66, 1978-02, 1978-44, 1978-97, 1979-89, 1980-55, 1981-02
    Music Library Association, 1969-22, 1970-34
    New Zealand Library Association, 1976-120
    placement, 1977-14, 1977-59, 1977-83, 1978-19, 1978-92, 1978-116, 1979-76, 1979-98, 1979-109, 1980-21, 1980-75, 1980-123, 1981-25, 1981-71, 1981-120
    public libraries, 1977-27, 1978-09, 1978-20, 1978-79, 1979-63, 1979-70, 1979-81, 1980-42a, 1981-02, 1981-115, 1981-131
    salaries, 1970-35, 1975-97, 1976-93, 1976-127, 1977-07, 1977-08, 1977-14, 1977-27, 1977-36, 1977-49, 1977-51, 1977-53, 1977-57, 1977-59, 1977-72, 1977-83, 1978-11, 1978-19, 1978-22, 1978-32, 1978-47, 1978-52, 1978-57, 1978-63, 1978-66, 1978-79, 1978-92, 1978-133, 1979-01, 1979-50, 1979-70, 1979-82, 1979-87, 1979-98, 1979-121, 1979-126, 1980-04, 1980-19,

Subject Index   183

1980-42a, 1980-48, 1980-59,
1980-114, 1980-123, 1980-133,
1981-02, 1981-115, 1981-120,
1981-129
Society of American Archivists,
1980-112
Southern California Association
of Law Librarians, 1979-82
Special librarians, 1978-79,
1979-126, 1980-135
Special Libraries Association,
1979-126, 1980-135
state library agencies, 1979-127
SUNY Library Association,
1977-08, 1978-63
Washington (State), 1980-88
Sweden, 1978-130I

"Teeth for the Professionally
Nameless," 1978-75
Temple University, 1977-77,
1977-78, 1977-84, 1978-17,
1978-46, 1978-86, 1980-20
Tepp, Linda, 1980-109
Texas Library Association,
1978-105
Training Appraisal and Promotion Program, 1980-94,
1980-95
Tucson Public Library, 1978-135

United States
  Department of Agriculture,
  1976-99
  Department of Labor, 1981-35
  Equal Employment Opportunity
  Commission, 1977-72, 1977-78, 1977-85, 1978-86, 1979-13,
  1979-36, 1980-20, 1980-78,
  1980-91, 1981-10, 1981-16a,
  1981-35, 1981-37
University of California, 1971-44, 1978-80
University of Georgia, 1977-45
University of Illinois, 1973-76
University of Michigan, 1973-72

University of Sheffield, 1975-96
University of Toronto, 1977-43,
1979-76
University of Washington School
of Librarianship, 1977-89,
1978-46, 1978-112
University of Wisconsin Library
School, 1980-10

Vermont Library Association,
1977-03
Virginia Library Association,
1978-134

W. L. Kellogg Foundation, 1979-83, 1979-90, 1979-94, 1979-100
Wallace, George, 1977-87
Walton, Genevieve, 1978-81
Warncke, Ruth, 1976-87
Washington (State), 1980-88
Weddington, Sarah, 1981-52
Wedgeworth, Robert, 1977-76,
1977-87, 1977-91, 1979-42,
1979-75, 1981-99, 1981-114
Weibel, Kathleen, 1976-97, 1977-46, 1979-88, 1980-50
West, Celeste, 1979-88
West Germany, 1976-122, 1978-130
West Virginia, 1977-72
Wheeler, Helen Rippier, 1978-140
White, Lelia, 1976-108
Whitlatch, Jo Bell, 1980-53
Winchell, Constance, 1976-87
Wilson, Betty, 1979-88
Wisconsin Women Library
Workers, 1979-02, 1980-50
WLW Journal: News/Views/
Reviews for Women and
Libraries, 1980-81
"Women in a Woman's Profession:
Strategies II," 1979-117 (letter),
1980-47, 1980-92, 1980-93,
1980-99, 1980-109, 1980-115
Women in Libraries, 1980-18
Women in Libraries, 1981-38A,
1981-72

Women's Equality Day, 1977-67, 1977-69
Women Library Workers, 1976-89, 1976-101, 1976-123, 1977-12, 1977-32, 1977-32C, 1977-48, 1977-62, 1977-92, 1978-28, 1978-34, 1978-64, 1978-67, 1978-83, 1978-124, 1979-36, 1979-47, 1979-88, 1979-114, 1980-54, 1980-81, 1981-35, 1981-97
Women's Information Service Award, 1979-114

Wood, Charlotte L., 1979-06, 1979-94
World War I, 1918-09, 1976-98, 1980-126, 1981-39
World War II, 1977-63 (letter)
Wyoming Library Association, 1977-74

X, Laura see Laura X

Yates, Elia Gaines, 1978-62

Index to Preliminary Pages

Adam, Margie, xxiv
affirmative action, vii, xii, xiv
Allen, Walter, ix
American Library Association
  1975 Annual Conference, xxiv
  1976 Annual Conference, xii, xvi
  1977 Annual Conference, xv, xvii, xxiv
  1977 Midwinter Meeting, xii, xiii, xv, xxiv
  1978 Annual Conference, xviii
  1979 Annual Conference, xix
  1979 Midwinter Meeting, xviii, xix
  1980 Annual Conference, xvii, xx
  1981 Midwinter Meeting, xx
  1982 Annual Conference, xii
  Association of School Librarians, xvii
  Black Caucus, xviii, xix
  Committee on Accreditation, xii
  Committee on the Status of Women in Librarianship, vii, ix, xiii-xv, xviii, xxi, xxx
    Pay Equity Project, xiv
    Profile of ALA members, xiv
    Salary range resolution, xiv
  Council, xiv, xviii, xix, xxi
  Executive Board, xviii, xix
  Library Administration and Management Association
    Personnel Administration Section
      Racism and Sexism Awareness Training Committee, xvii
    Women Administrators Discussion Group, xv-xvi
  Office for Library Personnel Resources, xiii, xiv, xxx
  Reference and Adult Services Division
    Women's Materials and Women Library Users Discussion Group, xv
  Resources and Technical Services Division
    Cataloging and Classification Section
      Racism and Sexism in Subject Analysis Subcommittee, xvii
  Social Responsibilities Round Table, xviii

186 Index to Preliminary Pages

ALA, SRRT (cont.)
  Feminist Task Force, xi-xiii, xv, xviii
    Committee on Non-Sexist Subject Headings, xii
  Task Force on Women <u>see</u> Feminist Task Force <u>above</u>
  Washington Office, xviii
  Young Adult Services Division
    Sexism in Adolescent Literature Committee, xvii
Anker, Anita, xix
Association of American Library Schools
  Women's Interest Group, xxii-xxiii
Association of Research Libraries, xxvi

Baer, Bob, xix
Barkman, Donna, xxvi
Beckel, Deborah, ix
Bergen, Polly, xx
Bergman, Sherrie, xv
Blake, Fay, xix
Blume, Edward, xxiv
Broadley, Pamela R., ix
Brothers, Joyce, xxvi
Brown, Rita Mae, xii
Bryan, Barbara, xix
Bryant, Dorothy, xii

career development, xxvii
Career Development and Assessment Center for Librarians, xxvii-xxviii
Carnegie Reading List Fund, xxi
Carpenter, Liz, xx
Carter, Jimmy, xx
Cassell, Kay, xv, xix, xx
Catalyst, xxi
Chicago, Illinois, xviii, xix, xx
COALITION, xiv, xviii-xix, xxxii n.11

Coalition for Women in the Humanities and Social Sciences, xiv
comparable worth, xiv, xxvii, xxx
Cooke, Eileen D., xviii
Cotner, Suone, xx
Crawford, Miriam, xviii, xxii

Dickinson, Elizabeth M., xvii
Dickson, Katherine, ix
<u>Directory of Library and Information Profession Women's Groups,</u> xiv
Donovan, Lynn Bonfield, xxii
Drexel Student Library Association, xix

Eakin, Sally Ann, iii, ix
Engle, June, xix
Equal Employment Opportunity Commission, xxx
Equal Rights Amendment, xi, xii, xiv, xvii-xxi, xxii, xxxi n.1
  dues checkoff, xix
  ERA Task Force, xix-xx
  mail vote, xviii
  Mother's Day March, xx
<u>Equality in Librarianship: A Guide to Sex Discrimination Laws,</u> xiv
ERAmerica, xix, xx
Erickson, Lynne, xv

Federation of Organizations for Professional Women, xiv
Florida Library Association
  Women in Libraries Caucus, xx
Fox, Marcia R., xii
Frederick, Janet, ix
Freedom to Read Statement, xix
Friday, Nancy, xxvi
Fuller, Muriel L., xxv
Fulton, Marsha K., ix
Futas, Elizabeth, xix, xxi

Galvin, Thomas J., xviii
Gates, Carol, ix
Goldhor, Herbert, ix

Goldstein, Rachael, xxi
Grant, George, xix
Griffith, Susan, xii
Griffith, Susan C., xxv

Haber, Barbara, xii
Hall, Mary A., xvii
Hecht, Dorothy, xx
Heim, Kathleen, vii, viii, ix, xix
Hiatt, Peter, ix, xxvii
Hildenbrand, Suzanne, ix
Hinshaw, Marilyn, xviii
Holloway, Johnna, ix
Horrocks, Norman, ix

Ihrig, Alice, xviii, xix
Illinois, xviii, xx
Ina Coolbrith Brigade, xxiv, xxv

Jackson, Karen, xix
Jemelka, Jorg R., ix
Johanson, Cynthia, viii, xxi
Jones, Clara S., xviii
Josephine, Helen, xv, xix, xxx
Josey, E. J., xviii

Kellogg Foundation, xxvii
Koehler, Julia, ix
Krummel, Donald, ix

LeBarron, Suzanne, xviii
Leita, Carol, xxiv
<u>Library Education Statistical Report</u>, xxiii
Library of Congress Women's Program Advisory Committee, xxiii
<u>Library of Congress Subject Headings</u>, xvii
library schools, xvi, xvii
Littlewood, John, ix
Lowe, Betty, xix

Mallory, Mary, ix
Marchant, Maurice, xvii
Marshall, Joan, xii, xxiv
Martin, Jean K., xxvii

Massachusetts Library Association, xxv
McClellan, William M., ix
Midwest Academy, xxiv
Midwest Federation of Library Associations, xxvi, xxxv n.65
Moon, Eric, xviii, xix
<u>Ms Archivist</u>, xxii
Muriel Fuller Memorial Day Brunch, xxvi
Myers, Margaret, ix, xiii-xiv, xxx

National Committee on Pay Equity, xxx
National Conference on Pay Equity, xxx
National Education Association, xxi
National Endowment for the Humanities, xxx
National Organization for Women, xxi
National Plan of Action, xiv
National Women's Conference, xiv
National Women's Studies Association, xiv
Nelson, Jim, xix

Oakland Public Library, xxiv
O'Donnell, Peggy, xx
Ohio Historical Society, xxii
<u>On Equal Terms</u>, xii, xxiv
<u>Our Bodies Ourselves</u>, xii

Pachuta, June, ix
Painter, Kathryn Ann, iii, ix
Palmer House, xix
Parikh, Neel, xix
Phenix, Katharine, vii, viii

racism, xvi-xvii
REFORMA, xviii
Reynolds, Malvina, xxiv
Rochester, Maxine K., ix
Rockefeller, Sharon Percy, xx

The Role of Women in Librarianship 1876-1976, vii
Royal, Norma, xix

SAA Women's Caucus Newsletter, xvii
San Diego Public Library, xxx
Scarry, Patricia, xxi
Schimmel, Nancy, xxiv
Schlesinger Library, xxx
Schuman, Patricia G., xviii, xxiv
sexism, xvi-xvii
Shank, Russell, xviii
SHARE Directory, xxiv, xxv
Sheehy, Gail, xii
Shulman, Alix Kates, xii
SMARTS, xvii
Smith, Janet, xxiv
Smith, Linda C., ix
Society of American Archivists
  Status of Women Committee, xxii
  Women's Caucus, xxii
Special Libraries Association
  Women's Caucus, xxi
Stanfield, Karen L., ix
Starr, Carol, xvii, xix
Stenstrom, Pat, ix
Stone, Elizabeth, xxx
Sullivan, Peggy A., xviii, xx
Szczech, Bernadette, ix

Temple University, xxx
Thomassen, Cora, xx
Tuttle, Helen, xix

University of California-Berkeley, xxx
University of Oregon School of Librarianship, xxv
University of Washington School of Librarianship, xvii

Vainstein, Rose, xix
Veaner, Allen, xix

Walker, Alice, xii
Washington State Library, xxvii
Weech, Terry, ix
Weibel, Kathleen, ix, xv, xxi, xxvi
Wisconsin Women Library Workers, xxv, xxxiv-xxxv n.63
WLW Journal, xxv, xxx
"Women in a Woman's Profession--Strategies II," xii, xvii
Women in Libraries, xii
"Women in the Community," xxx-xxxi, xxxvi n.78
Women Library Workers, xiv, xviii, xix, xxiii-xxv
  Chapter Action Fund, xxiv
Women's Action Alliance, xiv

Young Adult Alternative Newsletter, xix

Zubatsky, David S., ix